The Sacred Body

Studies in Christianity and Literature 4

EDITORIAL BOARD

THE SACRED BODY

Asceticism in Religion, Literature, Art, and Culture

David Jasper

BAYLOR UNIVERSITY PRESS

© 2009 by Baylor University Press
Waco, Texas 76798-7363

Cover Design by Cynthia Dunne, Blue Farm Graphics
Cover Image: Van Gogh, Self-portrait, 1889 (oil on canvas). Used by permission of Bridgeman Art Library.
Book Project management and composition by Scribe Inc., Philadelphia, PA

Library of Congress Cataloging-in-Publication Data

The sacred body : asceticism in religion, literature, art and culture / David Jasper.
    p. cm.—(Studies in Christianity and literature ; 4)
Includes bibliographical references and index.
ISBN 978-1-60258-141-8 (alk. paper)
1. Body, Human, in literature. 2. Body, Human—Religious aspects. 3. Asceticism in literature. 4. Asceticism in art. I. Title.

PN56.B62J37 2009
700'.4820447—dc22   2008052676

Printed in the United States of America on acid-free paper with a minimum of 30% pcw recycled content.

In memory of my father.

CONTENTS

List of Illustrations ix

Preface xi

Acknowledgments xxi

1 A Sunlit Landscape Amid the Night of Nonbeing 1

2 The Soul as Sacred Space 15

3 The Body, Sacred and Profane 31

4 The Word and the Body 47

5 Asceticism as a Way of Love, with a Modern Excursus 63

6 Asceticism, Imposed and Recovered:
Velázquez, Martha, and the Eyes of Faith 87

7 The Eucharistic Body in Literature and Modern Experience:
George Herbert and Simone Weil 109

8 Holiness and the Resurrection Body:
Meister Eckhart and James Joyce 135

9 Romanticism and the Recovery of the Sacred in Language 157

10 The Possibility of a Contemporary Theology 171

Notes 187

Bibliography 219

Index 227

ILLUSTRATIONS

Mathias Grünewald, *Isenheim Altarpiece: The Crucifixion.* Courtesy of the Musée d'Unterlinden Colmar.

Diego Rodriguez de Silva Y Velázquez, *Christ in the House of Martha and Mary.* Courtesy of the National Gallery Picture Library, London.

Diego Rodriguez de Silva Y Velázquez, *The Rokeby Venus.* Courtesy of the National Gallery Picture Library, London.

Georges du Mesnil de la Tour, *Repentant Magdalen.* Ailsa Mellon Bruce Fund. Courtesy of the Board of Trustees, National Gallery of Art, Washington, D.C.

Roger van der Weyden, *Mary Magdalene.* Courtesy of the National Gallery Picture Library, London.

Rembrandt, *Danaë.* Courtesy of the State Hermitage Museum, St. Petersburg, Russia.

Eric Gill, *The Nuptials of God.* Courtesy of the Bridgeman Art Gallery.

Luca Signorelli, *The Resurrection of the Body* (Orvieto Cathedral). Courtesy of akg-images, Berlin, London, and Paris.

Caspar David Friedrich, *The Monk by the Sea.* Courtesy of bpk / Nationalgalerie, Staatliche Museen zu Berlin. Photo: Jörg P. Anders.

PREFACE

I had originally intended calling this book *The Aesthetics of Asceticism*. Since Hans Urs von Balthasar's massive work *The Glory of the Lord: A Theological Aesthetics* was published some fifty years ago, there has been no small interest in books on aesthetics and theology.[1] However, to align myself to such works would be misleading, for my concerns and purpose are rather different from theirs, and so the title was changed. Rather, what follows is a continuation of my earlier book *The Sacred Desert* (2004), but with a focus given to the body and, in particular, the body in the traditions of asceticism as it began among the desert monastics of the fourth century. As with its predecessor, this will involve a journey through many texts of literature, through examples of Western art and the occasional film in its pursuit of the body in the Christian tradition as the Word made flesh, torn and crucified, resurrected and divinized in forms of beauty that embrace both deep suffering and profound joy in a celebration that is known finally in a form of existence that I will call liturgical living. At its heart is a theological journey on which I am still embarked, a journey that is incomplete and still struggling for articulation but whose history and alliances will, perhaps, gradually emerge, but which must finally stand alone before the God who is unknown, both absolute light and utter darkness. In a real sense, this book is a gift to me, even if to me alone.

The reader of this book will find experiments in different forms of writing—various conversations with self and others but, finally, with the Scripture by which the reader is, in the end, consumed. There will be moments of autobiography, and these, perhaps, are the hardest of all. Although academic, in a sense, I do not so much offer these pages for academic judgment (though that, too, has its crucial place) but for a form of response that is both simpler and much more difficult. Thus, *how* one reads this book becomes an issue that is explored most fully only in the concluding chapter, but you should be warned that the intention is, at times, to provoke and perplex rather than offer commentary or conclusion. Hermeneutics has ever been my passion, and here there will be made clear my own background as a teacher of literary theory, but the final imperative drives beyond this in the different registers of language and discourse, of light and dark, of harmony and discord. Often, references and echoes within the text will remain implicit or hidden, styles and voices will change, and contradictions will be left for the reader to absorb and deal with. My intention is not to persuade—rather, it is to offer and finally to begin to make possible (perhaps only for myself) a theological future to be celebrated fully and entirely only in mind, body, and spirit. And always there is a silent text that eludes both author and reader, but as yet an impossibility made, perhaps, possible by this text. This silent text is then the next book, maybe, for which this is but a grasping and a preparation.

* * *

Travelers in the desert have frequently remarked on its "indifference." The desert cares not whether we live or die. In the literature of the Christian desert fathers and mothers, this indifference is absorbed into the discipline that finds its conclusion in their own consciousness as, in Athanasius' description of St. Antony, "equilibrium," or sometimes "passionlessness"—a perfect balance between grief and pleasure, sorrow and joy, indifferent to the imbalance of all extremes. This cannot ultimately be disconnected from that disinterestedness that is at the heart of Immanuel Kant's aesthetics in the *Third Critique*, nor can that balance between exterior and interior (another desert characteristic) famously described in the *Critique of Practical Reason*: "Two things flood the mind with ever increasing wonder and awe [*Bewunderung und Ehrfurcht*], the more often and the more intensely it concerns itself with them: the starry heavens above me and the moral law within me."[2] But what is even more awesome than the starry heavens and the moral law, as Arthur C. Danto has noted, is the fact that Kant is aware of them; that his consciousness can reach into the universe, both outer and inner, and is open to that which is, in itself, unpictureable and even unintelligible. This is what the writer Vladimir Nabokov has called "the marvel of consciousness—that sudden window swinging open to a sunlit landscape amid the night of nonbeing."[3]

It is this marvel that reaches its perfect maturity in the equilibrium exemplified in the ascetic disciplines that are rooted in the desert, a pure match in the human spiritual consciousness to the indifference of the desert landscape. We find it perfectly described in the "phenomenology of consciousness" described by the seventh-century monk St. Maximus the Confessor "in which the mind can be detached by prayer from objects of sense and mental objects until its content is filled only with desire for God who, in one sense, can never be an object of consciousness, being beyond thought and language, yet who in other sense can fill the consciousness with his presence."[4] This utter balance of absence and presence, or being and nonbeing, is found on earth only in the fragile, pitiless purity of the desert, its profound spirituality described by the greatest Western chronicler of Arabia in the twentieth century, T. E. Lawrence, indicative of why Antony and his fellow ascetics in the fourth century had to leave the city for the wilderness:

> This faith of the desert was impossible in the towns. It was at once too strange, too simple, too impalpable for export and common use. The idea, the ground-belief of all Semitic creeds was waiting there, but it had to be diluted to be made comprehensible to us. The scream of a bat was too shrill for many ears: the desert spirit escaped through our courser texture. The prophets returned from the desert with their glimpse of God, and through their stained medium (as through a dark glass) showed something of the majesty and brilliance whose full vision would blind, deafen, silence us.[5]

Toward the end of this preface, we will travel to the dry rocks of the desert landscape through the immediacy of a journal that I kept during a solitary sojourn in the desert of West Texas in 2003, but for now it is important to relate this consciousness with a language that resonates with the desert landscape and that Martin Heidegger begins to formulate in his later writings as realizing and embracing the possibility of "poetic dwelling" on earth, a term to which we will return frequently and which I relate to the key word in John 1:14: "And the Word became flesh and dwelt [ἐσκήνωσεν] among us." Thus, to dwell is drawn from desert wandering, for it is literally, in the Greek, to "tabernacle" or "tent"—an ever-present being that is permanent and yet shifting, as the Ark of the Covenant moved with ancient nomadic peoples while they traveled with their tents [σκηνή] from place to place in the wilderness. The philosopher James C. Edwards sums up Heidegger's thought in this respect in this way: "To dwell poetically on the earth as a mortal is to live in awareness of the godhead, the clearing, the blank but lightening sky. It is to live so as to measure oneself against that Nothing—that No-thing—that grants the possibility of the presence of and the Being of the things that there are. Within that clearing, as Heidegger puts it, brightness wars with darkness. There we struggle against particular ignorances and incapacities to bring forth truth."[6] To dwell poetically is to live within the "space" that is at once a desert, an oasis and a space of literature. It is, in fact, nowhere, and yet it becomes the place of real presence beyond which is a mysterious infinity, a blank but lightening sky. In four essays from the early 1950s,[7] Heidegger asserts that "dwelling" is the fundamental form of human life and that to dwell is to build. Poetic dwelling is to acknowledge underlying conditionalities that constitute a fundamental condition of indebtedness: to live is to owe one's life—to be always in a form of giving—an attitude everywhere recognizable in the ancient desert ascetic. Furthermore, to live thus is to call attention to the underlying materiality of our being—what Heidegger calls "earth" (the horizontal axis) and, under the lightening sky, the recognition of "the beckoning messengers of the godhead" (the vertical axis). We are both and at once body and spirit, and in Heidegger's words, which might almost describe the *modus vivendi* of the desert fathers, who, in the words of the *Lives of Desert Fathers* (*Historia Monachorum in Aegypto*), lived here on earth yet as citizens of heaven, in perpetual expectation,[8] "mortals dwell in that they await the divinities as divinities. In hope they hold up to the divinities what is unhoped for."[9] Central to Heidegger's thinking here is the sense of our mortality—not merely our ceasing to exist but our awareness of our inevitable end and the acknowledgment of the necessary condition of death and our capacity to measure ourselves against that No-thing, to exist over the abyss of pure and momentary time. You see how the terms here are perfectly expressive of both dwelling in the interiority of being, which is Heidegger's concern, and the actual circumstances of desert existence. In Heidegger, and in the desert, this is to move toward a new way of thinking itself, and therefore of being, which finally constitutes what it is to be human, a possibility that is only present in the act of poetic dwelling.[10]

Such thinking, such dwelling poetically, has its origins for us in the biblical literature and its absorption into the lives and writings of the Christian ascetics. The scriptural basis for the evolution of the desert motif in Christian apophatic theology is Moses' encounter with God in the wilderness of Sinai, beautifully described by the Pseudo-Dionysius, in the fifth or sixth century C.E., in his *Mystical Theology*: "But then [Moses] breaks . . . away from what sees and is seen, and he plunges into the truly mysterious darkness of unknowing. Here, renouncing all that the mind may conceive, wrapped entirely in the intangible and the invisible, he belongs completely to him who is beyond everything."[11] Moses' disappearance into the desert for his theophany is a journey into the unknown and the unknowing, both physically and spiritually. At the same time, and throughout the Bible, the movement into the wilderness is regarded as a kind of golden age in the covenant between God and his people. Indeed, it is likely that Yahweh has his origins in the form of a desert storm god. Although the period of wandering for forty years after the escape of the children of Israel from Egypt is recorded as often a time of grumbling and backsliding; nevertheless, in the later prophetic literature, it is also often seen as a glorious time in contrast to the violent times that followed.

But perhaps the most mysterious desert encounter with God is in the story of Elijah in 1 Kings 19 in which the prophet is instructed to journey to Mount Horeb where the covenant had originally been established with Moses, and there he hears the divine voice speaking not in thunderous natural phenomena, but in what the King James Bible beautifully renders from the Hebrew as a "still small voice," though the Greek Septuagint and the Latin Vulgate suggest something closer to the "sound of a gentle breeze."[12] But the Hebrew, unlike Greek and Latin, a language born in the desert, captures perfectly the utter ambiguity and paradox of soundless sound, the still breeze that is alone both heard and not heard in the desert. It is a palpable silence known to the modern Egyptian poet Edmond Jabès when he writes, "You do not go into the desert to find identity but to lose it, to lose your personality, to become anonymous. You make yourself void. You become silence. It is very hard to live with silence. The real silence is death and this is terrible. It is very hard in the desert. You must become more silent than the silence around you. And then something extraordinary happens: you hear silence speak."[13] This exactly describes the silence of Elijah's still small voice, quite unknown in the interrupted worlds of our cultural dwelling. In the desert alone is truly known the God who both *is* and *is not*, a God of natural phenomena who is yet utterly transcendent, told in language that insists on distinct levels of meaning at once discontinuous and yet inseparable. Nor am I simply here writing as a theologian from the Bible or literature. For in my 2003 journal, there is a passage that echoes precisely this ambiguity drawn from my own experience, though I was not thinking of Elijah and I had not read the poetry of Jabès. I wrote,

> It hasn't been quite what I expected, but then things rarely are. I had a much more romantic image, absurdly constructed from myth, film, books. Of course, it is different. It has not been the grand desert of limitless sands and rocks and hills. But it has been something more than that—*a place which is neither exterior not interior, and remote.* I should have expected as much, of course—to travel all this way and find a place which has been familiar all along but hitherto largely unfrequented by me. It is a place we all know, individually, but rarely, if ever, visit. I don't think I could live here for *very long.*[14]

This strange sense of returning home in the desert is also found in the Bible, where the wilderness, which is not finally a place in which to live permanently but a landscape to be passed through (desert dwellers are nomads), is a place of renewal, a spot of secret tryst where the lovers first met and where it all began in innocence and hope. We find it in Hosea 2:14–16, when God speaks to Israel:

> Therefore, behold, I will allure her,
> and bring her into the wilderness,
> and speak tenderly to her.
> From there I will give her her vineyards,
> and make the Valley of Achor a door of hope.
> There she shall respond as in the days of her youth,
> as at the time when she came out of the land of Egypt.

So, beyond belief, the desert is the place of vineyards, and as in Isaiah 35:1, "the desert shall rejoice and blossom," and the parched wilderness becomes what it truly is, the garden of paradise. The image of the paradise garden is everywhere in desert literature, not only in the Bible, but also in the Qur'an, in the sayings of the Australian Aborigines, and in a beautiful Algerian saying that I shall drop into your mind and return to later: "The desert is the Garden of Allah, from which the Lord of the faithful removed all superfluous human and animal life, so that there might be a place where He can walk in peace."[15]

In the New Testament, the desert is also the place of John the Baptist, who literally incorporates its nothingness—another voice from the wilderness that speaks of God. And it is where Jesus begins his ministry, or, more properly, prepares himself to preach, at once tempted by Satan (did even Jesus have his inner demons to be fought, as all the desert fathers fought them?) and tended by angels. Jesus' forty days in the wilderness is the background to one of the most remarkable of novels on the desert, Jim Crace's *Quarantine* (1997). I will not attempt to describe it in any detail, but suffice to say that the "Jesus" of Crace's fiction (known as the Gally) is one of a small group of individuals who have gone out into the desert to fast and pray for their lost souls. There is also Musa, a merchant who is the embodiment of evil, madman and sadist, perhaps even Satan himself. Jesus is a young idealist who defies the desert, perhaps even to death. According to this version, did Jesus himself actually die in the wilderness making Christianity itself merely a story told, since, as has been attested with regard to the endurance of the human body, for the ordinary man "the forty days of fasting described in religious texts would not be achievable—except with divine help, of course?"[16] Finally, Crace's Gally is brought by the wilderness to a place between heaven and earth, both and neither the one nor the other: a place where the body meets the spirit in the desert wind, the *ruach*, the breath of the still small voice, a

citizen of the next world while still here on earth. Here, he meets the indifference of God, the nothingness. Here is the text:

> He'd almost welcome the devil more than god. For the devil can be traded
> with, and exorcised. But god is ruthless and unstable. No one can cast out
> god. It was too late. Jesus was already standing at the threshold to the trem-
> bling world which he had sought, where he would spend his forty everlast-
> ing days. So this was death. So this was pain made powerless. So this was
> fruit turned back into its seed.
>
> Jesus was a voyager, at last, between the heavens and the earth. There
> was a light, deep in the middle of the night. He tried to swim to it. He tried
> to fly. He held his hands up to the light. His hands were bluey-white like
> glass. The light passed through. The mountain shivered from afar. He felt
> the cold of nothing there. He heard the cold of no one there. No god, no
> gardens, just the wind.[17]

This extraordinary writing, is, let me assure you, utterly realistic. It is
the meeting of death in the indifferent desert. It is also the moment of deepest spiritual truth in the nothing, of which the Dominican Meister Eckhart
spoke when he said, "Man's last and highest parting occurs when, for God's
sake, he takes leave of God."[18]

On the final page of *Quarantine*, the evil merchant Musa thinks he sees
the figure of Jesus, who he knows has already died in the desert.

> Musa looked towards the distant scree again. He told himself this was no
> merchant fantasy. His Gally was no longer thin and watery, diluted by the
> mirage heat, distorted by the ripples in the air. He made his slow, painstak-
> ing way, naked and barefooted, down the scree, his feet blood-red from
> wounds, and as he came closer to the valley floor his outlined hardened and
> his body put on flesh.
>
> Musa raised his arm in greeting, but there was no response. . . . Nor
> could he contemplate the endless movements on the trading road, the
> floods, the rifts, the troops, the ever-caravans, the evening peace that's bro-
> kered not by a god but by the rocks and clays themselves, *shalom*, *salaam*,
> the one-time, all-time truces of the land.[19]

These words are capable of being read on so many levels, relating to the Passion Narratives and resurrection stories of the gospels, the perplexed mind
of Musa in the novel, but perhaps above all to the distortions of reality in a
landscape that seems as though it is at the end of the world. At the physical
level, the intense desert heat bends and manipulates the light rays to the point
that one actually sees things that are not there. Objects begin to float from the
ground, hard edges blur and ripple, and images present themselves out of thin

air. As a result of the shift in perceptions, we begin to respond at other levels than the physical—the psychological and even the spiritual. What, then, is truth? The familiar reversal of inner and outer is described by the artist Bill Viola after his experience of the Tunisian Sahara in 1979:

> I want to go to a place that seems like it's at the end of the world. A vantage point from which one can stand and peer out into the void—the world beyond—what would be above the surface to the fish. Where all becomes strange and unfamiliar. There is nothing to lean on. No references. It is said the mind plays "tricks." Standing there, a place where, after a long arduous journey, you realize you can go no further. Each time you advance towards it, it recedes further. You have reached the edge. All you can do is stand there and peer out into the void, watching. Standing there, you strain to look further, to see beyond, strain to make out familiar shapes and forms. You finally realize that the void is yourself. It is like some huge mirror for your mind. Clear and uncluttered, it is the opposite of our urban spaces. Out here, the unbound mind can run free. Imagination reigns. Space becomes a huge projection screen. Inside becomes outside. You can see what you are.[20]

Musa raises his arm in greeting, but there is no response. He has reached the edge, and it is, perhaps, a moment of judgment on this man, the moment when, in the distortions of the desert mirage, he realizes that the void is himself, inside has become outside, and a truth is known.

It was this terrible void that the desert fathers and mothers in the fourth and fifth centuries sought out and faced in their bodies and souls, beyond the endurance both physical and spiritual of ordinary beings. In the epilogue to the great work *The Lives of the Desert Fathers*, the *Historia Monachorum*, the travelers who visit the desert monks and describe their lives admit that they themselves do not dare to enter into the "deep desert" the *desert absolu*. And yet it is in the void, in the absolute desert, that the vision of the paradise garden becomes real in a true coincidence of opposites, a unity of being in perfect equilibrium that is one with the desert indifference.

You will remember my reference to the saying about the desert as the Garden of Allah where the Lord of the faithful might walk in peace. It reminds me of that verse in the book of Genesis when Adam and Eve, just after they have eaten the apple and made clothes for themselves to cover their nakedness, "heard the sound of the Lord God walking in the garden at the time of the evening breeze" (Gen 3:8). Surely this is the Lord's last peaceful walk in the garden, the moment when the desert becomes wilderness, the place of the dead, but through which alone can be recovered the lost Eden and the time when we did not hide from God for shame. Paul Ricoeur, in his early work *The Symbolism of Evil* (1967), translates this desert journey into the hope for a recovery of pure speech, the time when the silence of the desert is not the absence of speech but the fullness of all speaking so that finally, in the desert silence, as Jabès said, you hear silence speak: as Ricoeur put it, describing the hope for the recreation of language, "beyond the desert of criticism, we wish to be called again."[21] But this desert is also a real desert, and there our thinking becomes nothing less than pure being, Heidegger's poetic dwelling. There, pure detachment becomes a marvel of consciousness, a reversal of being into a recovered innocence that Ricoeur calls our secondary naiveté. Nor am I speaking here simply as a theologian: I am speaking of the real presence of the desert landscape as it meets the language of the Bible (whose literature emerges from the desert, for did not Abram, in the first instance, at the Lord's behest, leave his home and journey into the Negev—that is, the great desert to the south of the Holy Land?). This desert also becomes utterly inward in the greatest sermon of Meister Eckhart in the early fourteenth century, *On the Noble Man*, when, quoting the passage from the Prophet Hosea to which I have already referred, he says, "Now what is nobler than that which is born, on the one hand, from all that is highest and best in the creature and, on the other, from the most inward ground of divine nature and *the divine desert?* In the prophet Hosea our Lord says: 'I will lead the noble soul into a wilderness and there I will speak into her heart.' One with One, one from One, one in One and one in One in all eternity. Amen."[22] And, finally, in my own poor experience, I have glimpsed something of this desert unity, even Eckhart's "oneness," in the silence of West Texas, a very real place, beautiful and dangerous. Here is what I wrote after some time staying there on a solitary retreat:

> "Every person is by nature solitary." I think it was Thomas Merton who said that. Well, of course we are—in the end. All of us. And maybe it is important to be reminded of that now and then, and go back to our "nature" in silence, without communication, without communication or distraction. Because it is silent here, it means that it doesn't really matter *where* I am. Odd things are happening to my sense of time and place. I have travelled 5,000 miles to be in this strange place, but I don't feel remotely lonely or cut off. I am where I am, touching base. This is my home for the time being.[23]

It was truly a sunlit landscape amid the night of nonbeing.

ACKNOWLEDGMENTS

This book would not have been possible without the time and facilities granted to me as a Scholar in Residence at the University of Iowa's Obermann Center for Advanced Studies in the autumn of 2006. My thanks are due to Jay Semel, the director of the center, to David E. Klemm, Carin M. Green, Peter Manning, and all the members of the scholarly circle at the Center. I am grateful also to my colleagues and postgraduate students in the University of Glasgow, in particular, George Newlands, Heather Walton, Allen Smith, Jim Harold, and Ward Blanton, and to members of the Faculty of Theology at the University of Uppsala, especially Carl Reinhold Bråkenhielm and Mattias Martinson. But the one voice that is apparent throughout the book is that of Tom Altizer, to whom my gratitude for his work knows no bounds. There are too many others to name, but my chief thanks, as always, go to my family, Alison, Hannah, Ruth, and May.

An earlier version of chapter 3 appears in Deborah F. Sawyer and Dawn Llewellyn, eds., *Reading Spiritualities: Constructing and Re-presenting the Sacred* (Ashgate, 2008); of chapter 5 in Paul Middleton, ed., *The God of Love and Human Dignity. Essays in Honour of George Newlands* (T&T Clark, 2007); of chapter 7 in Natalie K. Watson and Stephen Burns, eds., *Exchanges of Grace: Essays in Honour of Ann Loades* (SCM, 2008); and of chapter 9 in Irene Visser and Helen Wilcox, eds., *Transforming Holiness: Representations of Holiness in English and American Literary Texts* (Peeters, 2006).

1

A Sunlit Landscape Amid the
Night of Nonbeing

Occasionally, in one's reading, one stumbles by accident across a phrase or a passage that throws a vivid light across other arenas of one's reflection, even though it is far distant from them. "The marvel of consciousness—that sudden window swinging open to a sunlit landscape amid the dark night of non-being": these are the words of Russian novelist Vladimir Nabokov when asked in an interview if he was surprised by anything in life.[1] Therefore, as one thinks about the wonder and awe of consciousness, beyond even the intelligible, one returns to that "phenomenology of consciousness" in the writings of St. Maximus the Confessor, with its detachment from the things of sense until one is utterly filled by a desire for the God who is beyond all consciousness. Later, we shall link Nabokov and St. Maximus with the tradition of phenomenology following the philosophy of Martin Heidegger, in thinkers such as Jean-Luc Marion and Jean-Yves Lacoste, as that tradition explores the possibilities of religious identity in the deepest recesses of what it is to be human, to "live liturgically."[2] These forms of consciousness, divided by so many years and such depths of cultural difference, seem to me to have a remarkable similarity, each celebrating a profound presence that is utterly realized yet beyond thought and even being.

I concluded my previous book, *The Sacred Desert*, with an image of what I called, after Thomas Altizer,[3] Total Presence, a oneness in which all opposites are reconciled. It was that which the desert fathers and ascetics sought, and it is the impossible possibility of the fulfillment of the human in the divine and the self-emptying of the divine into human, a point of pure being or Real Presence. It may come upon our consciousness in moments of sacramental sublimity, or through the discipline of contemplation and prayer—but it can finally only be enacted in the full realization of the body here and now, and it is only in such enactment that theology itself is finally real. My next task, then, after my reflections on the image of the desert in the Bible and tradition, was to contemplate the ascetic body, in the full acknowledgment that if asceticism means the disciplining and even repressing of the body, it is finally and truly its only proper realization. I pursue this task at the instigation of Altizer, who prompted me to develop the "desert" book into "the depths of the body itself, depths which are finally 'spirit' as well as body, and yet depths evoked by an absolute desert, and perhaps unreal and invisible apart from that desert."[4] Where this leads me is into a series of investigations of a radical understanding of the body as both sacrament and yet as "real," known finally in a liturgical celebration that embraces not less than everything.[5] Such discourse is rather different from the recent surge of interest in the social sciences and the humanities in "body," and not least, as Sarah Coakley has suggested, the "still lurking religiosity" of our present "bodily" interests,[6] perceived in a post-Christian and post-Enlightenment context. Yet it acknowledges Coakley's admission that it remains extraordinarily difficult to grasp what the "body" actually is—and the reason I suggest is because of our failure to admit its profound theological depths.

Thus, we turn to the ascetic body as perceived in Christian history and portrayed through art and literature. There have been a number of important, recent studies of asceticism: the huge multifaith survey edited by Vincent L. Wimbush and Richard Valantasis, published in 1998; Geoffrey Galt Harpham's *The Ascetic Imperative in Culture and Criticism* (1987), which traces the cultural importance of asceticism as a "discourse of resistance" for both ethics and aesthetics in the Western tradition; and finally, and most recently, Gavin Flood's study, *The Ascetic Self: Subjectivity, Memory and Tradition* (2004), which explores the ascetic element in the history of the Western tradition's construction of subjectivity.[7] What is extraordinarily lacking in all of these works, even Flood's, valuable though they are, is the acknowledgment of the utterly radical *theological* dimension of ascetic practice and its profound importance for our contemporary understanding of the body and embodiment. Let me come at this claim by some words of the artist Douglas Huebner, quoted by Arthur C. Danto in his book *The Abuse of Beauty*. These words express something in his art that is very close to the spirituality and purpose of the early Christian fathers and mothers of the desert as they literally "enacted" their theology in ascetic practices in the fourth and fifth centuries. Huebner writes, "I'm not trying to take anything away from the world. Nor am I trying to restructure the world. I'm not trying to tell the world anything really. I'm not trying to tell the world that it could be better by being this or that. I'm just, you know, touching the world by doing these things, and leaving it pretty much the way it is."[8] The remote desert ascetics, too, were deliberately touching the world with an embodied spirituality that meant little to it and that barely comprehended it, but it was, I would wish to say, by their deeply countercultural narratives, as *The Lives of the Desert Fathers* rather enigmatically expresses it, that "the world is kept in being . . . and. . . . human life is preserved and honoured by God."[9] In the Heideggerian phrase, dwelling poetically in the world, these extraordinary people opened to the world a window on eternity with their bodies in ways that few of us either can or would wish to follow. But precisely this impossibility opens up a central theme in my concerns—that is, the importance of hagiography, the textual representation of the impossible lives of the saints in ways that are precisely not ways to be copied in our own lives, but yet are metaphorically and symbolically radically transformative of how we ourselves perceive and exist in the world. Furthermore, in the hagiographic writings that we will be exploring later, the being of the saint is literally absorbed into a text, becomes textual in a final conjoining of word and flesh. *Textuality* is therefore a fundamental issue in this discourse—as the desert saints were almost literally consumed by the word of Scripture and became one with it in their lives,[10] so the body is also both and at once fulfilled and negated in the words and action of the sacrament. In St. Bernard of Clairvaux's *Sermons for the Feast of All Saints*, preached in the twelfth century, he explains that for Christ to nourish is to be nourished, and to eat the spiritual food of the Eucharist is at the same time to be consumed by Christ. "So it is that while he feeds others he himself is fed, and while he refreshed us with spiritual joy he himself joys in our spiritual progress. My penitence, my salvation are his food. I myself am his food. . . . I am chewed as I am reproved by him; I am swallowed as I am taught; I am digested as I am changed; I am assimilated as I am transformed; I am made one as I am conformed."[11] The Eucharist, then, is always central to this discussion of the saintly ascetic body, an impossible body that is both brought to nothingness (like Christ's body on the cross) and wholly fulfilled in material divinization in its consuming and being consumed by the real presence of Christ in a holy feast, which is also a holy fast.[12] The most acute and painful example of this near our own time, I suggest later, is to be found in the writings and life of Simone Weil.[13]

But before we move too far and too fast in a discussion that will continually swirl around its own still center, we need to ask the question, what is the nature of this radical theological imperative of the ascetic body? It begins in a radical reversal that is at once countercultural and practiced in defiance of the assumed "natural" currents of the body—a reversal summed up in the word "denial": the denial to the body of normal food, sleep, sexual activity, and so on.[14] But the point of this is neither to seek death nor the disposal of the body. Indeed, quite to the contrary, the Christian insistence on the resurrection of the body (and Jesus' bodily presence in the gospels after the passion) indicates that the end is a vision of the "body glorious," a transformed and transfigured body found in a theology that insisted—after Origen and others[15]—on the Song of Songs as a central text. In the desert tradition, there is a practical heart to the ascetic way, containing all the elements of simple survival in that inhospitable environment, practices then bleached onto the imagery of the Eucharist and its fragmentary and occasional presence in crumbs of bread and sips of wine. But the radical reversal in the body becomes the pattern for theology itself, with its Christian origins in the death and resurrection of the body of Christ, asceticism insisting on absolute negation to the point that scours clean all attempts actually to speak theologically as we have known them. Its focus is inevitably on the death on the cross, and it is on this that the true ascetic, in the deep desert, or on his crazy pillar for forty years, concentrates his whole being as the only possible touching point of the divine and the human. The ascetic way must therefore always be utterly solitary, and yet alone is the basis of true community, consumed and at the same time, in the proper Latin sense of the word, celebratory.

The theology of the ascetic pursues, not least in the very body itself, the negation of everything that we have known as God[16] in an incomprehensible and impossible landscape. The famed temptations of the ascetics are actually not so much the conventional demons of sex and fabulous food—but the deeper temptations of assumed spiritual perfection and, deeper still, the temptation to imagine that it is all a falsehood—even and especially God, him or herself. Asceticism lives within a series of radical contradictions: the rebirth in contemporary thinkers like Emmanuel Levinas and Jacques Derrida of a deeply radical Neoplatonism is a reminder of such an influence on the early ascetics and their goal of "divinization," or *theosis*, which is a becoming one with Christ, yet their insistence on the body and its continuances in the life of beauty was also at once a denial and an affirmation of this. There was never any sense of the shrugging off of the body to enjoy some kind of "pagan" union with divinity.[17] Rather, the ascetic insistence was upon the body, albeit a body rendered almost invisible and hidden, and yet it is in the body alone that the apocalyptic body of the Godhead is realized in the epiphany of the eucharistic body, both consumed and consuming. Thus, it was that the great saints of the desert, bequeathed to us in the narratives of hagiography, sought to become one with Christ at once in word and enactment, and lived truly eucharistic lives on the edge that was yet, finally, within the Total Presence, without remainder.

In the literature of asceticism the body is perceived within the context of a profound aesthetics—which is why I began with the insights of art and the revisionary aesthetics of the art theorist Danto in his book *The Abuse of Beauty*.[18] There are the haunting dreams of the two Cappadocian fathers, Gregory of Nyssa and Gregory Nazianzen, in the fourth century, of their respective sisters, Macrina and Gorgonia. In her brother's funeral oration for her, Gorgonia is seen in "garments bright with virtue alone," and on her deathbed, Macrina "refreshed her body as though with dew," while Gregory of Nyssa reports that even as she was wrapped in her grave shroud, "she shone even in that dark clothing, no doubt because the divine power added such grace to her body that, just as in the vision in my dreams, beams of light seemed to shine out from her beauty."[19] There are other examples of such bodies: St. Antony emerging from years spent in a tomb to appear in full vigor and youthfulness, or St. Mary of Egypt, who, despite forty years of wandering alone in the desert, proves as attractive as ever to the priest Zossimus.[20] The point is that if divinization is the goal of the ascetic life, following the pattern that if Christ became like us so we should thereby become like him, this is also a perfection of the body seen not in any conventional or culturally defined terms, but within a genuine theological and sacramental aesthetics. Thus, St. Maximus, at the heart of whose theology is the question of humanity's deification, understood as something that has already happened "in Christ," writes in his work *Ambigua* (*Difficulties*), "For God and man are paradigms one of another, that as much as God is humanized to man through love for mankind, so much is man able to be deified to God through love, and that as much as man is caught up in God to what is known in his mind, so much does man manifest God, who is invisible by nature, through the virtues."[21] For St. Maximus, we are already deified through the sacraments of baptism and the Eucharist by which we are incorporated (the word is to be understood literally) into Christ's death and resurrection. The ascetic life (the title of one of St. Maximus' works) is the disciplined realization of this present actuality, though ultimately our baptism is completed only at the final day when our bodies are raised from the dead. Meanwhile, through the reversals of asceticism, the invisible nonbeing of God becomes present in the phenomenology of consciousness as the ascetic body, disciplined to negation in human terms and which therefore participates wholly in the kenosis of God's impossible humanity in Christ that is only ever fully realized in his moment of death. At the same time, this is a supreme moment of transcendent beauty, a glimpse of a sunlit landscape amid the night of nonbeing. A recent study of St. Maximus on the body by Adam G. Cooper has linked his asceticism with the young, dying priest in Georges Bernanos' novel *The Diary of a Country Priest* (1936) and his reference to those "old monks, wise, shrewd, unerring in judgement, and yet aglow with passionate insight, so very tender in their humanity. What miracle enables these semi-lunatics, these prisoners in their own dreams, these sleepwalkers, apparently to enter more deeply each day into the pain of others? An odd sort of dream, an unusual opiate which, far from turning him back into himself and isolating him from his fellows, unites the individual with mankind in the spirit of universal charity!"[22] Thus, the ascetic in all things is a paradox, a life lived in reversal and yet fully lived in every sense: utterly isolated and yet a guarantor of universal community; a fragment yet whole, beyond the flesh, yet wholly of it; a theology that is only real in its enactment in the body, consumed and consuming. The ascetic is sustaining a continuous parting, that is Meister Eckhart's final and greatest parting from God and of all that can possibly be spoken of God for God's own sake, and enters into the silence of Total Presence, a truly Hegelian negation and a pure and necessary absence.

It is thus that, as a theologian, I take my particular leave of the theologians and enter the impossibility of theology through the actuality of the sacramental body, understood in the Eucharist and liturgical living but miraculously present in ascetic reversals. As my study progresses, it will be largely in the company of the bodies of individuals, some of whom, like Weil, have existed, but others who come to us only through the medium of hagiography or in the images of literature and art. But all of them, in one way or another, have lives that are realized for us in texts in which metaphor and reality are confused and conflated. My purpose is not so much to establish a careful academic narrative, but rather to explore, repetitively and in unlikely conjunctions, a profound understanding of the nature of the body recognized in theology and the religious life, and by artists and poets. Its truth gradually dawns only in moments of dialectic and dramatic reversal, a chiasmic structure such as is deeply embedded in the narratives of the New Testament: "Those who love their life lose it, and those who hate their life in this world will keep it for eternal life" (John 12:25). And this is to be understood not within a life-denying ascetic tradition, but at a deeper level of paradox that is sustained by the ancient spiritual fascination with the eroticism of the poetry of the Song of

Songs, or later in the poetry of St. John of the Cross, as a deep affirmation of the body, perhaps unreal and invisible apart from its death and resurrection in a deeply sacred and absolutely profane desert. Such apophatic moments of dramatic reversal call for the exercise of a crucially stretched energy of the imagination[23] that sees Christ's deepest glory even and especially, as we shall see later, in the hellish negations of the Mathias Grünewald's imaging of the crucifixion, and the most profound evocation of the eucharistic real presence in the anti-Scripture that is James Joyce's *Finnegans Wake*.

At the same time, it needs to be acknowledged that the argument holds the deepest intertextual discourse with the philosophical aesthetics of the last two hundred years of the history of European ideas and, above all, in Kant, Hegel, and Heidegger and the recent turn to phenomenology. But such discourse must be regarded as conversation, exchanges of metaphorical and narrative moments rather than as precise exegesis or close interpretation. Yet the exchanges are profound and important for all that. For example, at the very beginning of his great work on fine art, the *Aesthetics* (1835), Hegel draws a radical distinction between natural and artistic beauty. One might think that, reflecting from Kant and the Romantic tradition, greater stress would be placed upon the former, but it is the latter, artistic beauty, that Hegel prioritizes, granting it "superiority" inasmuch as it was "born of the Spirit and born again" (*Aus den Geistens geborene und wiedergeborene*).[24] I am drawn immediately and inevitably to what is perhaps ultimately my central, if largely silent, text, the Fourth Gospel, and the exchange there in 3:5–7 between Jesus and Nicodemus: "Very truly, I tell you, no one can enter the kingdom of God without being born of water and Spirit. What is born of the flesh is flesh, and what is born of the Spirit is spirit. Do not be astonished that I say to you, You must be born from above." If Hegel's suggestion was that artistic beauty was intellectual rather than natural, I would take the echoes of his phrase further and identify true beauty with a process of education and discipline, and a discipline that is as physical and spiritual as much as, though no less than, intellectual—a growing realization of what is and always has been most truly of the body, finally discovered, perhaps, only in its death and resurrection. Thus, in the third of his *Sermons for the Feast of All Saints*, St. Bernard articulates the three stages of the soul's existence—in the corruptible body, without the body and with the glorified body[25]—and yet the souls in bliss remain anxious until they receive their glorified bodies. Christianity has never not insisted on the *bodily* resurrection.[26] Furthermore, and to return to Hegel, Josiah Royce once suggested that his masterwork, *The Phenomenology of Spirit*, was structured like a *Bildungsroman*, a narrative of growth in which

Geist (Spirit) is educated to the discovery of its own identity. And born again in the Spirit, the body is glorified and fully realized in its potential.

Kant's seminal contribution to aesthetics cannot be disregarded, either, for do not the aesthetics of the *Critique of Judgment* have their origins, somehow and by devious, unknown routes, in the perfect equanimity and "passionlessness" of the desert fathers and the writers of the *Philokalia*?[27] And if our wonder begins in the starry heavens and the law within, the greater wonder is that our consciousness thus is open to depths beyond our understanding.[28] The point is that it is possible to become profoundly aware of and open to that which even our awareness has no means of grasping (one is immediately reminded of St. Maximus' phenomenology of consciousness, the mind and even the body having achieved detachment from objects of sense by prayer and the discipline of ascetic practice), and it is only then that we become truly human beings. The poet's sunlit landscape amid the night of nonbeing goes beyond even Kant in its concrete particularity and its realization of the universal in the particular experience—again and probably unconsciously reminiscent of John 1:5: "The light shines in the darkness, and the darkness did not overcome it." As Kant, for whom art was entirely representational, contemplates the presence in his mind of the starry heavens and the moral law, he could not have anticipated the advent of abstract art in the twentieth century, nor could he reflect upon the claim—made by the American artist Barnett Newman—that his great work *Onement I* "represents nothing but itself." But this is surely not so, for just as the true wonder is not the starry heavens themselves but that Kant is aware of them as awesome, Newman's work has a significance beyond itself—perhaps a sense of the oneness of God or, at least, of all being taken back to the central theme of unity in Eckhart himself. It is to this unthinkable moment that his abstract painting can bring our minds and our responses in a true marvel of consciousness. In this sense, to experience the beauty of art is the most profoundly religious experience possible, perhaps even beyond all experience (a moment known to the mystic), and makes possible an apocalypse such as we shall find in the impossible saints of the ascetic tradition, true artists of the body.

If Hegel and Kant have their contributions to make to this discussion of the ascetic body, so does perhaps the greatest thinker of the twentieth century, Heidegger. In his later essays, as we have seen,[29] and well after the writing of *Being and Time*, and long after the Fourth Gospel, Heidegger begins to formulate a language that realizes and embraces the possibility of "dwelling" on earth. Although Heidegger employs theological language, and powerfully so, for such dwelling, the references for the "divinities" for which we wait and hope may be poems, or pictures or even objects—that is, whatever holds the promise of our healing self-transformation.[30] In the Christian theological tradition, we might begin here to employ the language of resurrection. In Heidegger, the prelude to any theological possibility is to move toward a new way of thinking itself and a new way of being—that is, finally, what it is to be fully human. My sense is that within asceticism both in religion and culture, with its deliberate ambiguities of self, its reversals, and its capacity to structure oppositions without permitting of their collapse,[31] and in its enactment of a remembered tradition, there is a kind of prelude to theological possibility after the decay of theology itself—and a possibility that is only present in the act of poetic dwelling.

If deification is the goal of the ascetic life, and the ascetic body exists as far as possible on the cusp between the earthly and the already resurrected body, then what is the resurrection body? We might begin to answer that impossible question through another suggested analogy with modern art. When Marcel Duchamp submitted an inverted urinal to the Society of Independent Artists in 1917 as a work of art, was there any sense in which this was other than an ordinary urinal? Or what is the difference, if any, between a Brillo box and Andy Warhol's celebrated 1964 *Brillo Box*—an exact replica in art of the original design, meaningful only for that moment in time?[32] Or, in the realm of sound, how should we respond to John Cage's project of overcoming the distinction between music and mere everyday noise? The claim to art needs neither to be necessarily enlightening nor even acceptable. Notoriously and obscenely, the Holocaust has been described as the greatest work of art of the twentieth century, while more recently Karlheinz Stockhausen has called the destruction of the World Trade Center in New York as "the greatest work of art ever." Theology has always recognized the demonic possibility and problem at its own heart, how to distinguish God from Satan, and it is sometimes hard, and even impossible, to distinguish its darkest moments and the darkest abyss from the splendor of the divinized body, the body suffering on the cross. But my point here is that nothing in appearance or on the outside need distinguish the work of art from the normal and everyday, or the dark from the light. And yet it *is* different—the result of design and purpose and discipline—an object or a sound that is placed in a particular way and evokes a particular and universal response. Herein, too, is the mystery of the resurrection body—and furthermore, our commonplace body has already been touched by divinity, the divinized and deified body, through the sacraments, which are a genuine and present incorporation into the resurrected body of the ever-suffering Christ. Like the work of art that is apparently indistinguishable from the mere object, in a transfiguration of the commonplace,[33] the saintly body, a citizen of heaven though resident here on earth, through the absolute night of nonbeing, and with infinite discipline (*askesis*), perfects the flesh in a marvel of the final conjunction of the sacred and the profane, in Nicholas of Cusa's phrase, a *coincidentia oppositorum* of light and dark, body and spirit. The difference lies most profoundly in the opening of the abysmal possibility in the body of the nothingness itself, of the realization beyond comprehension of the absolute otherness that alone allows us to be what we are. Thus, St. Antony of Egypt, after years in the tomb, can emerge into the public light of day in Athanasius' account of his life, in full bodily vigor and beauty, sustained by an indifference to and detachment from every passion and partiality and his body already perfected in Christ.

It is this transformation from the mere object to the work of genuine art, and from the descent into flesh to the simultaneous ascent into the divinized body, that provokes the discipline that we know as the way of asceticism as a practice within the Christian tradition and as a continuing, if now largely hidden, feature within our own culture. In the world of art, it is a profound mistake to imagine that proper appreciation and understanding can come immediately and naturally. That is to forget Hegel's distinction between natural and artistic beauty. Just as Vincent van Gogh was utterly neglected in his own time (and among great artists he is by no means alone), we have also had to learn slowly and through the development of a necessary and new language of description to "see" the paintings of the New York School—Jackson Pollock, Newman, and others. But this learning comes not merely as a growth in cleverness or the development of a new theoretical language,[34] for in the same way, the spiritual discipline of asceticism is learned slowly and with infinite patience, as, in the Pauline phrase, the athlete preparing to win the race. The practice of such discipline is deeply physical and practical, an aesthetic education of the body. In the *Philokalia*, St. Gregory of Sinai, a fourteenth-century monk of Mount Athos, in his "Instructions to Hesychasts," emphasizes first the practicalities of physical attitude. The first instruction is "how to sit in the cell," and then in a strong image, "how to hold the mind," how to eat, how to read, and so on.[35] Thus the ascetic body becomes a work of art in the processes of an apocalyptic spirituality moving seamlessly from decay to splendor.

The ascetic body then becomes at once both as commonplace and as mysterious as the body of the risen Jesus in the episode of the Emmaus road (Luke 24:13–35). In Jesus' initial discussion on the road with Cleopas and his companion, "their eyes were kept from recognizing him" (v. 16). Jesus is perceived merely as an unidentified stranger, "as one unknown, without a name,"[36] extraordinarily so given their supposed familiarity with his pre-resurrection self. He is, in other words, utterly commonplace and utterly unknown. Then, in the common exercise of hospitality, Jesus transforms the meal into the sacrament—and immediately departs at the moment of recognition. "When he was at the table with them, he took bread, blessed and broke it, and gave it to them. Then their eyes were opened, and they recognized him; and he vanished from their sight" (vv. 30–31). Only then do they reflect on presence of Christ in the Eucharist, felt but not recognized, in his teaching of the word of Scripture.

This episode of Emmaus lies close to the heart of all my reflections on asceticism. If Hegel ultimately saw the task of philosophers as "to grasp their times as thought," then the task of the true "theologian" is to go beyond even this—that is, to articulate and embody that moment of sacramental realization that is at once a moment of Total Presence and utter negation, illuminated by the text, which alone gives it meaning. It was also Hegel in the *Logic* who equated Being and Nothing whereby "Pure Being and Pure Nothing are. . . . the same," and this only possible moment of true thought can finally only be instantiated in a eucharistic hermeneutic.[37] Recalling the effect of Christ's teaching of the text on Cleopas and his companion ("were not our hearts burning within us?" [v. 32]), the Word remains outside the text, for, in Marion's words, "The referent (unspeakable Word), transgresses the text to interpret it to us, as an interpreter authorized by his full authority (*exousia*): less explaining the text than explaining himself with it, explaining himself through it, he goes right through it, sometimes locator, sometimes referent, saying and said. . . . *The theologian must go beyond the text to the Word, interpreting it from the point of view of the Word.*"[38] Only in the moment of vanishing, a second death, is the Word at once saying and said, and the body, as Word made flesh, fully grasped in thought. Thus, it is in St. Bernard's sermons that the souls of the saints in their "city of rest" await the dissolution of their wills into the will of God, which is the final union of all souls and the realization of each. St. Bernard's two great images—both wonderfully social in their different ways—are the bed and the feast. On their beds of rest, each soul (and yet, the bed *is* the soul) longs for its glorified body for only thereby will their bliss be glorified.[39] And yet, like the solitary monk of the desert, they are individuals incorporated into true community. The image of the feast rather than the bed generates the conviviality of the eucharistic banquet whereby, out of pure love,[40] there is mutual consuming and consumption in the "glue" (*glutino*) of love. "Man and God, because they are not of one substance or of one nature, cannot, indeed, be said to be one; nevertheless, they are with sure and complete truth said [to be] one spirit [1 Cor 6:17], if they adhere to each other with the glue (*glutino*) of love. Certainly, it makes a unity not so much by a coherence (*cohaerentia*) of essence as by a sharing of wills (*conviventia voluntatum*)."[41] This convivial transformation of the will, which is the end of ascetic discipline as a discipline of the will and its offering up to the other, is also a transformation of the saved soul and a transfiguration of the body.

Deeply Origenist,[42] this is also a profound realization of the glorious body in eucharistic celebration—a realization of the body in both its death and its identity with the spirit. In the words of D. G. Leahy, "Before now the word was made flesh. Now the word is spoken in essence, that is, *Christ's imagination is now flesh*. . . . Now Christ suffers death in essence; now Christ is perceived to be embodied in God himself; now the world is seen to be the embodiment in essence of the transcendental passion of existence itself in essence. It is now the essentially transcendental perception of the body itself."[43] This full realization of the body can only be a pure theology, coincident with a pure philosophy, a coincidence of matter and thought that is "an enactment of the body itself in pure thinking."[44] Only thus can the absolute centrality of the Incarnation in the conjoining of body and spirit that is the full realization of both—body as spirit, and spirit as body—be realized. This is the beginning, and it is only and always a beginning, of what Leahy has called "the absolutely unconditioned body" in his book *Foundation: Matter the Body Itself* (1996), and it is the beginning and center of all art and every true act of the imagination. And it is realizable only in that single-minded asceticism in its recognition of the deep ambivalence in religion and culture itself that at once condemns and endorses every possibility in the human, and therefore touches upon what is deepest in our embodied humanity, its fulfillment and its loss.[45]

The French essayist and theoretician Paul Virilio has written of the desert, "The Hebraic tradition manifests two kinds of lack, expressed by two deserts, emerging one from the other, heart of everything, in its heart everything. One is named Shemana, despair and destruction, and the other is Midbar, which is a desert not of dereliction, but instead a field of uncertainty and effort."[46] Thus, we wander in the desert in uncertainty and with terrible effort, but the wandering is at least freedom and possibility, though it remains the freedom of the exile and of the God who remains hidden from us. Is this what it is to dwell poetically, or to touch the world, leaving it seemingly the same as before, for the world has not noticed, but still transforming everything— everything at once the same and yet utterly different?

The next two chapters will explore at more length the theme of dwelling—first in terms of the soul as sacred space, and then in the body, understood as at once profane and sacred, and the body not as a kind of container for the soul, but rather embraced by the sacred space of the soul, which alone opens the possibility of true being in the flesh and in the Word made flesh.

2

THE SOUL AS SACRED SPACE

This second chapter, like others in the book, will be in two quite distinct parts. The first is a kind of personal meditation on the Book and an initial reflection on the mystery of the Word made flesh as a way of establishing in my own experience the dynamics and dialectics of the ascetic way. In offering something of the perhaps inevitably painful appropriation of and by Scripture in the ascetic body (an utterly radical consumption that is quite other than our modern hermeneutical attempts to "understand" or even absorb the Bible), this will form a first attempt to engage with the absolute identification with the scriptural word that is found in the lives of the desert fathers and mothers, and later chapters will develop this more dramatically and fully in traditions of hagiography, art, literature, and poetry. The second part of the chapter will move, via a meditation on the nature of the icon, toward a contemplation of the suffering and sacramental body as the only possible place for the union of body and spirit, and the soul discovered only in the very depths of the body and at its very limit.

Aesthetics of the Word Made Flesh

The ascetic body always and necessarily enacts the deepest ambiguities of our human being and our culture.[1] In symbolic reversals, the ascetic becoming one with the flesh of Christ is simultaneously absolute suffering and its very opposite.[2] As Geoffrey Galt Harpham has observed, "asceticism neither condemns culture nor simply endorses it; it does both. Asceticism, we could say, *raises the issue* of culture by structuring an opposition between culture and its opposite."[3] The ascetic fathers and mothers of the desert simultaneously abandoned society and also sustained society in its deepest being in their solitude. They fought the body and its impulses and realized the deified body that is already present in the sacrament. They even abandoned the books of the church, and yet, in their own enactment of Scripture, they "brought the Book to the Desert, and served as apostles of a textual culture in the domain of the natural."[4] The temptations of St. Antony in the desert are, truly and most deeply, struggles with the Book. Michel Foucault, in writing on Gustave Flaubert, whose reflections on St. Antony's asceticism in his extraordinary work *La Tentation de saint Antoine* (1874), almost literally the work of his life, deeply underlie all that he wrote, above all, *Madame Bovary*, says, "The book—but not any book—is the site of temptation."[5] The book here is God's Scripture, the supreme Book, by which the saint is consumed, and which he consumes in his own bodily being. Creature comforts, indulgence in sexuality, and luxury—the usual and apparent places of human temptation—are but passing moments, finally to be set aside for the terrible sacred space of the ascetic, which is a place of perpetual resistance, reversal, and dialectic and an engagement with, even identification with, the Book in a silent struggle toward pure being, and therefore a pure silence that is alone and finally the true fullness of language in which each word is weighed in all its mystery and its actuality.[6]

The ascetic, like the mystic, continually falls prey to the temptation to write. Even Jesus himself writes, though it is in the sand and therefore unreadable, and now our only access to him is through the text of Scripture, a text finally to be absorbed and devoured. And the only pure writing is writing about writing—a writing that seeks a perfect balance between the outward and the inward in mysterious immanence. But is there another way, even though the end is always failure and disappointment, like the inevitable failure to read, though one reads always and compulsively? Can there be such a thing as pure writing, surely the purest of all temptations, and would that in any sense be readable? But yet its very failure is in the necessary resistance set up to the possibility of reading, a resistance to and in the very theory of reading itself. Absorbing the text, we are silenced by its imperfections, feeding upon it in the sufferings of interpretation until we are one with it in our necessary failure in the avoidance of the greater temptation that is to totalize. As Paul de Man once said, "Technically correct rhetorical readings may be boring, monotonous, predictable and unpleasant, but they are irrefutable."[7] But there, and this is what is so deadly, the struggle ceases. We cease to be, cease to acknowledge the virtuality of the text.[8]

What I am going to write now you might find vaguely embarrassing, or perhaps self-indulgent: a site of struggle. Exposure is always a risk. At the beginning of John Updike's novel *In the Beauty of the Lilies* (it is my favorite of all his titles, shockingly misunderstood, even by many Americans), the Reverend Clarence Wilmot struggles with the Word of his sermon, and loses the battle. He falls prey to temptation, the awful temptation of the preacher to abandon words and be silent. He is preaching in his church on hell—and is himself in hell: "The words seemed to parch Clarence's throat, which had become fearsomely dry. . . . Clarence felt his voice giving out, closing up. The effort to push words out into the great space of the church, with its clutch of unresponsive listeners, was taxing his chest; his lungs felt to be heaving within him. . . . He could speak no more. He felt strangled, his voice scorched to less than a whisper, a dry web stuck in his throat. . . . For moments that approached eternity he hung there, in the pulpit."[9] When I first read those words, I could hardly go on to read the rest of the words of the novel that filled another four hundred pages or so. I candidly admit, having myself been a priest for almost thirty years, to know absolutely that terrible experience of speaking or, should I say, enacting in blind obedience, the words of the Eucharist in public service (it only occurs for me with the Anglican liturgy in the Book of Common Prayer and not at all in the modern simplifications of its language) and finding my throat closing and my tongue almost unable to form the sounds. The sense is utterly physical, a moment of pure panic. It is the closest I know to hell, and not because of fear of public embarrassment, for that is the last thought in my mind. Here, and here only, one's whole being wishes to stop and cease speaking, to give in to the terrible negative mystery of the words. That I have actually given in as yet is neither cause for satisfaction nor a lessening of the anticipation that it will surely happen again. I do not say the words of the great thanksgiving prayer joyfully, for they are the stuff of nightmare. And that, perhaps, is close to the deepest moment of pure theological enactment, not an affirmation of doctrine of even belief—to say the words is terrible, but not to say them even worse and unthinkable. One realizes finally that, to be a priest, one must learn above all the dark truth of *kenosis*, of utter self-emptying, and necessarily to be a false priest—and the poet Friedrich Hölderlin teaches us this kenotic truth in his poem, *Wie wenn am Feiertage . . .* :

> The false priest that I am, to sing,
> For those who have ears to hear, the warning song.
> There.[10]

Or one begins to appreciate the extraordinary vision of Nikos Kazantzakis, whose novel *The Last Temptation* is a realization that it is not Jesus'
overcoming of temptation on the cross, but his perpetual bearing of it that
is necessary: that he must become the Christ whom even Paul, in the book,
rejects, and who is therefore utterly irrelevant. The greater and more inevitable blasphemy even than that is to crawl back onto the cross that Christianity
has constructed for him in its theological narratives.

I am ever more convinced that Fyodor Dostoevsky's novel *Crime and
Punishment* is one of the greatest works of theology ever written. Raskolnikov
is a murderer, utterly guilty, and we only know him in his punishment. The
text of the novel can never do more than suggest, in its very final words, the
possibility of a new story that cannot ever be told, for we do not know that
story. And even to reach the realization of the possibility that such a story
may be possible, though utterly silent, we must necessarily wrestle with the
complexities of the text of Raskolnikov's crime and its punishment. Like St.
Antony of the desert, like ourselves, Raskolnikov only has his present story,
for the next involves the passing into another world that even the penitent
yet still guilty soul can only know as an unknown reality, in the apocalyptic Christ known only to a few in the history of Christian theology. Prince
Nekhlyudov in Leo Tolstoy's *Resurrection*, his last and most deeply underrated
novel, like Raskolnikov, is finally left in Siberia with the New Testament in his
hands and only the vision of "hundreds and thousands of degraded human
beings locked in noisome prisons by indifferent generals,"[11] and only the possibility of a future locked within the eternal present. For Dostoevsky and
Tolstoy, that present must always present itself as something insuperable—a
temptation to be resisted, the resolution always and only enfolded in the as
yet untold story. As Ippolit in Dostoevsky's *The Idiot*, describes the ghastly
image of Hans Holbein's *The Body of the Dead Christ in the Tomb*, he reflects,
"And if, on the eve of the crucifixion, the Master could have seen what He
would look like when taken from the cross, would he have mounted the cross
and died as he did? This question, too, you can't help asking yourself as you
look at the picture."[12] Has Holbein realized that here is, in fact, a temptation
beyond our means: let us not be tempted beyond our capacity, but deliver us
from such evil? So we pray, but the truth is quite other.

Later in this chapter, we shall begin to encounter the eucharistic body
in its raw fleshliness, its insistent consumption of the broken body and its
bloody fluid. It is only through this body, consumed and consuming, that we
can know anything like a soul or spirit and, at the same time, any genuine
theological language. Yet is an honest theology in any sense even remotely

possible? I am now more than ever convinced that I can no longer honestly speak about theology or even speak theologically, but can only begin
to approach the possibility of entering into the place of temptation through
language that is at once and necessarily a full realization and an utter denial
of theology itself. In other words, such language can only be truly liturgical or
even approach the form of prayer itself as the language of pure being. Another
way of putting this might be to describe it as a poetics; but in any event such
language must provoke and instantiate a dialectical process of utter resistance
to the temptations of the book in an absolute *kenosis* of reading, which is
the only possibility of reading at all. That is to say, reading, and therefore, the
reader must deliberately divest him or herself of all possible claims over
the text, especially and above all the scriptural text resisting every possible
textual seduction of beauty or meaning, in order to enter into the text itself
and thereby overcome it, and be overcome by it in an utter defeat that is the
only possible means of victory. Thus, St. Antony and his fellow desert fathers
and mothers were perfectly prepared to sell even the Bible inasmuch as they
might claim, with perfect blasphemy, finally to embody it. One thinks also of
Meister Eckhart at his trial in Avignon and his "invitation to the soul to give
up the nothingness of its created self in order to become the divine Nothing
that is also all things."[13]

I am speaking here of nothing less than the spaces of the soul, incorporating yet also beyond both mind and body, as the only place of perpetual dialectic, a struggle that acknowledges at once and simultaneously both absolute
negation and absolute affirmation. But this is never to be regarded as in any
way a reconciliation, for it is the darkest of all places, and I am not speaking
here of that coordination of the apophatic and cataphatic as antithetical and
yet complimentary registers such as we find even in St. Maximus the Confessor and other irrepressible defenders of the faith, for in the dialectical soul of
the deep ascetic there is neither complimentarity nor any possible resolution.

Edith Wyschogrod, Caroline Walker Bynum, and others have written
on hagiographic texts as narratives between history and fiction that allow
the reader to experience the "imperative power" of the life of the saint.[14]
Hagiography, Wyschogrod insists, is not intended to elicit replication in the
lives of more ordinary people, but rather to contribute to the building up of
their moral and spiritual life as a kind of bridge between the earthly and the
heavenly realms in both body and soul. She refers explicitly to the life of St.
Mary of Egypt, which will be one of the subjects of chapter 5 of this book.
Even more anciently, the parable of St. Antony's life precisely and absolutely
denies us any participation in his Interior Mountain, which is utterly solitary;

though, at the same time, it necessarily confronts us with the solitariness of pure being as an absolute self-emptying that is the only possible ground of any true community divested of all those forms of discourse that serve only to comfort us in the face of our actual and real divisions. And only through language itself and its textual temptations is a true silence to be found, a silence that I can only faintly realize, and there alone, as I struggle and stammer with the terrible words of the Eucharist as they enact the being present here in our midst of a total absence. Who can dare speak such words but only the false priest? And herein, but only in the singular obedience of utter transcendence to the point of death, the final great temptation, is the final and painful leveling of the transcendent in an immanence that is the only possible advent of Total Presence. Thus, the greatest image we have in Western art of the true glory of God is to be seen in the unbearable suffering Christ on the cross of Mathias Grünewald, beyond which there is nothing, absolutely nothing. In his commentary on Grünewald's art, Harpham writes of its encouragement of "an ascetic practice of reading" that finally accomplishes a self-transcendence in the category of the unrepresentable. Whether it be in the sufferings of Christ or the temptations of St. Antony, art can only depict their unintelligibility in the sufferings of the body, so that "the *failure* of art, not its perfection, produces human figures that resemble angels: in such defeats we are closest to God."[15] In Eckhart's "abstractedness" (*Abgesheidenheit*), beyond even humility and charity, there is the spontaneous infusion of the Word and the soul as the soul gives birth to the Word. But it is a generation of and within a perpetual struggle even in the body that demands a totality to death itself, and only then, through such suffering, is the Word freed from the temptations of both body and spirit so that it can be pure Word, without any meaning or reference or illusion—a speaking of utter silence. Thus, St. Antony speaks to us most clearly from the silence of the Interior Mountain, from the book that initiates the flight of all possible temptations and, at the same time, is itself every temptation.

Even at this stage, I am perplexed as to how to proceed. The soul as sacred space longs for a silence that can only possibly be realized in the being of pure matter. Flaubert's Antony concludes triumphantly with these words: "Would that I had wings, a carapace, a shell,—that I could breathe out smoke, wield a trunk,—make my body writhe,—divide myself everywhere,—be in everything,—emanate with all odours,—develop myself like the plants,—flow like water,—vibrate with sound—shine like light,—assume all forms—penetrate each atom—descend to the very bottom of matter,—be matter itself."[16] Pure being is the very essence of incarnation. But for us the vision remains only in resistance, in the coincidence of opposites that remain stubbornly opposed in the being of matter, in the temptation to be what we are not and known only in what we are. It remains in the realization of an annihilation of everything into a Nothingness that is not the opposite of everything, but rather the realization of a totality of pure being, without remainder, without essence, utter facticity, pure joy in resistance. It is the darkest hell, and it is the brightest heaven of invention. As in the book opened by St. Antony that initiates the flight of all possible temptations, in Foucault's words, "Saint Antony was able to triumph over the Eternal Book in becoming the languageless movement of pure matter; Bouvard and Pécuchet triumph over everything alien to books, all that resists the book, by transforming themselves into the continuous movement of the book. The book opened by Saint Antony, the book that initiated the flight of all possible temptations, is indefinitely extended by these two simple men; it is prolonged without end, without illusion, without greed, without sin, without desire."[17] Perhaps the closest we have to the saints with whom I am concerned in modern literature is the figure of Sebastian in *Brideshead Revisited* (1945): a man finally who becomes nothing, yet of whom it is said, "I've seen others like him, and I believe they are very near and dear to God."[18] A fool, a failure, lost to the world, perhaps an ascetic in his way: "If he lives long enough, generations of missionaries in all kinds of remote places will think of him as a queer old character who was somehow part of the Home of their student days, and remember him in their masses."[19]

The Body as the Only Place of the Soul

Tom Altizer wrote to me of my book *The Sacred Desert* (2004),

> I think I detect one crucial potentiality that is here all too partially fulfilled. And that is the body, and the depths of body itself, depths which are finally "spirit" as well as body, and yet depths evoked only by an absolute desert, and perhaps unreal and invisible apart from that desert. Ultimately I think that this can only be an evocation of the depths of the Body of the Godhead, and if that Body is a Crucified Body, perhaps it can be most real to us through everything that you call forth as an absolute desert, and not simply a sacred desert in the common sense, but a sacred desert that is an absolutely profane desert.

It was from this observation that the present book eventually emerged as an all too inadequate response to Altizer's insights on the sacred and the profane: the body as desert, as book—and as icon. The body as the only place of the soul.

All my theological thinking to date has centered in one way or another on the theme of *kenosis*—that "emptying," which finds its primary Christian thinking in the great hymn of Philippians 2:6–11, that celebrates how God in Christ Jesus, "though he was in the form [ἐν μορφῇ] of God. . . . emptied himself [ἑαυτὸν ἐκένωσεν], taking the form of a slave." The reference is almost certainly to Isaiah 53:12–14, the account of the Suffering Servant who "poured himself out to death," an action recognized by St. Chrysostom as the sacrificial self-giving of the royal Son, "lived out physically on earth, but also revealing a quality intrinsic to divine love."[20]

This understanding of the great Pauline hymn finds its confirmation in the great iconoclastic debate that raged in Constantinople in the early ninth century C.E. and, in particular, in the second of the *Libri Tres Antirrhetici* of the patriarch St. Nicephorus (758–828). For St. Nicephorus, like his father before him, a staunch defender of images, the icon of the face of Christ is a memorial of *kenosis*, the word used by the Greek Fathers to describe the incarnation itself: to incarnate, to empty himself, to pour himself out into the physical form of a slave.[21] In describing the icon, the crucial distinction is between inscription and circumscription—in St. Nicephorus' words, "A man is inscribed in the image that represents him, but he is not circumscribed by it."[22] The image is unable to circumscribe the nature of the man, and Christ's *uncircumscribability* in the icon, his very absence acknowledged through the image, is the sign of his resurrection. The icon is not a representation of Christ's face, but rather a threshold, a "blessedly vacant object that respects the uncircumscribability of its object."[23]

The closest modern discussion to St. Nicephorus' discourse on the icon is to be found in Jean-Luc Marion's book *God Without Being* (1982), which acknowledges that in the icon, which is not the result of a vision, but rather provokes one, the invisible always remains invisible: "It is not invisible because it is omitted by the aim. . . . but because it is a matter of rendering visible this invisible as such—the unenvisageable."[24] This statement is made in the context of an argument that frees God, even as we perceive the face in the icon, from the horizon of being, a freedom realized for Marion in the realm of *agape*, or charity.[25] For now, I would link St. Nicephorus' perception of the icon to the most profound understanding of the mystery of the Word made flesh— that is, in the *sacrificial body* in its mysterious divine-human spatiality acknowledging the inscription of word, but even in that inscription transcending the circumscription, its deepest presence an absence and a freedom from being (i.e., the shift from the image [inscribed] to the likeness [uncircumscribed] of God without Being). All too frequently and in contradiction to this, the history of

Christian theology has too readily tended to pervert the iconic mystery of John 1:14, obsessed instead with the flesh made Word—that is, the circumscription of the body in the definitions of language—bodies perceived as trapped and controlled by defining words: male, female, virgin, hero, and so on.[26] In theology's obsession with the body in all its imperfections, its ancient suspicion of bodily functions and its corseting of what is regarded as acceptable bodily behavior, the mystery of the incarnation has been radically reversed. What needs to be recovered is a genuine and radical hermeneutics of the body, freed from the deathly impositions that have been laid on it and freed to be the proper temple of the soul with which it is one, embracing the soul but more deeply embraced by it.

The most profoundly Christocentric visionary of the past two hundred years in literature remains the poet William Blake, who presents us with an absolutely apocalyptic Jesus.[27] That is, he offers us a Jesus to whom we can relate only imaginatively, and who is therefore present (though simultaneously utterly absent) without a shred of ethical implication, imposition, or circumscription. In Blake's words at the beginning of *Jerusalem* (1804–20), "The Spirit of Jesus is continual forgiveness of Sin: he who waits to be righteous before he enters into the Saviour's kingdom, the Divine Body, will never enter there. I am perhaps the most sinful of men. I pretend not to holiness."[28] The truly imaginative system of Blake, in its very apocalypticism, separates him from almost all previous Christian theology but locates him as an artist in an aesthetic appreciation of the body that is most profoundly also to be discovered in the desert fathers and mothers of early Christian monasticism. The asceticism of the desert as a "training" and perfection rather than a destruction of the body gave rise to a "body of plenitude,"[29]—that is, a plenitude that overcomes not the degraded materiality of the body but signifies precisely a lack in it that is at once spiritual and corporeal. The consequence of the extraordinary acts of self-denial engaged in by the saints of the desert is not the decay or renunciation of the body but precisely the very opposite, its perfection in a bodily plenitude that overcomes the limits of time and space, and therefore, by *ascesis* or training, the body realizes the *kenosis* or self-emptying that is nothing less than the mystery of the incarnation itself. In Peter Brown's words, "through the Incarnation of Christ, the highest God had reached down to make even the body capable of transformation."[30] The body of the ascetic then becomes an exemplary body, capable of radical transformation and often described in the early literature of the desert fathers in metaphors of light (the face of Abbot Pambo, for example, shone like lightning[31]) exemplifying the glory that was lost in Eden and recovered in Christ, the light that enlightens the world. It was a transformation capable of breaking social order and changing culture itself and its very images.

In this aesthetics of asceticism is redescribed a bodily perfection, indeed a redescription of the body as signifier[32] that is a reimagining of how the body is to be *read* as a text, though it is precisely read as a dazzling absence, invisible and unreal apart from the absolute desert sought by the ascetic, both external and internal. It is thus absolutely the opposite of the constructions and deconstructions of the body that have constituted, for example, the history of sexuality and gender in Western culture. In his book *Making Sex* (1990), the historian Thomas Laqueur has described the "masterplots" of Western sexuality. In the first, and most pervasive, woman is perceived as an imperfect version of man, her anatomy and physiology construed and perceived accordingly, and the victim of medical thinking since antiquity.[33] The nature of sex and gender difference is not actually the consequence of our biology but of "our needs in speaking about it"—that is, they are linked closely to questions of perception and aesthetics (the cultivation of the "body beautiful"). Such aesthetics are precisely the very opposite of the aesthetics of asceticism, though historically the Christian tradition, with its historical obsession with the body of the perfect young man Jesus, has habitually been addicted to a false aesthetic—deeply, though it has to be admitted, often uneasily, gendered. We might think, for example, of the nineteenth-century fashion of the "pale Galilean," the epitome of Aryan beauty and preaching, in Ernest Renan's words, "*la délicieuse théologie de l'amour*,"[34] strangely though unobtainably attractive, its sexual ambivalence apparent to art in portrayals of the encounter with Mary Magdalene in the garden where the resurrection body of Jesus is proffered but with the sign "Do not touch" (John 20:17).

Christianity has always promoted an aesthetic of sex, though with a guilty conscience and terrible results, and buried its deepest insights into the incarnation of the Word as *kenosis* and the iconic image of Christ as empty of his presence and full of his absence.[35] Blake, as we shall see shortly, as both artist and poet stood in profound contradiction to this failure of the church in his achievement that Camille Paglia describes as the "violent yoking together of two opposing systems, the Bible and the visual arts."[36] Blake's radical vision is actually far more necessarily violent even than that, but the point will do for now, not least for its impact on the question of the hermeneutics of the body. For a recovery of an aesthetics of asceticism, we need to turn to the complexity of the sacramental body as it faces martyrdom, perhaps best portrayed in art in the fading form of Leonardo da Vinci's Christ of the *Last Supper* (1497) and the response to it of the disciples, finely described by the art historian Leo Steinberg. Here is the body on the very edge of human particularity, facing disintegration and completion in the universal, a body to be at once consumed and all-consuming. "Of course, the *Cenacolo* represents the announcement of the betrayal, the foreshow of imminent martyrdom, Christ signing the debt of his mortal nature. But in the collapsing duration which this picture is, the subject is as fully the grant of his sacramental body. The disciples, every one of them preordained, respond in accord with their natures, their faith, their forthcoming Communion, and the apostolate they inherit. . . . Leonardo's Christ gives himself to the world, as if the words *corpus meum* filled space itself, as if the space were the costume he wears."[37] The sacramental body seems to fill all of space itself, an *incarnatio continua* and a universal liturgical body invisible in the garments of space and time, and yet it finds its particular and specific Christian origins in the restrained gospel accounts of the passion and crucifixion. Martin Hengel, Stephen Moore, and others[38] have graphically indicated how the horrific, individual sufferings undergone by the victim of the Roman punishment of crucifixion are almost, though not quite, excised from the literary narratives of the gospels, and the terrible torture of the body virtually eliminated by the evangelists' almost bland phrases—"and after flogging Jesus he handed him over to the crucified"; "they crucify him"; and so on. What is going on here as the tortured body is embraced by the gospel text, almost eliminated, and reaches out to sacramental universality?

It is complex, highly ambiguous, and has had disastrous consequences within Christian theology and liturgy in what is ultimately a literary and artistic aesthetic that universalizes and finally undermines what the aesthetics of asceticism and the lives of the desert fathers recovered—a battle with their own bodies that realizes the absolutely necessary and particular *kenosis*, the "nothingness" that is at the heart of true being. In them the text is absorbed rather than vice versa. If the writers of the gospels (perhaps understandably) allow us too easily to grasp the narrative of the passion, making it too bearable because readable, then other clues in the New Testament properly return us to a more deeply profane, sacramental moment—the sacred meal as eating human flesh and drinking human blood: the Word made flesh, the bloody flesh governing the text, and not its opposite in literary aesthetics. This insistent consumption of broken body and bloody fluid, ultimately utterly and horrifyingly specific, is met in the symbolic nature of the deed: the specific and the symbolic is what makes it sacramental, a "real presence" only by virtue of its absence. Elaine Pagels makes the point powerfully in her book *Beyond Belief* (2003), reminding us that even "Tertullian cannot dispel the shocking fact that the Christian 'mystery' invites initiates to eat human flesh—*even if only symbolically*. Pagans might be repelled by the practice of instructing newcomers to drink wine as human blood, but devout Jews, whose very definition of *kosher* (pure) food requires that it be drained of all blood, would be especially disgusted."[39] Pagels acknowledges that indeed the Eucharist might be seen as typical of ancient cult worship, though Justin Martyr gets around this in his first *Apology* by suggesting that the cults are actually only imitations of Christian worship: the Eucharist was insistently the real thing! This was the real consumption of a real body—symbolically and in the enacted text of the liturgy—the enactment of what Paul calls the "scandal," the paradox that in the depths of human defeat is found the victory in death of God.[40]

But it is precisely at this paradoxical point that almost the whole of the Christian theological tradition has failed in its retreat from a genuine apocalypticism, which is the revealing of what remains at the same time absolutely hidden, and possible only in the utter tragedy of the God who alone can enter into the darkness of his own Being, and thereby become utterly other than himself, utterly Godless in an act of "ultimately inner divine devolution."[41] This is possible only in the body of Jesus, flayed, dissected, and lovingly eaten. If Tertullian remains committed to the shocking fact of the mystery of the Eucharist, eaten symbolically and sacramentally, its dreadful actuality is revealed more shockingly in the perverse freedoms of fiction, from Euripides' *The Bacchae* to the consumption of the body of Jean-Baptiste Grenouille at the end of Patrick Süskind's novel *Perfume* (1986). "In very short order, the angel was divided into thirty pieces, and every animal in the pack snatched a piece for itself. . . . When the cannibals found their way back together after disposing of their meal, no one said a word. . . . to eat a human being? They would never, so they thought, have been capable of anything that horrible. . . . Though the meal lay rather heavy on their stomachs, their hearts were definitely light. All of a sudden there were delightful, bright flutterings in their dark souls. . . . For the first time they had done something out of Love."[42] Even to read this passage is hard enough, shocking and indigestible to the sensitive reader. But if to consume an angel (and a murderer) is utterly nauseating, what of Christ himself? Yet only in this utterly profane, liturgical moment of pure *kenosis*, of pure consumption as sacrament of the actual body, can be glimpsed the kingdom of God as "not a royal sovereignty, not an imperial nor even a messianic reign, but rather a full abolition or reversal of all given conditions."[43] This is indeed the marriage of heaven and hell and the root of Blake's demand that all humankind be one and identical with Christ (only possible in the fleshly consuming and being consumed that is

Eucharist) and only possible in the purest of all aesthetics, in the purity of the *desert absolu,* in the body of the soul enlightened and free from blemish and "neither constricted by grief, nor relaxed by pleasure, nor affected by either laughter or dejection."[44] This is why Blake is the most Christocentric of our poets, following in the path of the dialectical mysticism of Meister Eckhart and Jakob Boehme.

But it is necessary to translate these meditations on the body further into a moment's reflection on that favorite subject of contemporary art theory— that is, the gaze. Feminist criticism, in particular, has acclimatized us to the tradition of the male gaze that has coded the female body for display, just as gender, as we have seen in the work of Laqueur, has been coded to ensure the dominance of heterosexual procreative sex.[45] But when art dares to be transgressive of its own aesthetics and presents us, the viewers, with the very simulacrum of the real body, then viewing becomes a problem, an indecency. How then do we truly look at ourselves and the gendered, decoded body of the other when provoked and paradoxically at the same time unprotected by artistic rules of the aesthetic, the body seen in an uncomfortable act of appro-priation that "is not one that takes place in Spirit, but is conditioned by its quality as an external object"?[46] Peter Brooks, in his book *Body Work* (1993), recounts his experience of attending the opening of an art show of the works of the artist John De Andrea in Paris:

> At which it became evident that the spectators, myself included were embarrassed by their own looking. Here were a dozen or so sculptures of nudes, mostly women. The poses were casual, everyday postures, the bodies young and attractive. They were reproduced with astonishing fidelity: flesh tones, folds of the skin, fingernails, pubic hair . . . This art reminded one of Madame Tussaud's waxworks, but without the illustrational, anecdotal aim of the waxworks . . . Such was not, of course, the standard of judgement for classical sculpture, where the body is conceived to be the vehicle of expres-sion. . . . The very simulacrum of the real body makes you ask what you are supposed to do with them. They almost appear to be full-sized dolls for some sort of regressive adult play.[47]

I am reminded in this disturbing description of human figures, seen purely externally and for what dark purpose, of the crucified Christ standing glossily on Christian altars, or hung around the neck on delicate silver chains, cosily aestheticized and preserved from the bloodied body of the crucified that "sat-isfied the primitive lust for revenge and the sadistic cruelty of individual rul-ers and of the masses."[48] Only through the deliberately reversed, ambiguous and contradictory aesthetics of the ascetic can we even begin to gaze with love on such a bloodied figure. De Andrea's figures, on the other hand, render us embarrassed by our own looking—on their purely external realism we look with fascination, not love, seeing what is forbidden and unclothed, and there is an inarticulate, obscene, necessary truth in their almost banal naturalism. All the more hermeneutically problematic, though entirely reversed, is the particular profane obscenity of the lacerated body of Christ, prompting an indecent theology that must first endure the collapse of the grand narratives of the Christian tradition, just as Marcella Althaus-Reid has recounted the collapse of the grand narratives in Latin America: "Precisely, the resolution of perplexity (plurality) in Latin America was done in material ways. 'From some people the buttocks were cut, to others the thighs, or the arms. . . . cutting hands, noses, tongues and other pieces from the body, eaten alive by animals and (cutting) women's breasts.'"[49] All of these body parts belong to individual people and their physical and deeply interior sufferings. And yet the tendency of the religions of the book, though steeped in the blood of wholesale slaughter and darkly fascinated with the body as object, has been to feel queasy when faced with the blood of life: "Our tradition has helped to rub out the living bodies." Seeing bodies as objects, merely externally, we forget the body as it rejoices and suffers in its carnality, as the temple of the soul, and embraced by the soul, and that "at the heart of the creation, there takes place always, in endless quantities and qualities of difference, deformation and transformation, the *incarnation*."[50] Therefore, the early Christians, seemingly, and with deep wisdom, preferred and stuck to the stories of the sacramental eating flesh and drinking blood (however absorbed and dried in the later ceremonial traditions of the church), to the tamer versions to be found in noncanonical works, such as the *Didache*.[51] The fathers and mothers of the desert *became* in their own ascetic flesh the eucharistic body, consumed and consuming. At the same time, the earliest art of the Christians, on the walls of the catacombs, was not aesthetically refined images of the cross—they came much later—but pictures of Jesus the deliverer and images of bodily release and transformation: Jonah emerging from the whale, Daniel freed from the lions, Lazarus leaping new-born from the tomb. In the *Apocalypse of Peter* (a Gnostic work discovered at Nag Hammadi in 1945), we read of Jesus "glad and laughing on the cross," an apocalyptic image of the soul being of light hidden and revealed in the obscenity of suffering: sick, too hard to bear, lost for two thousand years in the sands of the deep desert.[52] Yet the poet Blake knew of this apocalyptic Jesus; in Altizer's words, "Already in the *Songs of Innocence* there is an underlying vision of the omnipresence of the passion of Jesus, and as Blake gradually but decisively came to see that passion in every concrete pain and sorrow, he was prepared to celebrate the naked horror of experience as an epiphany of the crucified lamb of God."⁵³ In a supplementary and abandoned plate designed for the *Songs of Experience* (1794), Blake describes "A Divine Image," the words within an engraving showing Los, poet and craftsman, forging the sun as the symbol of imagination, into the words of the poem.

> Cruelty has a Human Heart
> And Jealousy a Human Face
> Terror, the Human Form Divine
> And Secrecy, the Human Dress
> The Human Dress, is forged Iron
> The Human Form, a fiery Forge.
> The Human Face, a Furnace seal'd
> The Human Heart, its hungry Gorge.⁵⁴

Into this abyss and gorge of humanity alone plunges the Godhead, emptying the self in a truly kenotic venture that is the death of God and an obliteration that is at the same time the Total Presence of the body. It is an absolute self-consumption, a realization of flesh and blood memorialized in the impossibility of the eucharistic feast. It is the wholly ascetic and necessary meeting of the universal and the particular that can only be an apocalyptic event freed from the demythologizing of the theologians who have transformed the "apocalyptic Jesus into a mysterious and humanly empty Word"⁵⁵—the flesh made Word. At its heart there is a dialectical mysticism that Blake and some others of the Romantic poets and thinkers knew, and has surfaced only now and then in the traditions of Western art but has almost universally been absent from what Steinberg has described as the "profound, willed, and sophisticated" oblivion of our modernity: "It is the price paid by the modern world for its massive historic retreat from the mythical [mystical] grounds of Christianity."⁵⁶

In his two volume work *The Art of the West* (1970), Henri Focillon suggests that the age of the "Baroque Gothic" was coterminous with the birth of the mystical experience.⁵⁷ Tom Conley, in his foreword to Gilles Deleuze's book *The Fold*, referring to Focillon, describes it thus: "It is characterized. . . . by an individual's account of his or her voyage to and from an ineffably universal event, which set the body in a trance, and which has left marks, scars, or other physical evidence that confirm the individual's tale of passage. The mystical venture convinces because no language can be said to represent what it means. It is tantamount, in part, to what . . . might [be called] an *event*: it may not have an empirical or historical basis, but it happens to be the virtual sensation of a somatic moment of totalization and dispersion."[58] This description of baroque art, folded and enfolded in hidden places that reveal and conceal, strangely echoes the literature and experiences of the desert saints, whose lives truly embodied Christ and who found the true union of the body and spirit in the actuality of the deep desert and the interior mountain, the meeting of the particular and the universal, citizens of heaven though here on earth. Here, in their bodies and souls and in the aesthetics of the ascetic, they realized the utter darkness of God,[59] revealed in the crucified and consumed body of the apocalyptic Jesus, who is the realization and negation of the individual in the universal and the final meeting of the profane and the sacred. To confess this is to return to St Nicephorus' recognition of the icon not as a representation but as a threshold that respects the uncircumscribability of its object, rendering visible the invisible and the unenvisageable. It is to realize the true silence of love, "man revealed to himself by the originary and radical modality of the erotic"[60] in a language that moves beyond the tautological into pure silence, attempting the impossible.

3

The Body, Sacred and Profane

I do not love by proxy, nor through a go-between, but in the flesh, and this
flesh is one only with me. The fact that I love cannot be distinguished from
me, any more than I would want, in love, to distinguish myself from that
which I love.
                                    —Jean-Luc Marion, *The Erotic Phenomenon*

Any truly genuine experience of the body must be a genuinely dialectical
experience, a realization or enactment of embodiment and at the same time
a total transfiguration of incarnation, always and at the same time what it is
not and thereby realizing its proper being beyond being. The body is utterly
soul, the soul body. Origen was aware of this in his pure heterodoxy, which is
nevertheless the only total theological system created by the ancient world.[1]
At the same time, there is no possible division between myself and my flesh
and, even more importantly, between myself and the beloved other. As John
Donne writes of lovers, profane and sacred, in his poem "The Ecstasy,"

> To our bodies turn we then, that so
> 　　Weak men on love revealed may look;　＼
> Love's mysteries in souls do grow,
> 　　But yet the body is his book.
>
> And if some lover, such as we,
> 　　Have heard this dialogue of one,
> Let him still mark us, he shall see
> 　　Small change, when we'are to bodies gone.[2]

Thus, the soul is read in the text of the body in a revelation of love seen in
pure, erotic embodiment. There can be no division between the sacred and

31

the profane body, or in the relationship between body and spirit. This is to acknowledge the endless ambiguities of being "in the body" and the disturbing, dark connection between life and death in eroticism and, at the same time, the Crucified Body that remains fixedly at the heart of Christianity, the religion of the incarnate Word.

At the beginning of her essay "Holbein's Dead Christ," Julia Kristeva quotes at length from Fyodor Dostoevsky's novel *The Idiot*, referring to the description by Ippolit, a minor character in the book, but with traits similar to Prince Myshkin himself, of Hans Holbein the Younger's 1522 disturbing painting *The Body of the Dead Christ in the Tomb*. The picture is of a cadaver just after the moment of death and before *rigor mortis* has set in, and the narrative emphasizes the utter desolation such a body, now offered to us in art, must have brought on those who had taken it from the cross and now gazed on it. "Looking at that picture, you get the impression of nature as some enormous, implacable, and dumb beast, or, to put it more correctly, much more correctly, though it may seem strange, as some huge engine of the latest design, *which has senselessly seized, cut to pieces, and swallowed up—impassively and unfeelingly—a great and priceless Being*."[3] Even here, in this deadly industrial image of nature, we find the sacrificial body torn apart into pieces and consumed, an image of the Eucharist even here, the divine being dying into an implacable creation. The image of the tortured body caught between life and death, says Ippolit, is beyond what is bearable, beyond any possible contemplation, beyond even the bearing of God. We see in the painting a disfigured body that has just passed from life to death by the most ghastly means imaginable, an image so awful that even Jesus himself would have rejected the enormity on which we are asked to gaze and avoided the cross. Yet we are reminded also of the first revelation to the fourteenth-century anchoress Dame Julian of Norwich, when she sees "the red blood trickling down from under the garland, hot, fresh and plentiful, just as it did at the time of his passion when the crown of thorns was pressed on to the blessed head of God-and-Man, who suffered for me"[4]; or her contemporary Richard Rolle's image of the wounds as text—"More yet, Sweet Jesu, thy body is like a book written all with red ink; so is thy body all written with red wounds"[5]; or Isaac Watts in the eighteenth century bidding us, "*See* from his head, his hands, his feet / Sorrow and love flow mingled down."[6] In this terrible contemplation, have Holbein and Dostoevsky hit on the true horror that simply asks too much of us—a true descent into hell wherein the necessary gaze on Christ's dereliction is our participation in his own Godforsakeness, his total *kenosis*, an impossible gazing at the absolutely sacred, the absolutely profane, and indeed, therefore, a radical reversal of Christian consciousness?

This radical reversal is in fact a deep return to the spirit,[7] precisely in its very insistence on the body in a manner of Eckhartian detachment that the Christian tradition itself has rarely, if ever, been able to tolerate beyond a small company of ragged mystics, poets, or idiots, like Prince Myshkin. It is realized, as Kristeva puts it, in a body that is "inaccessible, distant, but without a beyond."[8] In this lack of a beyond, utterly immanent yet wholly transcendent, lies the sacramental heart of the insistent "real presence" of the Eucharist in which, even from the time of St. Paul, the followers of Christ took the intolerable flesh into their own bodies in the Eucharist even as they were consumed by it. Yet the oblivion of theology itself has tended to obliterate this scandal, the scandal of the crucified, unwatchable body, the body in hell, that yet we take into ourselves. Against the background of reflecting on the images of Holbein, Mathias Grünewald and Dostoevsky, I first encountered the final words of Margaret Miles' recent book *The Word Made Flesh: A History of Christian Thought* (2005) on the unity of the body and the soul. She writes, "The religion of the incarnate Word consists of the struggle to 'keep body and soul together.' It is a *project* of comprehending, incorporating, and participating in the 'Body of Christ.' Addressing the deep human longing for integrity of body and soul, Christianity makes the wildly counter-evidential, counter-cultural claim that 'in my flesh shall I see God.' The meaning of that claim can never be definitively articulated, but it forms and informs historical and contemporary Christians who seek to understand it, not only conceptually, but also, and more importantly, *in the life*."[9] I find myself at once attracted and repelled by this statement, for it contains profound truth, but at the same time, its claims for the Christianity of the church and Christendom must be almost wholly untenable. For this struggle, this *project*, involves a being in the depths of the body that is profane beyond belief if salvation is to remain for us in the absolute self-emptying, or *kenosis*, of Christ's body. What then is this struggle for the integrity of body and soul? What does it mean?

"In my flesh I shall see God." The words are, of course, from Job 19:26: "and after my skin has been thus destroyed, then in my flesh I shall see God." Job's meaning seems pretty clear—Job will see God with his own eyes, even after his skin has withered away. But in the English we can read the phrase in at least two ways: "I shall see God in this flesh of mine." Or, "When I see God I shall be clothed in my flesh"—either way (as in Job), there is the Christian insistence on the resurrection and persistence of the flesh, the odd perversity of which is beautifully caught by the American poet Jorie Graham in her poem "At Luca Signorelli's Resurrection of the Body":

> See how they hurry
>   to enter
> their bodies,
>   these spirits.
> Is it better, flesh,
>   that they
>
> Should hurry so?[10]

This fleshly rush to see God ("Is it better?"), even when evildoers assail and seek to devour the poor flesh, is caught also by a much earlier poet than Graham, the writer of Psalm 27:

> Hear, O Lord, when I cry aloud,
>   be gracious to me and answer me!
> "Come," my heart says, "seek his face!"
>   Your face, Lord, do I seek.
>   Do not hide your face from me.
> (vv. 7–9a)

No doubt these words have a liturgical and cultic origin in Jerusalem, as suggested in, for example, Hosea 3:5: "The Israelites shall return and seek the Lord their God, and David their king; they shall come in awe to the Lord and to his goodness in the latter days." But the problem verse is 8: "Come," my heart says, "seek his face!" The Hebrew can be translated literally as, "To thee my heart has said, 'Seek [plural] my face,'" while the *Oxford Bible Commentary* suggests,[11] "From thee my heart conveys the message 'Seek my face'": whatever that means![12] In the midst of scholarly confusion, we might have recourse to literary guides, in this case, John Updike's novel *Seek My Face* (2002), observing that, at the very least, Updike seems to be more sensitive to the effects of language than the scholarly translators of the New Revised Standard Version of the Bible.

In Updike's novel, Hope Chafetz, by now an old woman, is seeking for God, her life as an artist permeated by her "susceptibility to beauty."[13] She recounts her life with an impossible genius—the novel is clearly based on the domestic life of the artist Jackson Pollock, with possibly something also of Andy Warhol—and now sees herself no longer beautiful but an old, aged, and lonely woman. Knowing all too well that modern art has abandoned the task of creating things of beauty, she seeks what is hidden by life—and in the final few pages, she reenters her childhood with her grandfather, who "saw into her life." Hope views her aged body, without compromise, with surprise, and even as something separate from herself, and "reads" it almost as Rolle once read Christ's scarred and bloody body on the cross: "The back of her hand is mottled and scarred by sun and age as if once scalded, the more prominent veins making patterns like wiggly letters she can almost read, random little rivers that have stayed in their courses all her life. The swelling of arthritis in a number of joints has caused the top segments of her fingers to deviate from the straight. She marvels that this gnarled crone's hand is hers."[14] With her grandfather, however, she regards herself as a young child again, seeing him physically, always watching. Everything is in the seeing: and it is the game with the coins that she remembers—how he would hide two coins down the side of the chair so that she had to push her hand down and feel for them and seeing for the first time the markings on a fifty-cent piece. Throughout her life she would continue to search for the lost coins, feeling for them in the chair—her chair that had been his chair—searching for the trace of the forgotten face, until now her body was too stiff to bend down. But her fear is more than that: "Hope thinks of exploring between the two big plaid cushions right now, but her back and hip hurt in anticipation of getting down, grunting, on her knees on the oval rag rug, and she is afraid of finding nothing."[15] These are the last words of the novel. We seek, defeated by the aging body, and we are always afraid that we might find nothing and that everything is an illusion. Yet the body that we see, the body that is ours, is at the same time intolerable, subject to decay, damaged, unlovely. We are afraid, even as we utter the words, "Do not hide your face from me." And yet we seek, searching for the lost coins. At the end of a very different work, Elie Wiesel's *Night* (1958), the young boy recently liberated from the nightmare that was Buchenwald sees, for the first time, his own face in a mirror. It is his face, and yet it is also the face of the other, that other, the corpse with whom in our deepest sufferings we are never reconciled and is our deepest self. Yet he wants and needs to gaze on himself, to know who he is, and to know his own body, even as a corpse:

> I wanted to see myself in the mirror hanging on the opposite wall. I had not seen myself since the ghetto.
> From the depths of the mirror, a corpse gazed back at me.
> The look in his eyes, as they stared into mine, has never left me.[16]

Or again, in fiction, as we read the last pages of Joseph Heller's *God Knows* (1984), and the aged King David reflects on his dying condition: "I think of Saul in his wordless gloom and torment every time I came to his chamber to play for him, and I realize as I remember that I never saw a sadder face on human being until a little while ago, when Abishag the Shunammite held a mirror up for me to see and I looked into mine."[17] Oneself is always another, seen in the mirror, and the place of deepest sorrow, but where alone and in the flesh, even in its decay, is found the God who is utterly absent, intolerably present.

The seeing, of self and other, and of self as other, is absolutely necessary yet utterly intolerable. It is at once to know, and yet not to know—seeing the self as familiar and as wholly other and alien; and yet still we are afraid of finding nothing, a hunting for lost coins, though the finding is almost as terrible as the fear that there is nothing there. And yet to *see* the broken body is as devastating, as destructive of all faith, as Dostoevsky's description of the unseen but still present gazers who behold the dereliction of Holbein's *Body of the Dead Christ in the Tomb*: "The people surrounding the dead man none of whom is shown in the picture, must have been overwhelmed by a feeling of terrible anguish and dismay on that evening which had shattered all their hopes and almost all their beliefs in one fell blow."[18] We, like these viewers, are always the unseen, haunted because the body that we see is always finally our own—the inevitable corpse gazing back at us, and yet there is the insistent "in my flesh I shall see God." With all the vitriol and despair of Jacobean tragedy, we ask in words from John Webster's *The Duchess of Malfi* (1612–13), "What thing is in this outward form of man to be beloved?"[19] Yet we remain still standing at the foot of the cross, watching with the mother and caught between the two verses of the medieval hymn the *Stabat Mater*:

> For his people's sins, in anguish
> There she saw the victim languish.
> 　　Bleed in torments, bleed and die:
> Saw the Lord's anointed taken;
> Saw her Child in death forsaken;
> 　　Heard his last expiring cry.
>
> May his wounds both wound and heal me,
> He enkindle, cleanse, anneal me,
> 　　Be his Cross my hope and stay.
>
> May he, when the mountains quiver,
> From that flame which burns forever
> 　　Shield me on the judgement day.[20]

The seeing is at once a wounding and a healing, the ascent also and at once a descent into the deepest hell. It would be an easy transition from here into the familiar sadomasochism of the eroticism of wounds and bondage and its theological equivalent, all that stuff about the wound of knowledge, or even the wound of reason. But this is different, and in the seeing of the body as both absolutely sacred and utterly profane, I am seeking to retrieve another way, a different and darker narrative than the customary defenses of the necessary resurrection of the body and, in Archbishop Rowan Williams' terms, "a Jesus concretely continuous with the earthly leader and friend of the days of the ministry."[21] It is, I think, both simpler and much, much more complex than that, and only the most profound practices of asceticism have begun to know this.

Consider, if you will, that early and continuing Christian obsession with the Song of Songs, that great cry of erotic longing for the beloved that is also an unfulfilled search, another searching for lost coins, perhaps, its eroticism embedded in both presence and the absence that provokes the power of metaphor. However spiritual the interpretation of the text, the obsession with it and the poem itself are deep acknowledgments that, like Christ himself, we are according to the flesh and its mysterious incentives.[22] One of the first great Christian commentators on the Song was Origen, to whom we shall return, indirectly, later in this chapter though by another route, and while my reservations about that great scholar are immense, in the context of the present discussion, he remains profoundly important.[23] For if, for Origen, the body and the material world are bestial and a prison house, yet it is still through corporeality alone that revelation is possible—the light shines *in* the prison house.[24] There is undoubtedly a dark side in the interpretation of the tradition that begins here. Leaping across the Christian centuries to St. Bernard of Clairvaux (1090–1153) and his great sermons on the Song of Songs, I find myself at one with the Cambridge theologian Don Cupitt in his suspicion of a particular kind of Christian piety (though it is not that of St. Bernard or even Origen) that finally misunderstands profoundly what is going on here *bodily*—a false escape into soul-talk though couched in the heated metaphorical language that indulges in a specifically female sexuality with the accompanying images of "thralldom, bondage and ravishment."[25] In his book *Mysticism after Modernity* (1998), Cupitt is reading Williams as *he* reads St. Bernard's sermons. St. Bernard comments first as, in sermon 3, he meditates on the Song of Songs 1:1, "Let him kiss me with the kiss of his mouth." He famously makes a distinction between the three stages of kissing—Christ's feet, his hand, and finally his mouth. The first is reminiscent of the penitent kiss of the sinful woman in the gospel, and from it we wait patiently for forgiveness.

> Though you have given first a kiss to the feet, do not presume to rise at once to kiss the mouth. You must come to that by way of another, intermediate kiss, on the hand. This is the reason for that kiss: "If Jesus says to me, 'Your

sins are forgiven,' what is the good of that unless I cease to sin? I have taken off my filthy garment. If I put it on again, what progress have I made?" (Sg 5:3)[26]

The union of the self with God, for St. Bernard then, is progressive toward the ultimate bliss of the final kiss on the mouth. Now Williams, in his book *The Wound of Knowledge* (1979), writes, "Bernard compares the union of the self and God with the mixing of water in wine." We seek "ever greater openness to the pressure of God's love" and (with a reference also to Meister Eckhart's startling image), "having arrived at that nakedness where the naked reality of God can enter, the soul is fertilized with divine life."[27] Cupitt responds to this language with one word: "Hm." And rightly so, for it represents an all too common misreading of St. Bernard (and, I think, Eckhart[28]) in his tradition, with its much more subtle, more powerful, and even erotic but finally less offensive understanding of the body in the mystical union with God.

St. Bernard indeed advocated what he called a "carnal love for Christ," yet it is a love that is rooted deeply in humanity itself. "Notice," he said, "that the love of the heart is, in a certain sense, carnal because our hearts are attracted more to the humanity of Christ and the things he did while in the flesh."[29] He expands this, in his Sermons on the Song of Songs, in terms of the three, progressive kisses, and begins with the by now familiar verse from Psalm 27:

> My heart rightly says to you, Lord Jesus, "My face has sought you; your face, Lord do I seek." In the morning you showed me your mercy. When I lay in the dust to kiss your footprints you forgave my evil life. Later in the day you gave joy to your servant's soul, when, with the kiss of your hand, you gave him grace to live a good life. And now what remains, O Good Lord, except that now in full light, while I am in fervour of spirit, you should admit me to the kiss of your mouth, and grant me the full joy of your presence.[30]

The point here is that for St. Bernard, drawing on the Song of Songs, there is no false dichotomy or distinction between the body and soul in the search for the Lord's face. The one embraces the other perfectly. "In my flesh I shall see God." St. Bernard does not indulge in rather false, and perhaps misogynistic, metaphors about the soul being fertilized into divine life, having entered God's naked reality. But, we might object, do not his sermons yet see Christ as the bridegroom of the soul and the church, a common enough theme in twelfth-century mysticism? Indeed, but the point is that this, for him, is not merely a metaphor. Rather, the image takes its life and reality from the experience of the body and the erotic experiences that also contain an element of profound and originary unknowing, beyond the profane and beyond knowledge, in spite of the sacred. One of St. Bernard's favorite texts was 2 Corinthians

3:18: "And all of us, with unveiled [unhidden] faces, seeing the glory of the Lord as though reflected in a mirror, are being transformed from one degree of glory to another; for this comes from the Lord, the Spirit." Through St. Bernard, we are not so far from the author of the Fourth Gospel, and then to the metaphysical poets George Herbert, to whom we shall return in detail in chapter 7, and Donne, again at his most fleshly in his poem "The Good Morrow" in the enchantment and reenchantment of the self.

> My face in thine eye, thine in mine appears,
>   And true plain hearts do in the faces rest,
> Where can we find two better hemispheres
>   Without sharp north, without declining west?
> What ever dies, was not mixed equally;
> If our two loves be one, or, thou and I
> Love so alike, that none do slacken, none can die.[31]

Before we begin to weave back to the awful and yet strangely beautiful body of Christ in Holbein and Dostoevsky, one further brief excursion into Christian theology and the power of the icon is perhaps required to further provoke the narrative. St. John of Damascus' (655–750) *Three Treatises on the Divine Images*, written in the eighth century against the iconoclasts or "those who attack the holy images," are a passionate defense of icons and their veneration. St. John establishes the centrality of the terms image and icon in the Christian tradition, through, for example their presentation of Trinitarian relationships—the Son as the image of the Father[32]—to the nature of the relationship between God and the created order in which visual images give us clues and intuitions of invisible realities. Attacking the *materiality* of images is, for St. John, tantamount to attacking the whole of Christian theology. This is not to deny at the same time that, in St. John's words, "it is impossible to depict God who is incommensurable and uncircumscribable and invisible."[33] Rather, he says insisting on the incarnation wherein the invisible becomes visible: "I am emboldened to depict the invisible God, not as invisible, but as he became visible for our sake, by participation in flesh and blood. I do not depict the invisible divinity, but I depict God made visible in flesh."[34] Now at this point I presume not so much to diverge from St. John as to revise his relationship between terms. He concludes, "For if it is impossible to depict the soul, how much more God, who gives the soul its immateriality." But, I would wish to say, this immateriality is not separate from but utterly co-inherent[35] in the human body's materiality, its mystery and the cloud of unknowing traced in the mysterious extremes of erotic longing, on the one hand, and the utterly unbearable horrors beyond imagining that the body can provoke, on the other. Dostoevsky's character Ippolit precisely describes the body only just taken down from the cross: "still retaining a great deal of warmth and life; *rigor mortis* had not yet set in, so that there was still a look of suffering on the face of the dead man, as though he were still feeling it." And this is the face on which we gaze, a face still suffering yet beyond all suffering, which is not hidden from us, and from which, in its awfulness, even Christ himself might have spared us and not mounted the cross. Such is the final temptation, perhaps.[36]

This looking beyond all knowing and beyond toleration and circumscription is an experience that is given commentary in more theological terms, as we have already seen in the previous chapter, by another participant in the iconoclastic debate, slightly later than St. John, the patriarch St. Nicephorus in his *Libri Tres Antirrhetici*. For St. Nicephorus, you will recall, the icon is a memorial of *kenosis*, the word used by the Greek Fathers to describe the incarnation: to incarnate, to empty. The icon, then, is not a representation of Christ's face, but rather a physical threshold, in Marie-José Baudinet's words, "a blessedly vacant object that respects the uncircumscribability of its object."[37]

So far we have looked in this chapter, as at an icon and as physical thresholds and boundaries, at bodily images of excess within the theology of the Christian tradition: the ravaged body of the crucified Christ, and the eroticism of St. Bernard in his Sermons on the Song of Songs. They are at once images of the deepest darkness and the brightest light imaginable. In them there is a darkness of exile, and beyond each there is an absolute desert, utterly profane and deeply sacred where alone becomes possible the body of the Godhead that is also the body of our deepest humanity. But before we touch on that deepest abyss, let us pause once again for a moment before another image of the ascetic body—that is, the famous and even familiar description of St. Antony of Egypt, in the *Life* by St. Athanasius, of the moment when he emerges in full and balanced health and vigor from his tomblike prison after nearly twenty years of unceasing struggle with demons and psalm singing:

> This was the first time he appeared from the fortress for those who came out to him. And when they beheld him they were amazed to see that his body had maintained its former condition, neither fat from lack of exercise, nor emaciated from fasting and combat with demons, but just as they had known him prior to his withdrawal. The state of his soul was one of purity, for it was not constricted by grief, nor relaxed by pleasure, nor affected by either laughter or dejection. Moreover, when he saw the crowd, he was not annoyed any more than he was elated at being embraced by so many people.

He maintained utter equilibrium, like one guided by reason and steadfast in that which accords with nature.[38]

It is easy to be frustrated by or even dismissive of this clearly fictionalized description of the body schooled in asceticism. It stands in utter contrast to the description of Holbein's *Dead Christ*, the ravaged Christ of the passion. And so, in the text of the hagiographical narrative, what face of Antony here are we being asked to see? It cannot be an historical portrait, but in our reading of it, it provokes puzzlement, awe, and perhaps even a little weariness with its good order, its sense of balance and harmony, its reason even. Antony's "equilibrium" is far beyond our reach, perhaps even beyond our desires, though we can see the point of showing us the saint as humanity deified, as the body seen as it truly is "in Christ," and, as it were, already ascended, the body as described by St. Maximus the Confessor. And as a legend, the portrait has a plausibility, even and perhaps especially in its impossibility. As Edith Wyschogrod in her version of the life of St. Mary of Egypt, derived from a twelfth-century French source, has suggested this is not a life actually to be *lived*—though its excessive demands may be profoundly disruptive, disturbing, and even destabilizing to our own lives, leaving us "no longer at ease here, in the old dispensation."[39] So it is with St. Antony. What St. Athanasius' legendary account has done is narrativize a life of immense struggle and physical endurance so that, in the narrative, the deepest conflicts are sequentially resolved in that "equilibrium" that actually provokes them. The narrative mirrors that of the canonical gospels (with the exception, perhaps, of Mark, which ends properly with the empty tomb), which restore for us the face of the yet Crucified Christ in the calm perfection of the resurrection body, the body that Mary in the garden was forbidden to touch though it is seen restored to her.[40]

We will come back to St. Antony and St. Mary of Egypt again before we finish this chapter, but for now I want to redescribe this narrative, moving away from the hagiographic and "proto-novelistic" sense of forward movement and resolution in lives not to be lived, in Wyschogrod's terms, "not intended to elicit replication but to inspire a new catena of moral events appropriate to the addressee's life."[41] Rather, it is to see the end or resolution rendered impossible in the immediate and actual enactment of a life lived over an abyss that makes it, in St. Nicephorus' terms, iconic—that is, a life that is inscribed in an image that represents its intolerable impossibility and in its abjection admits an uncircumscribability, an absence that is the true sign of resurrection, even and only possible in the very depths and the darkest deserts of profanity.

Perhaps the most profound illustration of this in Western art is Grünewald's staggering *Isenheim Altarpiece* (1512–16), already briefly referred to in the previous chapter. It is a work of art that is too often misunderstood and trivialized because the central, folded panel of the crucifixion is almost always taken in isolation. In fact, the whole work, in ten panels, has a painted surface that is over fifty feet in width, and when closed, it is nine feet high and sixteen feet wide. Here I can only scratch the surface of its complexity, built on various levels and physically in three layers of ten panels, some of which must be deliberately hidden in order to see others. St Antony appears more than once: in a nightmare version of his Temptations, which lies opposite a quiet image of him in conversation with Paul the Hermit walking in a wildly tormented natural world, while on the right of the crucifixion itself Antony appears as the patron saint of the Antonines, the religious community that ran the lazar house for whose chapel the work was completed, because he was invoked against the curse of "St. Antony's fire" or the terrible and disfiguring skin disease of erysipelas. When the wing panels are fully opened, we see on the left an Annunciation scene; in the center, an allegory of the nativity with, in the sky above the Holy Family, an image of heaven and God the Father; while on the right there is a resurrection, Christ rising gloriously from the tomb.

Thus, biblical scenes interplay with vivid scenes from the lives of the saints— but at the very center of all, and always visible, is the terrible crucifixion itself. Even when the panels are closed we see it. There is no relief, yet it hides and embraces all these other scenes, all of which are literally enfolded within the suffering body, and only through the contemplation of it are they accessible at all. On Christ, and in a sense also on the very viewer, are inscribed the wounds, an emptying of the body in the deepest suffering that renders all else unreal and invisible apart from itself. Here is the true sacred desert seen in the depths of the crucified body of the Godhead. Grünewald's vision of the crucifixion is, of course, itself far from simple. On the viewer's left, the Virgin, her eyes closed, is supported by St. John, while at their feet a kneeling Magdalen looks up in agony at the face of Christ. On the right (our right, though Christ's left) stands John the Baptist, book in hand and elongated right forefinger pointing at the Christ, at the very Word made flesh. We see what he reads. In the bend of his arm are the words from the Fourth Gospel (John 3:30): "He must increase but I must decrease." Christ's very emptying into the body, his *kenosis*, is at the same time an "increase." At his feet is the Lamb, blood flowing from its wounded heart into the eucharistic chalice. Thus, the picture is at once a teaching about the sacrament, a visual Bible study, a practical lesson in salvation for the suffering inmates of the lazar hospital—a reminder that he became like them so that they might become like him, indeed that in the dreadful condition of their bodies they *are* Christlike—but above all it is a stunning vision of bodily agony and horror, for the figure on the cross is central to all in its terrible physicality. Nothing is spared the viewer—from the impaled hands and feet, the gasping mouth and chest, the bloody wounds and the dreadful crown of thorns. A few hours later, this same figure would become Holbein's *Dead Christ*. We are caught here in the moment and crevice between death and life, a universal moment, and as Dostoevsky's Ippolit was to remark, "it is nature itself, and, indeed, any man's corpse would look like that after such suffering." Yet this deepest moment of human being, when the body is most human because at the absolute edge of human possibility, is also the most radical moment of *kenosis*—of emptying, of pouring out, and of incarnation. Nor is this a revisionary act, as Harold Bloom describes *kenosis*, an act of strong poets that takes place in a relationship to what has gone before "and makes possible a kind of poem that a simple repetition of the precursor's afflatus or godhood could not allow."[42] It is, rather, the moment of *absolute kenosis*, a making nothing and a self-emptying, without any other reference, when the divine and the human become one and absolutely other than God and all humankind so that the only cry possible is "My God, my God, why have you forsaken me?"—another voice from the Psalter echoed and repeated in the gospel narrative. Grünewald's Christ, despite the other figures at his feet, is utterly solitary, without narrative relationship to past or future—in human terms, this is the moment of absolute *metanoia*; that is, not repentance, but a total reversal of consciousness, the descent into hell that alone makes possible all the other scenes that are depicted in the *Isenheim Altarpiece*, Antony's vicious nightmares and also the vision of heaven above the nativity. There is no possible profanity greater than this, for it is the death of God, a descent into hell and a perpetual self-annihilation, that alone makes possible the presence of the universal and cosmic Christ. For Grünewald, the resurrected Christ *always* remains the Christ on the cross, that is, the unique body of the incarnate God who has totally identified himself with any and all possible experience. Grünewald's Christ is physically disproportionately large beside the other four human figures in his painting—literally, in his descent into hell, he grows and increases while John grows less.

    This radical insight into the totality of experience was to have a deep aesthetic impact on Western art in ways that the church and its theology have largely chosen to ignore in its attempts to articulate reassuring narratives and their obsession with the past of history and the particular body of Jesus. Geoffrey Galt Harpham, in his essay on the *Isenheim Altarpiece*, writes of the "counterforce of unintelligibility. . . . that defines the ascetic as distinct from both the metaphysical and the worldly."[43] Later in Western art the beautiful and aged peasant women of Velázquez and Rembrandt or the deeply haunted eyes of Van Gogh's self-portraits[44]—are portraits of the human soul that is utterly *of* the body, and they are images that are deeply, radically Christian, revealing of what remains deeply hidden and radically sacred in their tragic inscription that goes no further—like the desert fathers and mothers, and the Eastern practitioners of hesychism who simply repeat the name as the path to salvation. That is all: nothing else, without past or future, but in and beyond all time. They utter the profound truth that the divine presence is never a way to avoid human beings taking absolute responsibility for everything here and now on earth. It is, incidentally and as an aside, a truth utterly forgotten or deeply reversed in the nauseating obsessions with what Polly Toynbee has recently called "the worst elements of Christian belief"[45] in C. S. Lewis' Narnia stories, and the dreadful, inhuman figure of Aslan as pure, raw power—a figure whom children are supposed to fall in love with, but yet full of dark, neofascist implications.

And so, finally, we return to the wisdom of the desert: St. Antony, St. Mary, and others went far beyond the *imitatio Christi* to a radical *cultura Dei*—which is the earliest Latin translation of the Greek word *askesis* in the *Life of Antony*—actually instantiating in themselves the totality and Total Presence of the incarnation: in a sense, in their bodies, extravagantly and eucharistically, they even *became* Christ. Their wild ascetic struggles, however, were not a flight from their humanity, but rather the very opposite, that is an immense journey into its very depths. As Peter Brown has well expressed it, "the ascetic brought with him into the desert fragile tokens of an enduring humanity that he had to defend tenaciously if he was to survive at all and maintain his humanity. He could not sink like an animal into its alluring immensity."[46] The stories of *The Lives of the Desert Fathers* are full of extraordinary, indeed legendary, physical endurance and pain—the cell of the monk is even referred to as the "furnace of Babylon"—but yet seen as a wrestling with God in darkness, like Jacob at Penuel, and therefore an inevitable wounding; yet, Jacob's story continues in Genesis, for Jacob returns to his brother Esau, whom he has betrayed, with the words, "Seeing your face is like seeing the face of God" (Gen 33:10).

"Do not hide your face from me." In the *Apophthegmata Patrum*, or *The Wisdom Sayings of the Desert Fathers*, it is written of Apa Pambo "that just as Moses had taken on the likeness of the glory of Adam, when his face shone with the glory of the Lord, in the same way, the face of Apa Pambo shone like lightning, and he was like an Emperor seated on a throne." Here is indeed a description of the body deified, a realization that Christ in his self emptying became like us in order that we, in our poor bodies, may become truly like him. These desert ascetics did not despise or reject their bodies: quite the contrary. Rather, they sought their mystery to their deepest depths. They sought absolute participation in the body of the Godhead at its deepest depths of humanity, at a point so far beyond the bearable, in the absolute desert, that its own deepest being met God as truly total absence wherein alone is Total Presence. In this utterly profane moment there can be no severance of spirit from body, for the body, in all its physicality now is nothing but spirit, always unreal apart from that deep desert. In the *Sayings* we can thus find a radical reversal of imagery in a daring celebration of the sacred found only in the profane body—yet it is not that either. It is a realization that only in the deepest depths of the body, embraced by the soul, can be found spirit as an abyss that is utter negation and therefore pure presence. Whose face do we seek? A final story in this chapter, and a little lighter in tone, if not implication, from the *Sayings*—this one from John the Dwarf. (It looks forward also to chapter 5, which has a more detailed reading of the life of St. Mary and her sisters.)

> There was in the city a courtesan who had many lovers. One of the governors approached her saying, promise me you will be good, and I will marry you. She promised this and he took her and brought her to his home. Her lovers, seeing her again, said to one another, let us go to the back of the house and whistle for her. But the woman stopped her ears and withdrew to the inner chamber and shut the door. The old man said that the courtesan is our soul, that her lovers are the passions, that the lord is Christ, that the inner chamber is the eternal dwelling place, those who whistle are evil demons but the soul always takes refuge in the Lord.[47]

Well, I suppose you can take that in many ways! Like so many of these little stories from the desert, they have knowing and a sharp edge—and seem to be told with a twinkle in the eye. The allegory works all right, but then again, is this just another story about St. Mary or one of her kind—and which version? For most of this chapter, we have been out in the desert with the body crucified and profaned, and, I think, necessarily so—absolutely necessarily: but maybe the governor in the story, whoever he was, had the right idea. Perhaps, with Origen, St. Bernard, even St. John of the Cross, and not a few others, he learned a bit of true wisdom from the Song of Songs—before he blew out the candle in the inner chamber.

4

THE WORD AND THE BODY

> Let him kiss me with the kisses of his mouth!
> For your love is better than wine.
> your anointing oils are fragrant
> your name is perfume poured out.
>
> —Song of Songs 1:2–3

As we have already noted, from the very earliest days, the Christians produced commentaries on the Song of Songs. As in the Jewish tradition of interpretation, it was customary to read the poem as an allegory, in this latter seen as a description of God's love for Israel. At the same time, there is evidence that it was also sung as a secular song, performed in banquets and there, presumably, taken quite literally as an erotic text.[1] The earliest surviving Christian commentary is St. Hippolytus of Rome's *Fragmenta in Cantica Canticorum* (ca. 200 C.E.), which clearly influenced Origen's slightly later *Commentary*, which was to exert an influence on later scholars, such as Jerome and Augustine of Hippo.[2] From the very outset, Origen's work is ecclesiological, the Song read as a wedding song or epithalamium written in the form of a play and celebrating the heavenly love of a bride for her bridegroom "who is the Word of God." "For whether she is the soul made after His image or the Church, she has fallen deeply in love with Him."[3] But at the same time, and referring to Hebrews 5:12, Origen warns his reader that the Song of Songs is not milk for infants, but rich fare, fit only for spiritually mature adults and, in particular, unsuitable for anyone "impelled and moved to the lusts of the flesh."[4] He is perfectly well aware that this most spiritual of books is at the same time necessarily and dangerously "bodily." Exactly the same

47

point is made some nine hundred years later in the sermons of St. Bernard of Clairvaux, his strict Cistercian brother. He begins his first of no less than eighty-six sermons on the Song with the words, "And so be ready to eat not milk but bread."[5] But the *Doctor mellifluus*, as St. Bernard was called, takes the sensuality of the poem to the very heart of his theology with an almost postmodern reading of the second verse of the Song, "Let him kiss me with the kisses of his mouth," in the progression through the three stages of the kiss until, through the processes of repentance and forgiveness, the final erotic divine rapture and "a joyous contemplation finds rest in him in the rapture which is the kiss of his mouth."[6]

The words of the Song of Songs are at once at the heart of Christian spirituality and utterly also embodied. In the late fourteenth-century macaronic poem, "In the vale of restless mind," Christ suffering during his passion utters in Latin the words from Song 2:5, "*Quia Amore Langueo*" (I am faint with love), his dying on the cross at the same time a fainting away with love. Thus, the literal reading of the poem, with its detailed descriptions of physical beauty and desire, its words of love, feeds our reflection on divine love. In the same way, perhaps, at the end of his extraordinary and intimate exploration of the landscape of human eroticism, Jean-Luc Marion concludes with a meditation: "In the end, I not only discover that another was loving me before I loved, and that this other already played the lover before me, but above all I discover that this first lover, from the very beginning, is named God. God's highest transcendence, the only one that does not dishonor him, belongs not to power, not to wisdom, not even to infinity, but to love. For love alone is enough to put all infinity, all wisdom, and all power to work."[7] For love is nothing without the body, and that body is spoken, enrapt and realized in the word. As one of the most recent commentaries on the Song of Songs, following the work of Origen and St. Bernard, says of chapter 1:2: "A disembodied voice speaks, giving birth to a poetic Edenic world, as in those first moments of creation."[8] The poem is then likened to the first words spoken by God in the act of creation, "Let there be light" (Gen 1:3), and their Christian echo in John 1. A voice speaks a word and a world comes into being and the Word becomes flesh, its fullness found in the silence of being.[9]

The Fourth Gospel opens with a singular Word—the Logos. This word is more than mere speech; it is divine action. From the creative word, everything comes into being as celebrated by the psalmist:

By the word of the Lord the heavens were made,
and all their host by the breath of his mouth.[10]

God's utterance and his spirit—his very breath or *ruach*—brings all things into being in heaven and on earth, and it is this Word that finally, and in an act of pure *kenosis* and divine self-emptying, becomes enfleshed and dwells among us. And if, as the neoplatonists of the Renaissance believed,[11] God is both beauty and the source of beauty, and God's image is man, then the beauty and glory of this Word made flesh, which we have beheld, is indeed divinity itself. Furthermore, in the last of the so-called Johannine writings of the New Testament, the Book of Revelation, God proclaims himself at the outset as embracing *all* words and *all* text—the alpha and the omega—the first and last letters of the alphabet. God is all words, and all things have their being through the Word, embracing all time and space, for this is the Lord God "who is and who was and who is to come, the Almighty" (Rev 1:8).

But if herein lies, perhaps, the clue to what I would wish to call the textuality of all being, at the same time the last verse of the Fourth Gospel sounds a warning note in our ears: "But there are also many other things that Jesus did; if every one of them were written down, I suppose that the world itself could not contain the books that would be written" (John 21:25). The shift then is from the creative Word to the plethora of books, words tumbling over words, and recordings of multitudinous and endless facts and doings in an image of both the miraculous plenitude of Jesus' deeds, but also the incapacity of the world to hear and sustain the unedited version. And do we even need such excess? Does not the creative Word bring order out of chaos? Does not the text and the essence of textuality truly select and convey meaning and significance, giving structure to our human being and guaranteeing our human community in its ultimate silence?

This chapter is a kind of exercise in hermeneutics, exploring the nature of *textuality* and the place of the Word as it flows from the mouth of God in creation, to the flesh of Christ in the incarnation and in sacrament, and into the texts of Scripture and literature, and from there necessarily back into the lives of those who write and read, who engage with the Word in the daring, perhaps even blasphemous poetic repetition in the finite mind of the divine and infinite I AM,[12] whose bodies are written on, and who both consume and are consumed by the words of Scripture and in the liturgy. Texts are certainly not always intended as channels for the communication of meaning and understanding but as containers of secrets within time and as parabolic guardians of mysteries. Daniel, as guardian of the sacred text, is dismissed with the words, "Go your way, Daniel, for the words are to remain secret and sealed until the end of time" (Dan 12:8). Jesus says to his uncomprehending disciples in St. Mark's Gospel that to them has been given the secret (τὸ μυστήριον) of the kingdom of God, "but for those out-side everything comes in parables" (Mark 4:12).[13] But if texts are not to be understood, then they may well be consumed, and the physical experience of consuming the word of Scripture is well documented. "So I went to the angel and told him to give me the little scroll; and he said to me, 'Take it, and eat; it will be bitter to your stomach, but sweet as honey in your mouth.' So I took the little scroll from the hand of the angel and ate it; it was sweet as honey in my mouth, but when I had eaten it, my stomach was made bitter" (Rev 10:9–10).[14] From here it is but a short step to the biblical hermeneutics of the early Christians of the desert, as found in texts from *The Sayings [Wisdom] of the Desert Fathers*, to the hagiographical writings and as late as the texts of the *Philokalia*.[15] It is important to remember that this broad textual tradition has oral roots, texts transmitted by word of mouth, so that words once literally resided in the mouth and stomach. Walter Ong has emphasized the power of the word as event in oral cultures, a power that our widely literate and text-based culture has tended to flatten: "Deeply typographic folk forget to think of words as primarily oral, as events, and hence as necessarily powered; for them, words tend rather to be assimilated to things, 'out there' on a flat sur-face. Such 'things'. . . . are not actions, but are in a radical sense dead, though subject to dynamic resurrection."[16] The desert fathers and mothers wholly internalized and devoured the words of Scripture and projected from the text of the Bible a "world of meaning," which they strove to appropriate in the manner of their lives.[17] It was often emphasized that, as in the case of St. Mary of Egypt, they were illiterate, but this is no barrier to their appropriation by the word of Scripture, and their appropriation of the word of Scripture. Nor do the biblical texts have "meaning" for them as such, but rather, just as the secret or mystery of the Kingdom of God was entrusted to the disciples, they yield a surplus of physical and spiritual energy in their lives, which spills over in significances that are far beyond any initial or later moments of under-standing. For example, the moment when the young Antony responds to the scriptural call to sell everything and give the money to the poor (Matt 19:21) is defining for his whole life and opens up for him a whole expansive "world of meaning." According to St. Athanasius' *Life*, the power of the text is by virtue of its being a channel for the fulfillment of "God's design" for the saint. When Antony hears the text read aloud in church, "It was as if by God's design he held the saints in his recollection, and as if the passage were read on his account."[18]

Hardly to be described as interpreters of the texts of Scripture, the desert monks were engaged in a process of appropriation, a "conversation" with its

words whereby they sought to digest them and transform their bodily existence into a form of holiness that was both practical and a lived metaphor in
the world. This power of the lived metaphor is never to be underestimated
as a form of presencing in the world by which the world is touched in ways
it barely perceives and recognizes, or knows itself. Douglas Burton-Christie,
in his study *The Word in the Desert* (1993), has pointed out that the origins
of the life of withdrawal and asceticism do not necessarily have a religious or
spiritual impulse.[19] Retreat (*anachoresis*) and the adoption of a solitary and
simple life in the desert may have been adopted before the origins of monasticism in Egypt for various and sometimes quite practical reasons: as a flight
from civil oppression, as a kind of primitive countercultural statement, as
an act of desperation in the face of poverty. Furthermore, the rule of simple
living and sparse diet was probably not altogether a choice, at least for many,
and certainly not a religious or spiritual one, but a basic necessity for survival
in the harsh conditions of the desert. In my book *The Sacred Desert*, I made
much the same point about the "asceticism" of the twentieth-century desert
dweller and soldier T. E. Lawrence. For him, the ascetic life was pursued,
at least to a large degree, as a discipline to enable him to survive as a desert fighter against the Turkish army, though his practices of abstinence and
"indifference" are remarkably similar to the ascetic spiritual disciplines of the
monks. Lawrence lived with the Arab who attained "intense condensation
of himself in God by shutting his eyes to the world, and to all the complex
possibilities latent in him which only contact with wealth and temptations
could bring forth."[20]

Wherein lies the difference, then? We are back to the question asked in
the introduction—how do we distinguish the work of art from the most ordinary of everyday objects? How do we distinguish a practical exercise in bodily
survival in a harsh environment from a willed spiritual discipline that follows
the same pattern? The point is that, in one sense, we cannot distinguish them.
Many are the stories of the ancient fathers and mothers of the desert who
lived the simple and practical lives of basket makers or were employed hidden away from the world in the humblest of tasks—as mad scullery maids,[21]
(repentant) prostitutes, or simply subsistence farmers. Many did not appear
as spiritual giants (except, perhaps in later hagiography) but as distinctive
only by their unremarkableness or, at most, their unattractiveness. And, as
with Meister Eckhart later, they exemplified a union between the life of contemplation and the life of activity.[22] But, even more, as with Jesus on the
Emmaus road, once their simplicity and anonymity is uncovered, they simply
vanish in body and cease to be, lost in the mysteries of the inner desert. But

actually, the difference lies in the overwriting of Scripture as a text mapped onto their lives so that as their lives, though barely touching the world,[23] realize the Word in action, and text and life converge and become indistinguishable. They are those who, in the discourse of asceticism, have succeeded in a radical decentering of the self,[24] a "reversal of the flow of the body"[25] in order to lose themselves and at the same time find themselves more profoundly in their bodies. There are, then, stories of the Fathers who happily sell or give their copies of the Scriptures away—for they have no need of them as their lives are the same, one with Scripture and one with Christ. If this begins with sometimes spectacular struggles with the demons of temptation, it often ends with simple and often repetitive and mundane deeds in lives that are characterized by renunciation. At this point, the life of the monk becomes the sacramental meeting place, so insignificant as to be most easily missed and dismissed (and its tiny particularity is the guarantee of universality), between the universal and the particular, the world as is and the world to come, time and eternity. In the life of the ascetic, time touches eternity and is thereby sanctified. Written on by the text, the life, wholly lived in body and spirit, becomes itself a text in which reality and metaphor, the miraculous and the mundane, even heaven and hell, become one and indistinguishable.

In what sense might all this be called a hermeneutics? These desert dwellers understood the interpretation of Scripture solely in terms of the process of transformation and holiness. In no sense was it an intellectual search for meaning (though it might become so in some and as the monastic tradition developed[26]), but it was an art that involved the whole life of the mind and body. As the fourteenth-century Nicephorus the Solitary of Mount Athos wrote, "Monastic life is called the art of arts and the science of sciences; for it does not bring perishable blessings akin to the things of this world, which drive the mind from what is best and engulf it; but monkhood promises us wonderful and unspeakable treasures which the 'Eye has not seen, nor ear heard, neither have entered into the heart of man' (I Cor. ii. 9). Hence, 'we wrestle not against flesh and blood, but against principalities, against powers, against the rulers of the darkness of this world'" (Ephes.vi. 12).[27] This, indeed, is a hermeneutics of the Word made flesh—of the word endlessly realized in the flesh of the interpreter and validated only there in wrestlings that far exceed the flesh, beyond thought and language, yet filling the consciousness. It is a hermeneutics that entertains a possibility that might be defined as "*the impossibility of impossibility*."[28] Thus, it sustains a sense of textuality that transcends the practicalities of communication but maintains a necessity that finally ensures a universal sense of the oneness of all things, perhaps a sacramental sense of the absence/presence of that unity of being/ non-being that may even be apparent only in despair, and in absolute despair. It is quite possible to see this in the texts of the poets.

On September 17, 1982, the Russian poet Irina Ratushinskaya was arrested and charged with "anti-Soviet agitation and propaganda." She was sentenced to seven years hard labor in a "strict regime" labor camp, with five years of internal exile. Her crime was writing poetry.[29] The poem "Pencil Letter" was composed in the KGB prison in Kiev in November 1982 as she awaited trial, inscribed on a scrap of paper and without hope that it will ever be read by her husband, to whom it is written. Yet it is a communication where communication is impossible, a physical affirmation of her presence through the living form of words. Many of Ratushinskaya's later poems written during her imprisonment became literally a part of her and her continuing identity as they were written on bars of soap with the sharpened ends of burnt matchsticks and then committed to memory. The words of "Pencil Letter" convey to the absent reader a meaning not in what they say, but in what they do not say—a reading "between the lines," a silence of understanding between two beings that is sustained in hope by the hopelessness expressed in text, a presence in forsakenness. It is a silence realized only in the fullness of language.

> I know it won't be received
> Or sent. The page will be
> In shreds as soon as I have scribbled it.
> Later. Sometime. You've grown used to it,
> Reading between the lines that never reached you,
> Understanding everything. On the tiny sheet,
> Not making haste, I find room for the night.
> What's the hurry, when the hour that's passed
> Is all part of the same time, the same unknown term.
> The word stirs under my hand
> Like a starling, a rustle, a movement of eyelashes.
> Everything's fine.[30]

The physical text, the word that stirs to the touch, is fragile, but enters into and transforms being and time, at once a monologue and a dialogue, a guarantee of physical attachment (through the word, the feeling of the "warmth of my hand" is realized), word flowing into the impossible body, the body sustained by the sacrament of language. And the text of the poem does survive miraculously, smuggled out of prison, and is read as a memorial both to the poet's physical survival and spirit.

* * *

Georges Bernanos (1888–1948), novelist and polemical writer, writes with a violence that seems to be belied by the simple and even commonplace nature of his fictional narratives. In his 1936 novel *The Diary of a Country Priest* (*Journal d'un curé de campagne*), the relationship of the reader to the text and its hermeneutical challenge is highly complex as Bernanos writes through the fragmentary diary and private reflections of his young priest of Ambricourt, written as a form of confession and for no particular eyes. The result is a deeply solitary, interior monologue (and yet texts are always communal, inviting us into their world), deliberately reflecting a fragmentary and often highly confused mind, though one through which his own text is drawing the reader into a deeper spirituality even as his physical grip on the world and others' understanding of him become darker and less assured. Bernanos himself regarded his vocation as an author as a priestly one in the etching of a spiritual adventure that can only finally end in martyrdom. As it becomes ever clearer to the reader that the young narrator, convinced also of his failure as a priest—a priest must always face the impossibility, the necessary falsehood of the attempt at priesthood—is also dying, so his naïve innocence becomes an ever more painful absorption and consumption in his own body of the misery and evil that inhabits his utterly average and therefore universal parish. Emptying himself, he enters into the suffering flesh of his people. In a letter, Bernanos wrote, "He will have served in the same measure that he believes he has *failed*. His innocence wins out over all before he dies peacefully of cancer."[31]

The narrative of actual events in *The Diary of a Country Priest* is hardly worth recounting, for the "story" is almost entirely interior within the young priest's mind. Bernanos' model for his priest was, to some extent, the French Carmelite nun St. Thérèse de Lisieux (1873–97), whom he admired for her "hiddenness" and the fact that she was almost unnoticed by her Carmelite sisters, a sanctity hidden deeply within the common order of things.[32] Profoundly ascetic, St. Thérèse's short life quickly attracted hagiographic attention in miracles of healing and prophecy as a realization of her promise, "*Je vais faire tomber un torrent de roses.*"

From the beginning of Bernanos' novel, it is made clear that the parish of Ambricourt is utterly commonplace—"like all the rest. They're all alike." What happens simply reflects a universal human condition, deliberately and drearily average in its characters and their interaction. The young priest writes, "My parish is bored stiff; no other word for it. Like so many others!"[33] And yet the drama works intensely at other levels than that of the social landscape. On the first page of his diary, the priest uses the image of the cancerous growth to describe the boredom all around him: "Some day perhaps we shall catch it ourselves—become aware of the cancerous growth within us." In fact, as we learn later, he is himself dying of a cancerous growth, the image becoming a literal reality in his own body, a cancer that at once kills him and confirms his "failure," and yet at the same time through the written text of his diary becomes the paradoxical moment of growth in his spiritual life, bringing him to a sense of universal grace in the very moment of death itself. Early in his writings the priest writes, slipping into an absolute reality that is beyond both thought and reason,

> I have been looking over these first few pages of my diary without any satisfaction, and yet I considered very carefully before making up my mind to write it. But that is not much comfort to me now. For those who have the habit of prayer, thought is too often a mere alibi, a sly way of deciding to do what one wants to do. Reason will always obscure what we want to keep in the shadows. A worldling can think out the pros and cons and sum up his choices. No doubt. But what are *our* chances worth? We who have admitted once and for all into each moment of our puny lives the terrifying presence of God? Unless a priest happens to lose his faith—and then what has he left, for he cannot lose his faith without denying himself? He will never learn to "look after number one" with the alert common sense—nay, with the candor and innocence of the children of this world. What is the use of working out chances? There are no chances against God.[34]

These lines define the whole nature of the diary—which is a mixture of reported narrative of events and meetings, unfinished thoughts and questions, doubts and affirmations. They are defined by prayer rather than "reason"— prayer as a kind of conversation with an almighty God against whose providence there is no "chance." The point is that anything can go either way, and in a sense it does in the life of the young priest in a simultaneous utter failure and total "victory"; that is, at one level nothing can be changed and all things are defined within both freedom and responsibility—or, in his dying words, reported by a friend, *Does it matter? Grace is everywhere.*[35] The priest's cancerous tumour is his crucifixion—the sign of the inevitable decay and indeed self-consumption of the body to the point when its annihilation and death is the moment of final affirmation of God's absolute dispensation—the breaking into a sunlit landscape amid the night of nonbeing. In the tragic text of the priest's dying body is held the final realization that God is both before and after, transcending us in love as we finally "rest in him in the rapture which is the kiss of his mouth."[36] Throughout the young priest's diary, there are references to a physical closing on and unity with the eucharistic presence—his diet becomes an ever more sparse one of sour wine and bread, so that para-doxically, as we become more aware of his decaying body, the body becomes less relevant and more real, more universal.[37]

How do we become a reader of *The Diary of a Country Priest*?[38] Through Bernanos' narrator we are granted an utterly privileged position and a curi-ously uncritical one. The stumbling fragments of his reports and reflections impel us to read between the lines—as perhaps always, what is *not* there is more important than what is yet defined by and held within the mundane and physical. What we read are the shards of the impossible heap of words referred to in John 21:25—to read everything would be both impossible and irrelevant—and it is in the gaps, the physical shreds, the poor, tattered text of the body and the implied metaphorical connections with the sacrament and the spiritual life that we "see" the "true story." Thus, only in the reader does the young priest actually live—his life literally a text that maps a geog-raphy of grace on his feeble and forlorn pastoral efforts and dying frame.[39] There is only one moment of seeming strength in his long conversation with the bitter Madame la Comtesse and her impossible daughter and sham mar-riage, but that becomes also the moment of his final rejection and misunder-standing by the world around him. By then, it might be said, he was not even of this world, and his touch brings about the death of the Comtesse herself. To read his diary is to enter into a Passion Narrative, just as to read the gos-pels is to realize, in a sense in the reading itself, the real presence of Christ. It is a Total Presence, possible only in an absolute absence, both in "reality" and in the physical events narrated in the text. Words then eliminate, and alone make possible and even inevitable the impossible ubiquity of grace, truly thereby even an impossible impossibility. In worldly terms, the priest's life and death, like that of St. Thérèse, and like many another foolish saint, must be hidden and commonplace for only then is it possible for the body to be unified with all things and thereby become the medium for true resurrec-tion. Bernanos writes, "My death is here. A death like any other, and I shall enter into it with the feelings of a very commonplace, very ordinary man. It is even certain that I shall be no better at dying than I am at controlling my life. I shall be just as clumsy and awkward. So often have I been told to be 'simple.' I do my best. It is so hard to be simple. Worldly men talk of 'simple people' as they do of 'humble people,' with the same indulgent smile. But they should speak of them as kings."[40] To be simple, to know the Truth, is the hardest thing of all. It is unknowable.

The priest's death is an absolute scaling down, a moment of true *keno-sis*, and he is inadequate even in the business of dying. It too is an art to be

learned, a controlling of life in death as in all asceticism and spiritual discipline, an artistic beauty[41] that is yet indistinguishable from the commonplace
with which it identifies, so that in this extreme humility (like Christ mocked
in a purple robe by the soldiery in John 19:2–3 and on the cross), "we should
speak of them as kings."

To read *The Diary of a Country Priest* is literally to follow the discipline
of the priest's own ascetic journey in the body. The overt occurrences in the
parish and at the end of his life are almost inevitably matters of failure, even
his diet is unable to sustain him and yet is the only food that is harmonious
with his failing body. To read his narrative, therefore, is to read between the
lines, to see as if in negation and not to know except in the evocation of
human sympathy with the body, until what is abstract becomes the most
concrete and vice versa. Thus, as Rémy Rougeau has suggested, "the subtext
of the novel is about a steady rise to holiness"[42]: only the subtext is, in the end,
the only text. Like the body of the ascetic, it is the merest, barely discernible
trace on the earth's surface that is the clue to the being of all things, a Total
Presence while almost completely absent.

Thus, we need ever to be learning to read, to decipher the text and relate
to it both in body and mind. We need to develop ever more remote hermeneutical ways in the appropriation of the text, which is the only articulation
of the body, but a consuming of the body that also consumes the reader.
For in the text and its event the bodily presence is realized as sacramental,
utterly negated, and therefore utterly realized and divinized. One of the most
remarkable modern fictional explorations of this process is to be found in
the writings of the Serbian poet and writer Milorad Pavić. His novel *Landscape Painted with Tea* (1990) is written in the form of a series of clues in a
(real) crossword, which is embedded, as a kind of subtext, in the fabric of the
novel's text. The reader is left pursuing the search, which is the subject of
the narrative, in the very form of the narrative itself. Ostensibly, it is the story
of an architect in Belgrade (Pavić's own city) who is searching for his father,
an army officer who vanished in Greece during World War II. In the first half
of the novel, which becomes increasingly fragmented, devious, and slippery
as it progresses, the key location is Mount Athos—the ancient monastery on
the Aegean where we both disappear and are found. It is at once a place and
no-place.

The book opens with a rooting of place in the remoteness of premonastic
prehistory, buried deep in biblical literature. When the ancient fathers of the
monks first appear, "they dispersed across the wilds of Syria, Mesopotamia,
and Egypt, hid in graves, in pyramids, and in the ruins of onetime fortresses,

wearing their long hair wrapped under their arms and tied across their chests to keep them warm at night."[43] They divide into two groups, those who live a communal life (cenobites, or solidaries) and those who live in isolation (idiorrhythmics, or solitaries), described thus:

> For idiorrhythmics each keep their own silence, whereas cenobites foster a common quiet. The solitaries work silence like a field of wheat; they plow it, give it space, extend the furrow, water it so that it may flourish, so that it may grow tall, because with silence you can reach God, with your voice you cannot, no matter how hard you shout. . . . The solidaries, in cultivating their quiet, do not direct it toward God but, rather, extend it like a dam toward the part of the world that does not belong to them and that has yet to be conquered; they surround and enclose themselves with quiet, and protect themselves with it or send it to catch their game like a hunting dog. And they know that there are good hunting dogs and bad.[44]

Given that the book is in the form of a crossword puzzle, here is the first clue offered to the reader, the purpose of the puzzle being to learn how to read. The reader, then, is to be, so to speak, monastic—both and at once communal and solitary (as is true of all reading). Central to each is the use of silence, which is at the very heart of and embraces all language and all texts. Each silence is directed differently—the one toward God, the other as a protective wall. The reader, then, is to cultivate or build silence as a necessary response to the words of the text. That text is shaped, chapter by chapter—like a crossword, the text moves not in a linear narrative, but down and across, vertical and horizontal, metaphorically and metonymically.[45] Thus, the reader must also learn to move down and across the text—yet not to bombard it with words, but rather with the silence of one kind or another. And, like hunting dogs, some may be good and some may be bad.

In the extraordinarily difficult (not to say perverse) response of silence to the wordy demands of reading (the temptation is always to ask questions, What does this *mean*? What is this *saying* to me?), the reader of *Landscape Painted with Tea* will eventually become its ideal reader, like the solitary lost in the deep desert, a mere trace on the mind and imagination—as identified by the author.

ALL READERS OF THIS BOOK
ARE ENTIRELY IMAGINARY.
ANY RESEMBLANCE TO ACTUAL READERS
IS COINCIDENTAL.[46]

What the reader, like every true monastic (as hagiography insists), must learn is to cease to be at all—to become entirely imaginary, utterly decentered, and only then can he or she become a "true" reader. In the act of reading, we must also learn an absolute *kenosis*, which is alone the guarantee of true incarnation, or enfleshment, and then, in the *imagination*, consumers and consumed, we can be free to be interpreters of the hidden text. Of course, in the actual text, and necessarily, the author will continue to test and defy us, realizing our unwillingness to let go and our inability to stop asking the wrong questions. Texts remain dangerously seductive to the mind. Almost at the end of the book, Pavić continues to play his games. "In the meantime, the author will amuse himself one last time with the hero of this book, architect Atanas Razin. Because Razin's notebooks beckon both to us and to him. Landscapes painted with tea are waiting for us."[47] The texts beckon, though their landscapes actually cannot be seen. Furthermore, to the very end, the author continues to chide and discipline the reader. The last words of the novel read, "The reader cannot be so stupid as not to remember what happened next to Atanas Svilar, who, for a time, was called Razin."[48] The text is followed by a totally and deliberately pointless index—a further joke against the stupid reader who cannot give up the search for immediate meaning and significance. Entries in the index include, "what, *passim*" and "who, *passim*."[49] Of course, we are inveterately, all of us, stupid readers, searching for knowledge and missing the truth.

To read *Landscape Painted with Tea* is finally to acknowledge, perversely, its unreadability. Yet its many words, and their puzzles and games, lead us back ineluctably to the beginning, and to the silences of the old monks, solitary and communal, the silences embedded, and only embedded, in the long discipline of words. The only true landscape is the landscape of heaven, and that is entirely imaginary, known only in text—as we must be as readers, for "heaven cannot be expressed or represented: the mind can grasp it only by recognizing its own limitations and the necessity of coming to terms with it."[50] Since Jacob's dream of the ladder to heaven, we should have realized that words can only be steps in the ascetic ladder of divine ascent, and we as readers must actually become physically one with them in their imaginative movements.

The text redeems by our participation in it, our becoming one with it, as the ascetics became one with Scripture. After the unspeakable horror of the Holocaust, which invalidated any possible excuse of theology and which Theodore Adorno believed brought language itself to an end, the poets did, of deep necessity, speak, and in their words, however painfully, memory is sustained and the body, in its terrible beauty, continues to be envisioned even in death and annihilation. Paul Celan was the son of Romanian Jews who both died in a concentration camp after the occupation of Romania by Germany in

1941 to 1942. Surviving the camps himself, Celan took his own life in 1970. His most well-known poem, "Todesfuge" ("Death Fugue"), tragically and with extraordinary beauty resonates with the complex rhythms and structures of the musical fugue perfected by J. S. Bach, Germany's greatest composer, defining the sufferings of the Jewish people as they breathe the smoke of the ovens that burned and devoured their bodies. The music and the physically powerful, insistent rhythms of the poetry and its images are evident even in the English translation.

> Schwarze Milch der Frühe wir trinken dich nachts
> wir trinken dich morgens und mittags wir trinken dich abends
> wir trinken und trinken
> Ein Mann wohnt im Haus der spielt mit den Schlangen der schreibt
> der schreibt wenn es dunkelt nach Deutschland dein goldenes Haar Margarete
> Dein aschenes Haar Sulamith wir schaufeln ein Grab in den
>   Lüften da liegt man nicht eng.

> [Black milk of daybreak we drink you at night
> we drink in the morning at noon we drink you at sundown
> we drink and we drink you
> A man lives in the house he plays with the serpents he writes
> he writes when dusk falls to Germany your golden hair Margarete
> your ashen hair Shulamith we dig a grave in the breezes there
> one lies unconfined.][51]

The text realizes the bodies of the two women in the ghastly context of the death camp. The man, the officer, writes with the pen of the great German poet Goethe, recalling the beautiful, innocent, golden-haired Margarete of his masterpiece, *Faust, Part 1* (1801). But the epitome of Aryan beauty is matched by the raven-haired beauty of the Jewish Shulamite girl, Abishag, who was brought to warm the aged King David as he lay dying (1 Kings 1:3). Yet her hair is now ashen, turned gray by the falling ashes of the Jewish bodies in the smoke. The physical beauties of the two races are brought together as the music sweetly plays—"*der Tod ist ein Meister aus Deutschland*" (death is a master from Germany).

Yet the poet speaks, mysteriously, in words the bodies made flesh and emptied. There is no justification and no meaning, but a terrible beauty in the meeting of opposites. Nothing is justified, but the impossibility and the possibility of its negation are sung in words. With the poet, then, we move from these torn and annihilated bodies to the body that is at the center of Good Friday in its descent into hell, and back again to its impossible love known only in the flesh, only in words. The poem is Geoffrey Hill's "Canticle for Good Friday" of 1956:

> The cross staggered him. At the cliff-top
> Thomas, beneath its burden, stood
> While the dulled wood
> Spat on the stones, each drop
> Of deliberate blood.
>
> A clamping, cold-figured day
> Thomas (not transfigured) stamped, crouched,
> Watched
> Smelt vinegar and blood. He
> As yet unsearched, unscratched,
>
> And suffered to remain
> At such near distance
> (A slight miracle might cleanse
> His brain
> Of all attachments, claw-roots of sense)
>
> In unaccountable darkness moved away
> The strange flesh untouched, carrion-sustenance
> Of staunchest love, choicest defiance,
> Creation's issue congealing (and one woman's).[52]

The music and the physical density of the poem, its attention to the singular occasion, is extraordinary, words effecting in the reader the very stuff of action and substance. Here is the crucifixion seen from the witness of the disciple Thomas—doubting Thomas, the one who will later seek tangible proof of the risen Lord's reality. Poised on the cliff-top of Calvary, Thomas staggers and is staggered by the burden and mystery of the cross. Words explain nothing, look both ways—but bring into being. Thomas, like us, is a frail human figure, not transfigured as Christ has been and seen in glory before the passion, and subject to the suffering of watching, smelling, and feeling the agony that is so close and yet utterly beyond the reach of sense, "at such near distance." Here, at this crucial moment of agony, there is not even the slightest of miracles to relieve him from the "unaccountable darkness" of the death of Jesus on Good Friday. The body on the cross is already a cadaver, "carrion-sustenance," universal and utterly particular, seen by Mathias Grünewald and soon to be the body portrayed by Hans Holbein and described by Fyodor Dostoevsky—"Creation's issue congealing (and one woman's)."

This is the body of the icons and of Grünewald—the body of utter desolation and Christ in glory. It is the finally ascetic body. And what of us? We remain, perhaps, still like the prisoners in Kafka's story *In the Penal Settlement*, ever straining to read what is beyond our gaze, because it is the text that is inscribed on our own bodies. We are like the condemned man at the beginning of that story, caught as in the web of Piranesi's *Carceri d'Invenzione*, "a stupid-looking wide-mouthed creature with bewildered hair and face" bound in a "heavy chain controlling the small chains locked on the prisoner's ankles, wrists and neck, chains which were themselves attached to each other by communicating links."[53] It is only in leaving such inscribed and circumscribed bodies can we fully realize the uncircumscribed body of the true incarnation in utter negation and the silence that is the purity of the resurrected, divinized flesh and is the final overcoming of all words in the silence of the Word.

5

Asceticism as a Way of Love, with a Modern Excursus

> Never has any thing in this World loved too much, but many things have
> been loved in a fals way: and all in too short a Measure. . . . We should be
> all Life and Mettle and Vigor and Lov to evry Thing. And that would Poys
> us. I dare confidently say that evry Person in the Whole World ought to be
> Beloved as much as this.[1]

The English poet and spiritual writer of the seventeenth century, Thomas
Traherne speaks of "poise"—a balance in life that is born, he suggests, of
mettle, vigor, and a love for all things. It is perhaps, and seemingly paradoxically, a quality that is not far removed from that rest or "passionlessness"
sought by the fathers and mothers of the desert tradition, which was the fruit
of a striving for purity of heart and a losing of oneself in the otherness of
God in Christ—a true finding of the self. This quality in asceticism will be
found by the end of this chapter, but by a somewhat unexpected route, and
one characterized, I suggest, by mettle, vigor, and a deep and true love for
all things, realized finally in what the Christian tradition has known as the
resurrection body. The subjects of our reflection will be a group of women
whose lives have come to us by a tradition of storytelling that might be called
hagiographic, certainly graphic, and clearly fictive in its narrative form. They
are lives told in stories and texts through extremes, lives ostensibly of conversion from the carnal to the spiritual, but lives shot through with the language
and textuality of the erotic, lives of love experienced and transfigured yet still
known through the body as both desert and place of fulfillment. Texts into
bodies and bodies into texts: the lives of these ascetic women which we will
follow in our reading are not to be read *literally*—although perhaps at some

deep and profound level that is also not true. They are best understood in an *absolutely* literal sense, depending on what we mean by the word literal.[2] Certainly, as Benedicta Ward has rightly reminded us in her book *Harlots of the Desert*, the stories of their lives, which have come down to us from an initially oral tradition, are not to be read as biographies, or reports of events that have actually taken place, or taken as psychological narratives of relationships.[3] Rather, they are *theologies*, realized through a sense of the sacred found only within the experience of the body as loved and realized, disciplined and ruled. But in the end the language that sustains their stories loses its location specifically in *either* the physical and erotic *or* the spiritual and sacred, and not as exclusive options, for it carries easily from one to the other, with easy, loving, though sometimes harsh, transgression. The forerunner and Mother of all such women is Mary Magdalene, *apostola apostolorum*, who bears the myth and metaphor of her story without compromise in her flesh.[4] For though a text more or less banished from the canon of Scripture (which treats Mary in a rather different way, distanced and pushed beyond physical reach—*noli me tangere*—"do not touch me"[5]), still we read in the Gospel of Philip that she is the most intimate of Christ's companions and that "Christ loved her more than all his disciples, and used to kiss her often on the mouth."[6] As the beloved of Christ she is truly a woman of flesh and blood. Yet, as remembered in a recent fictional life of Mary, Michèle Roberts' *The Wild Girl* (1984), like every true ascetic, she finally vanishes from this world, her decaying mortal remains hidden in obscurity and she living on only in her story as it is passed from generation to generation. "No trace of her has ever been found. Nor have we received news of her death. We do no know where her body lies. We have uncovered and copied and passed on what she wrote in her book, as we have passed on by word of mouth the stories and songs that came from her. Pray for us. Amen."[7] Like Moses and St. Antony, her grave is unknown, and she lives, like her sisters, in the mouths and songs of others, her life a text.

A model of repentance, Mary Magdalene provides the pattern for subsequent literary figures behind whom are perhaps shadowy historical personages now lost in the mists of time, merged into the stories and the impossible, often sacramental, ascetic visions that they have become. The first of these, St. Pelagia, is, like Mary Magdalene, a legendary figure who is the merging of a number of originals. Her earliest incarnation is from the early fourth century, and is mentioned by both St. Ambrose and St. Chrysostom. Here, Pelagia is a fifteen-year-old girl who flings herself from a window into the sea to escape the soldiery in Antioch during the Diocletian persecutions. In a later incarnation, Pelagia is from Tarsus and is burned to death for refusing to become the mistress of the emperor. But it is in her middle persona, and certainly the most mythic, between these two images of sexual resistance, that Pelagia is most fascinating and most developed within the context of the ascetic tradition. Her story is told by the self-styled Deacon James from the fourth century, translated into Latin by Eustochius,[8] and readily available to English readers in both Helen Waddell's *The Desert Fathers* (1936) and the work of Ward. It is a tale of beautiful reversals.

The story begins with a convocation of bishops in the city of Antioch, among them Nonnus, "the most holy man of God [says the narrator], my bishop, a marvelous man and a most observant monk of the monastery called Tabennisis."[9] As the bishops discuss theological questions, the city courtesan, Pelagia, rides by with the chorus of the theater, "dressed in the height of fantasy"—that is, wearing nothing at all except jewels, pearls, and gold ornaments, her perfume filling the air with sweetness. The good bishops avert their eyes "as if from a very great sin," except Nonnus, who gazes at her in rapture. Has he fallen prey to the lust of the flesh, or is it indeed love at first sight? In subsequent debate with his ascetic, and no doubt scruffy colleagues, Nonnus "buried his face on his knees over the holy Bible" and then speaks, as if from the very word of Scripture itself:

> What do you think, beloved brothers, how many hours does this woman spend in her chamber giving all her mind and attention to adorning herself for the play, in order to lack nothing in beauty and adornment of the body; she wants to please all those who see her, lest those who are her lovers today find her ugly and do not come back tomorrow. Here we are, who have an almighty Father in heaven offering us heavenly gifts and rewards, our immortal Bridegroom, who promises good things to his watchmen, things that cannot be valued, "which eye has not seen, nor ear heard, nor has it entered into the heart of man to know what things God has prepared for those who love him" (I Cor. 2:9). What else can I say? When we have such promises, when we are going to see the great and glorious face of our Bridegroom which has a beauty beyond compare, "upon which the cherubim do not dare to gaze" (I Pet. 1:12), why do we not adorn ourselves and wash the dirt from our unhappy souls, why do we let ourselves lie so neglected?[10]

Pelagia, then, becomes for Nonnus an image for the beauty of the soul before God. Subsequently, it is her turn to fall in love as she listens to the bishop preaching, and she is bewitched by the spiritual beauty of his words. As a result, she reverses her way of life, selling all her wealth and taking the way of the ascetic after her baptism by the good bishop, quoting to him the incident of Jesus' encounter with "the harlot in Samaria" in John 8. Physical and spiritual beauty are merged, each rooted in texts of Scripture, in the love story between Nonnus and Pelagia. She withdraws to the solitude of the desert, and they never meet in this life again, though they continue joined in mutual prayer. As she leaves Antioch for her cell on the Mount of Olives, outside Jerusalem, Nonnus likens her to the Mary in the gospel story (Luke 10:42), who "has chosen the better part" in preferring the *vita contemplativa* to the *vita activa* of her sister Martha.[11]

Therefore, Pelagia withdraws to a solitary ascetic life, even renouncing her gender, and content to be known as the monk Pelagius until her death. But what is remarkable about this narrative is that it remains a story of love and even affection between Pelagia and Nonnus, as her beauty inspires his vision and his spiritual insight prompts her repentance—and their love is fulfilled rather than lost in their solitary lives. Indeed, if the demon of lust is a frequent subject in *The Sayings of the Desert Fathers* (the *Apophthegmata Patrum*), then the image of the beauty of the courtesan and its capacity to bring people to the divine vision is also startlingly present, as John the Dwarf compares the soul to a courtesan: "One of the old men said, 'John you are like a courtesan who shows her beauty to increase the number of her lovers.' Abba John kissed him and said, 'you are quite right, father.'"[12]

* * *

An altogether edgier story is that of another repentant prostitute, Thaïs, also a legendary figure emerging out of fourth-century Egypt, though perhaps linked with the Egyptian mistress of Alexander the Great, who bears the same name. She appears briefly in Jacobus de Voragine's hagiographical collection *The Golden Legend* of the thirteenth century, and is notoriously reincarnated in Anatole France's novel *Thaïs* (1890), which I will discuss shortly. But perhaps her most fascinating literary appearance is in the play *Pafnutius* by the tenth-century canoness of the Saxon Imperial Abbey of Gandersheim, Hrotsvit. Thaïs' very persistence in the literary tradition is not without importance, and her story is not without parallels among other women of the ascetic tradition.

According to the Latin translation of the earliest Greek text that recounts her life,[13] Thaïs is a beautiful courtesan, so attractive that many "for her sake sold all that they had" and engaged in quarrels and fights for her favors.[14] Finally, the monk and ascetic Paphnutius, seeking her salvation, disguises himself as one of her prospective lovers, and, offering her money, enters her bedchamber. It is she who admits that God watches everything, allowing Paphnutius to prompt her to penitence and forsake her way of life, casting herself on God's grace. Immediately burning all her goods, she allows the monk to incarcerate her in a small cell, walled up so that she has to endure the stench of her own excrement, and fed only occasionally. After three years, Paphnutius "began to be anxious" for her welfare, and consults the great Father Antony inquiring of him if her sins had been forgiven by the Lord. In a vision, Paul, one of Antony's disciples, sees a glorious bed made up with rich cloths and guarded by three virgins—and was told that this was for the harlot Thaïs. Realizing that she has indeed received God's forgiveness, Paphnutius hurries to Thaïs' cell only to find her unwilling to emerge. Eventually, she does come out, forgiven not because of the rigor of her penance but because she had never forgotten her sins, thus calling down divine grace upon herself. After two weeks, she dies peacefully.

What is it in this stark and deeply uncomfortable story that endures in literature and has kept its place within the traditions of asceticism? France was appalled by it, changing the saintly Paphnutius into Paphnuce, a young Alexandrian nobleman, himself promiscuous in his youth, but then converted to a fierce, harsh asceticism. But he is to learn only when it is too late that his treatment of Thaïs is governed by his desire and pride as finally he returns to her in her cell in order to bring her back from her life of death to the world of love and beauty. It is, indeed, hard not to be revolted by Paphnutius' harsh behavior as it crushes the life out of the one whom he seeks to "save." But that is to misunderstand the complex nature, and the literary structure of the hagiographic tradition, and the parabolic demands of its abnormalities within social narratives. In what possible sense is the story of Paphnutius and Thaïs a love story and a celebration of the beauty of the ascetic body redeemed by the pure love of God's grace offered in excess of any possible confession or penance?

To answer this we must turn to the extraordinary dramas of Christian saints and martyrs by Hrotsvit of Gandersheim. Hrotsvit takes as her literary model the Latin comic dramatist Terence, and seeks to beat him at his own game (an early example of not allowing the devil all the best tunes), turning his comic rhetoric against itself in dramatic portraits of the monastic ideal, which are both intellectual and emotional in their appeal. She writes in spirited manner:

> Many Catholics one may find, and we are also guilty of charges of this kind, who for the beauty of their eloquent style, prefer the uselessness of pagan guile to the usefulness of sacred Scripture. There are also others, who, devoted to Sacred lecture and scornful of the works of other pagans, yet frequently read Terence's fiction, and as they delight in the sweetness of his style and diction, they are stained by learning of wicked things in his depiction. Therefore, I, the Forceful Testimony of Gandersheim, have not refused to imitate him in writing whom others honor in reading, so that in that self-same

form of composition in which the shameless acts of lascivious women were phrased the laudable chastity of sacred virgins be praised within the limits of my little talent.[15]

In her play *Pafnutius* (or, *The Conversion of the Harlot Thaïs*), Hrotsvit tells a love story in which the events of the narrative are to be read at the level of metaphor, the initial "secret location" of Thaïs' love chamber finally realized in the heavenly vision of "a bed with white linen beautifully spread" of Antonius' disciple Paul.[16] The ascetic life, understood as a way of love, sustains the Terentian imagery of the erotic, and is finally fulfilled in the resurrection of the body whereby, in Pafnutius' concluding words, "Thaïs be resurrected exactly as she was, a human being, and joining the white lambs may enter eternal joys."[17] Thaïs, by God's grace, remains beautiful, celebrated like Pelagia before her, her filthy cell an image of her sinful life, mired in its own excrement, from which she emerges in all her glory, quickly divinized in her resurrected and perfected body.

In Hrotsvit's play, Pafnutius first visits Thaïs in lover's disguise, employing language from the Song of Songs. His call to contrition is also a wooing, as the flames of her "illicit passions" are forsaken for the flames caused by the public burning of all her goods. What never varies is the language of love in a series of reversals between body and soul (through what Pafnutius calls "the medicine of contraries"[18]) through which Thaïs *becomes* what she at first only *seems* to be—that is, a being of beauty in both soul and body—"having cast aside the rough pelt of a goat, she will be clothed with the soft wool of the lamb."[19] In Hrotsvit's play, the cruel penance that so revolted France, is tempered by repeated comments made by Pafnutius to the great Antonius expressing concern for her welfare, until finally Paul's vision of the great bed and "the beauty of this marvelous brightness" takes Thaïs full circle to the glory of her bedchamber, now perfected in the vision of heaven.

Hrotsvit opens her play with a long and highly complex discussion between Pafnutius and his disciples on the mathematical and musical principles of world order, the ensuing drama being played out according to the number symbolism of the "music-lesson" wherein the discordances in Thaïs' life are brought into a proper harmony.[20] In the heavenly vision of Paul, Thaïs' place within the celestial harmony is assured as from her emanates the spheral tone that ensures the *musica mundana* and celestial harmony. Hrotsvit dramatizes beautifully the ancient sense of this tale as theology told as a love story, the extremes of asceticism irrigated and concluded in a vision of the resurrection body that perfectly unites body and soul in pure being, a realization of the sacred in the pure profanity of the ascetic's prisonlike cell from which Thaïs, like St. Antony, emerges in her full glory.

* * *

But perhaps the greatest of these ascetic women whose narratives follow that of Mary Magdalene and for whom asceticism is a way of love, revealing gloriously, and even profanely, the works of God in the resurrection body known only in the body of the desert, the body denied and realized,[21] is St. Mary of Egypt. In her, connections are made in the religious life that are too often kept apart and made in a spirit of profound generosity. The impetus for this theme of generosity within asceticism emerges from a book written some years ago by a Glasgow colleague of mine, George Newlands, titled *Generosity and the Christian Future* (1997). Much of the remainder of this chapter will be in the form of retellings of the story of St. Mary, seemingly at alarming variance with one another, but actually, and like the lives of Pelagia and Thaïs, all the same in a reappraisal of what it means to live the ascetic life in full generosity of both body and spirit.

St. Mary is also, like her sister courtesans, probably largely the stuff of legend, though we hear of her frequently in the literature of the lives of the early Christian desert saints of the fourth and fifth centuries, and she became widely popular in the Middle Ages throughout Christendom. According to the legend, Mary left home at the age of twelve, and spent seventeen years in the city of Alexandria as a prostitute, until, at the age of twenty-nine, she joined a pilgrimage to Jerusalem, paying her way by offering her sexual services to the sailors. In Jerusalem, an invisible power holds her back from entering the church with her fellow pilgrims, and as she gazes at an icon of the Blessed Virgin, she is told to cross the Jordan where she will find rest. Taking three loaves with her, she vanishes into the desert, where she remains, almost unseen by the world for the rest of her long life, covered only by her hair, which grows to hide her body as her clothes wear out. Unable to read, still she is instructed in the Christian faith by divine intervention. One day, a devout priest, Zossimus, stumbles upon Mary by accident and listens to her story. Promising to meet her in the same place during the next Holy Week and bring her the holy sacrament of communion, he duly returns eagerly, almost like a lover to his beloved, only to find her dead. A passing lion helps him to bury her body.

There are the simple essentials of the story of St. Mary, which we will now look at more closely in various literary versions, both ancient and modern, for her narrative also is capable of bearing levels of literary weight and retelling, a theological fiction that acknowledges the robust persistence of the hagiographic myth.

Mary truly was a gentlewoman and a generous one, and I want to suggest, in an appeal to your imagination, that her life, divided by her great act of repentance in Jerusalem, is actually a much more sustained and fully embodied example of the ascetic life than is usually acknowledged. As we recall again the early Christian fascination with that great erotic poem of the Hebrew Bible, the Song of Songs, read as an account of divine love, we begin to see Mary as lover, transfiguring her early indulgences into a deeply moving love affair with Father Zossimus as each of them seek the perfection of divine love in true generosity of spirit. Did (or does) Mary exist except in the text of her story? Is her life not one of reversal, but transfiguration in the life of love, an impossible instantiation of theological claims lived to the full in body and soul?

In addition to "generosity," we need to keep in mind two other words that will sustain the narrative of Mary's story, and they are "culture" and "memory." Let us take *culture* first. The third volume of Michel Foucault's *History of Sexuality* is titled *The Care of the Self* (*Le Souci de Soi*; 1984), and it is concerned to explore the relationship between culture and sexuality—the latter being an important item in Mary's life, at least (though perhaps, as we shall see, by no means exclusively) in its early stages. Foucault revisits the traditional Christian distrust and even dismissal of sexuality, and recasts sexual behavior as within the arts of culture, an "art of existence" that redefines the nature of self and therefore also the nature of the body. Foucault writes, "This art of the self no longer focuses so much on the excesses one can indulge in and that need to be mastered in order to exercise one's domination over others. It gives increasing emphasis to the frailty of the individual faced with the manifold ills that sexual activity can give rise to. It also underscores the need to subject that activity to a universal form by which one is bound, a form grounded in both nature and reason, and valid for all human beings."[22] With a culture of self-care that includes sexuality, Foucault seeks a proper *balance* or equilibrium between self-control, on the one hand, and a pure enjoyment of the self on the other, a balance that is free from exaggerated practices of either prohibition or indulgence. In short, he seeks the "development of an art of existence" that expresses a perfect balance between the individual and the universal, the self and the other, the horizontal and the vertical planes. It does not deny an ethics of pleasure or participate in what Foucault sees as the fatal Christian tendency to regard sexuality as "linked to evil by its form and its effects." Nevertheless, he roundly asserts, "in itself and substantially, it is not an evil."[23] Such a culture of existence does not merely find its natural fulfillment in

monogamous marriage, which has been the standard form of cultural protection and balance in the West, at least (often theoretically) for women, against
the vicissitudes of sexuality and kinship.[24] Certainly, the monastic tradition
has provided a way out from a potentially crippling and patriarchal marriage
system for some admittedly generally affluent and independent women, since
its early days. But there is also a radical alternative, strangely we may think
at first sight, found in the asceticism of the desert saints, and the story of
St. Mary is a perfect example of this, not least because it is precisely that, a
story of which the elements of fabulation or storytelling actually endorse the
practiced, cultured discipline that is the ascetic rule—a rule of the highest art
of living that is actually belied by the image of the ascetic as a skinny, scruffy
waif whose only concern is to abandon the body for the assumed good of the
soul. Actually nothing, I have been suggesting, is further from the truth of a
genuine asceticism, of which St. Antony (and before him the Christ of the
resurrection) is the founder. And St. Mary, indeed, like Pelagia and Thaïs,
remains gorgeous, even sexy in her body, to the end. For her, also and perhaps
above all, asceticism is truly a way of love.

So much for *culture*: the second word is *memory*. I go back to the seventh-
century text by St. Sophronius, patriarch of Jerusalem and also a monk—a
life of St. Mary that is endlessly beguiling and fascinating, a fiction with a
deep theological, indeed liturgical, soul. Sophronius' *Life of St. Mary of Egypt*,
the text used, after its translation into Latin, during the fifth week of Lent
in the Western liturgy, read at matins on the Thursday morning, to celebrate
Mary as a model of repentance,[25] is certainly a work of miraculous excess. I
will come back to it in detail shortly. Edith Wyschogrod, as we have already
noted,[26] considers also a much later, twelfth-century version of Mary's life
and its linking—again liturgical—of three narrative strands: the narrative of
Mary's life itself, the "true story" that is told by the narrator-witness who is
distinct in his own time from the tale's characters, and the "we" of the present community who look back and pray for Mary's intercession. For this last
community, which includes ourselves as readers—as generous readers, Mary's
life is to be taken as a whole, at once both as prostitute and as saint—"Mary
is retrospectively interpreted as always already sinful and always already
redeemed, a life making and unmaking itself." [27] As hagiography, again, her
life is precisely not presented as a model to be copied, for it is deliberately and
fabulously beyond our reach, but as a story to be read and meditated on in
the imagination and in true liturgical living.[28]

The reading of Sophronius' *Life* becomes, then, a liturgical memorial,
an act done in memory of her in which her life is recreated and reassembled
both and at once as an icon of repentance *and* as a way of love. The excess

of sainthood provides a pattern not to be reenacted in our poor lives, but like the eucharistic memorial, to be "done (the Greek verb in 1 Cor 11:24 is ποιεῖτε [*poieite*], from which we derive the term "poetry") in remembrance" in the generosity of our reading and, one hopes, action. In Sophronius' text, Mary's final act before her death is to receive the blessed sacrament from the hands of the priest Zossima, truly a consummation of her own eucharistic life of giving. Before this, Zossima had marveled that all her speech to him had indicated an intimate knowledge of Holy Scripture, only to be told that she was illiterate and had been instructed directly by the Word: "Never in any way did I learn letters [she admits] nor have I ever heard any one reading or singing them, but the Word of God living and active itself teaches man knowledge" (Heb 4:12).[29] At the end of Sophronius' *Life*, we are informed that the monks preserved the story of St. Mary without writing it down—it was preserved as an act of loving memory in their lives—and the author has "told in writing what I heard orally."[30] We see clearly, then, the three strands of narration—from oral to written until, finally, we, the community of readers, the interpretive community,[31] are called to remember the living and active words of the saint's life that is wholly embedded in Scripture, and recreating in our lives, in the generosity of the poetic imagination, the miraculous arts of her existence.

Mary's life is only finally completed in her singular participation in the Eucharist in which alone she is perfected in death. Like Pelagia and Thaïs, she dies but in her death realizes the full integrity of body and soul. But the narrative of her ascetic life in the desert is an ever-changing scenario in which her loving relationship with Father Zossima is a central element. Zossima, the monk who had become spiritually muscle-bound by his perfection in his religious calling, meets the true ascetic in Mary, charming and fascinating to the end, whose charity, as always in the true ascetic, rests in her refusal to presume in her own perfection of virtue. If the Cappadocian Gregory of Nyssa saw the perfection of the spiritual life as an *epektasis*, or continual growth,[32] more immediately in the traditions of desert asceticism, the fifth-century *Ascetic Discourses* of Abbot Isaiah of Scetis emphasize the life of love as central, and each must find his or her own way in their journey. Giving the scriptural example of Martha and Mary, and unlike later tradition, at least in the West, which tended to prioritize the contemplative way of Mary, reducing Martha to the role of the anxious drudge (Luke 10:38–42), Abbot Isaiah, like Meister Eckhart after him, gives both ways their due, writing, "Then the zeal of Mary and Martha was shown. Lazarus found the others free from anxiety, reclining at table with Jesus. While Martha carries out her duty with diligence and joy,

Mary carries the alabaster jar of myrrh and anoints the Lord's feet."[33] This image of the two contrasting women in these most ascetic of discourses is peculiarly relevant for St. Mary of Egypt. First, in monastic circles, Mary was quickly compared, even confused with, the figure of Mary Magdalene, the repentant prostitute who is linked also in tradition with the sister of Martha and the woman with the alabaster jar of ointment (Luke 7:37–50). Second, there is a cultured, relaxed quality about the image of the two women in the gospel narrative reclining at table with Jesus—something almost *risqué* (this point is later discussed in the context of the art of Velázquez)—and yet here the image is set up as an example of the ascetic life well lived, and linked by Abbot Isaiah (who was no slouch in the practices of asceticism, and still was well aware at the same time of the challenges to interpersonal relationships that the monastic life presented) to the great hymn to love of 1 Corinthians 13: "If I speak in the languages of men and angels, or give away all my possessions and deliver my body to be burned but do not have love, I am a noisy gong or a clanging cymbal. Love suffers long, is kind, not jealous, is not proud, or arrogant or rude. It does not seek its own things, is not provoked. It does not resent evil."[34] The way of love is indeed central to the ascetic tradition.

And so, turning in more detail now to Sophronius' *Life*, let us take a final glance at Foucault as we carry into our reading the three terms—*generosity, culture,* and *memory.* Foucault has been called a "theoretician of resistance,"[35] interpreting against the grain in revisionary rewritings as resistances to the flow of text that have the characteristics of ascetic principles. They are, we might almost say, examples of writing in the gospel tradition of the revisionary principle of "you have always thought, but I now say to you" (Matt 5:21–22). With cenobitic rigor, all claims to particularity, even all forms of consciousness, suffer mortification in the absolute suppression of nostalgia and self-indulgence. What emerges then, paradoxically and strangely (and we see it in Foucault's reading of Gustave Flaubert's strange work, *The Temptation of Saint Anthony*), is the refusal of the body to be reduced by the text. Asceticism is a way of perfection that is actually expressed in the irrepressible nature of the body, in the bodily embracing of the Word and its capacity always to be resurrected. The generous reader reads in resistance to any textual closure, embracing the text, like Mary herself, in a move even more radical than the Derridean shift from the book to writing,[36] but rather into a liturgical orality that the monks who first preserved her story well understood, and of which Sophronius preserves the memory in his written narrative.

The story of St. Mary of Egypt is often read simply as a tale of lust turned into love.[37] Like her distinguished predecessor Mary Magdalene, with whom she bears so many comparisons, including, like the English Lady Godiva in a later age, a habit acquired late in life of wandering around naked and using her hair as her only garment,[38] Mary became in the church an icon of repentance, and now, without in the least wishing to deny the importance of repentance, I want to give another, perhaps more modern and mettlesome (though infinitely ancient and by no means contradictory), turn to her story. In her desert wanderings and what I want to call her love affair with Father Zossima, she becomes truly what she always had been, her body, finally deified and consumed in her consuming of the sacrament, a place of generosity and love, her asceticism a cultural and religious perfection of her youthful excesses.[39]

The story, as told by Sophronius, actually begins not with Mary, but with Father Zossima, a self-satisfied and altogether "good" monk who seems to have the godly life all sewn up, while Mary, on the other hand, is sewing her wild oats with a vengeance. It is a theme fairly common in the literature of the desert: for example, there is the saintly Father Piteroum in the fourth-century *Lausiac History*, who similarly revels in his own spiritual perfection until he meets a idiotic scullery maid who is streets ahead of him in the sanctity stakes precisely because it never occurred to anyone to think that she was anything but a mad kitchen maid and the lowest of the low.[40] The shift in the narrative from Zossima to Mary through the priest's desert wanderings, pursued tirelessly and eagerly "as if he were hurrying towards a well-known inn,"[41] to his first encounter with the wild woman Mary, her naked body scorched black by the sun and her hair now white and cropped, anticipates Roman Jakobson's bifurcated tropes of the metaphorical and the metonymic. The initial metaphorical axis is the vertical, "based on a similarity between a word and its invisible, often transcendental, meaning,"[42] represented in Father Zossima's isolated life of spiritual perfection. In a metonymic structure, on the other hand, multiple terms coexist on a horizontal plane, represented in Mary's highly social existence (despite her years of solitude) and the horizons of the desert, a landscape that flattens the vertical, making the transcendent irresistibly present in its utopic spaces.[43]

Sophronius is a good storyteller. He begins by encouraging his reader in the arts of literary generosity and the imagination, a necessary precondition for the reader of the hagiographic tradition, writing, "If, however, such readers of this narrative are found, who are so overcome by the miraculous nature of this account that they will not want to believe it, may the Lord be merciful to them! For they consider the infirmity of human nature and think that miracles related about people are impossible."[44] Indeed, we should be prepared to believe in miracles. In any good narrative there must be an element of the willing suspension of disbelief[45] on the part of the reader, a willingness to accept the excess of the tale and the likely impossibility in preference to the unconvincing possibility.[46] The story begins in Palestine, with Father Zossima bored with his superlative achievements in the monastic life. His life, lived entirely on the vertical plane in relation to the transcendent and isolated inasmuch as no one can touch him in his spiritual perfection, seeks further afield, in the vast mystery of the desert, for new challenges and the desired, necessary disapproval. He wants a new challenge, and he is to find one in Mary. But first, he sets out across the holy river Jordan to a monastery where he encounters, much to his edification, "old men, glorious in the life of action and also of contemplation, fervent in spirit, serving the Lord."[47] The monastery is utterly lost in the desert, unknown to all in the world. Its monks, at the beginning of each Lent, observe a rule whereby each monk leaves the monastery confines to seek solitariness in the desert in primal destitution, for each "had nothing but his own body and its tattered clothing and when his nature demanded food, he fed on whatever grew in the desert."[48] Their one rule was not to know about each other, and thus there was no spirit of competition among them—and in this worthy, if somewhat dry, spirit, Father Zossima sets out, ever hurrying as if to find a familiar place of refreshment. It is then that he meets Mary as it were as in a vision, a mere shadow of a human form, and his prayers cease, overcome by a more demanding presence. "At first he was troubled, thinking that he saw the appearance of a devil and he trembled. But he protected himself with the sign of the Cross, and chased away fear (his prayers now were over) and he saw that there really was some kind of being walking along at mid-day. It was a woman and she was naked, her body black as if scorched by the fierce heat of the sun, the hair on her head was white as wool and short, coming down only to the neck."[49] Mary, the harlot, is seen by the priest as she was always seen by her lovers, naked and without shame though her hair is like that of the lamb, an image used also of Thaïs, and he, just like Mary's lovers of old, chases after her protesting that he is merely an old man and a sinner. They eventually stop at a strange place, the bed of a dried-up stream though no stream could ever have flowed naturally in that barren spot. As Ward, in her commentary on the narrative, remarks, it is a place full of intricate symbols—but she restricts herself to the overtly religious signs; Mary's loaves, which sustain her and remain undiminished, like the loaves of Elijah, her walking on the water in the manner of Jesus, and finally the lion who effects her burial, the sign of the prince of peace. But there are also other signs, more deeply hidden in the textual body of the story. As always in these narratives, reading must be against the grain and parabolic, a "medicine of contraries." At this dried up river, Sophronius asks, "Where could a stream have come from in that land? The ground there had that appearance naturally."[50] But the place—any place—of encounter with Mary is a natural oasis, her very presence always a source of refreshment in a parched land and for the famished soul of the priest.

Before she will speak to Zossima, Mary insists that he gives her a cloak, which "partially hid the nakedness of her body." She is perfectly conscious of her body and its effects on the monk. She asks him for his blessing so that he performs the proper function of the priest, after which she in turn blesses him, "since grace," he insists, "is recognized not by office but by the gifts of the Spirit." Still, Zossima is full of fear and confusion before this strange being and, as if faint from love, falls to the ground, until Mary, with simple efficiency, helps him to his feet and assures him that she is just a woman: "I am not a spirit but earth and ashes, entirely flesh, in no way calling to mind a spirit of phantasy."[51] From the beginning to the end of her story, Mary is just a woman, and in this spirit she tells her tale to Zossima. Considering her forty-seven years of solitary struggle in the desert, she has retained a pretty lively sense of narrative, sustained as she has been only by one washing in the waters of the Jordan and three loaves of bread. She cuts no corners in recounting the sexual exploits of her youth, when her excesses as she comes up out of her native Egypt to Jerusalem are nothing if not spectacular. She was, we are told, a huntress of "the souls of young men"[52] until, at the festival of the Exaltation of the Precious Cross, she enters the cathedral in Jerusalem, and after hearing the voice of her namesake, the Mother of God, calling her to cross the Jordan (an image of baptism), she enters into her restless wanderings in the desert wherein she finds rest, the true reality of her body as flesh and spirit called forth in the sacred desert that is at the same time an absolutely profane desert.[53]

Her journey, of course, is not without its struggles, like those endured by St. Antony and all other desert wanderers: with "the wild beasts of irrational desires,"[54] the longing for food and drink, and for lewd songs. Meanwhile, her body is tempered by the extremes of the physical conditions of the wilderness, matching in their extremity the excesses of her previous indulgences. Yet through it all, and in her natural embracing of Scripture, she remains the same Mary—her sexuality and physicality both and at once consumed and fulfilled, her nourishment real and effective, though now described in sacramental terms.

And then she meets Father Zossima, the last and most perfect of her human lovers. She fascinates him with her story, so much so that she has to restrain him, impetuous as he is, from bowing down and kneeling before her, just like a young man in love. She sends him away for a year, almost like a test of his constancy, during which he is to stay within the walls of the monastery, returning on the same day as all the other monks return from their solitary desert journeys, while she meanwhile and typically, with bewitching mystery, "disappeared very swiftly into the depths of the desert,"[55] leaving Zossima absurdly kissing the ground on which her feet have trodden, having just met a girl named Mary. Was she real, he wonders, and who would believe him if he told them? A year later he sets out as anxious and impatient as any lover to see his beloved, tormented by understandable doubts. These are expressed in Zossima's excited thoughts in Sophronius' story: "What will happen if she does come? How will she cross the Jordan since there is no boat? How can she come to me, unworthy as I am? Alas, I am wretched; who is keeping such beauty from me?"[56] Mary, it would seem, has not lost her capacity to charm the boys—but it is a charm transfigured, her asceticism a way of love, as she crosses the Jordan to her lover—but in the miraculous manner of her Lord, walking on the water. She is, to the priest, a dream woman, but in her romance she is finally absorbed in the mystery of the sacrament as she eats but three grains of the lentils that he has brought for her sustenance as, for her, "the grace of the Holy Spirit is sufficient to keep whole the substance of the soul."[57]

But as in all true love stories, and the stories of all ascetics, the idyll cannot last, at least in this world. As she lies dead in the sand, her lover sees words written above her head giving instructions for her burial, a final miracle as she herself could not write, but lives now in the words of her story, which is her memorial, a truly cultured lady who brings the complex stuff of her life to fruition not in the sterile perfection of solipsistic transcendence, but in the harsh, real and lovely planes of the desert. In a final symbol, the true touch of the mythic, a princely lion helps her frail, aged priest and lover to bury her naked body, while he returns to the monastery to tell the story that "kept the memory of the saint in fear and love."[58] The memory remains in the telling from generation to generation of monks, until Bishop Sophronius commits it to writing for us as hagiography, written for our learning and liturgical celebration.

And what have we learned? In the final part of this chapter, which has read these narratives of the ascetic harlots of the desert, we will look at two more recent, cultured reflections on the impossible life of St. Mary of Egypt, one a deliberate retelling in a work of modern fiction, the other connected with her only in my own imagination—in a painting from the early seventeenth century by the Spanish artist Velázquez of an old woman cooking eggs.[59] In this peasant "Mary" of the Counter-Reformation, we see her in the figure of a beautiful, dignified old peasant woman engaged in the humblest of culinary tasks, providing simple food for her "Zossima," here a young boy who is holding under his right arm a honeydew melon that has a cord threaded about it so that this simple fruit seems to resemble an imperial orb. "It is good to keep close the secret of a king, but to reveal gloriously the works of God" (Tobit 2)—those are the words from the apocryphal text that preface Sophronius' *Life*. The glorious revelation is not in things representing earthly power and wealth, but in the woman's gesture of generosity and her steadfast, firm look as she prepares her three eggs—a reminder to us of the three loaves of the woman of the desert. Hers is a life well lived, her beauty undimmed in age against a dark, mysterious background.[60]

The second retelling is a deliberate fictional recreation of Mary's life by the English novelist Michèle Roberts, in her book *Impossible Saints* (1997). Here we see, in this deliberate narrative of reversal, the saint in all her glory. In Roberts' modern version of the story, Mary's life is, indeed, in a sense, reversed, though in a reversal that illustrates her true transfiguration. The first half of her now-contemporary life in the novel is spent as "a maiden lady of uncertain age,"[61] housekeeper to the rather dull Father Zozimus, an English parish priest, the highlight of whose year is a rather monastic two-week holiday in the staid seaside town of Blackpool in the company of a group of other priests. This is his version of the monastic community visited by his ancient predecessor Zossima. But like the Zossima of Sophronius, the Reverend Zozimus of Roberts' version of the story tires of the boring spiritual perfection of his life in England and, in old age and retirement, gets a wanderlust and sets off for Egypt and the Holy Land. The life of the tourist, however, does not suit him, until one day, quite by accident, he is left behind by the tour bus and finds himself walking along a road that "led away from the river Jordan into the desert. He had somehow come the wrong way. He was lost."[62]

At this point, his journey significantly crosses the path of old Zossima, who, in much the same situation, "went on tirelessly, as if he were hurrying towards a well-known inn."[63] At the end of the road for each of them, Mary is waiting, naked, gloriously suntanned and utterly desirable—for whom both priests have a desire and a longing, like soul and the flesh of the pilgrim for the courts of the Lord in Psalm 84.

> How amiable are thy dwellings: thou Lord of Hosts!
> My soul hath a desire and a longing to enter into the courts of the Lord: my
> heart and my flesh rejoice in the living God.[64]

The words of the psalmist fit perfectly Father Zozimus' experience. Like his illustrious predecessor, he encounters what he at first takes to be a mirage—a naked woman, tanned by the sun, with gray hair. But there is a difference; this time he knows her. She is, in fact, his virginal housekeeper of old whom he last seen years before boarding a train in the dull midlands English town of Swindon "destination unknown."[65] Now she is, indeed, an innkeeper, her inn called *The Oasis* being a beautiful place of sanctuary in the depths of the desert where all restraints are cast aside, a place of true culture that stirs stronger memories in the soul than ever the beach at Blackpool could do. In short, it is here that Mary turns her talent for love to its proper use. She had left her chaste life as a housekeeper because, she admits, "I discovered I had this brilliant talent for sex. . . . I really loved it and I was really good at it."[66] Paradoxically, Mary becomes thereby the true ascetic, putting to good use all the language of erotic longing, the obsession with the poetry of the Song of Songs that litters the writings of Christian spirituality. Even Origen, who rather disqualified himself in matters of sex, in his *Commentary on the Song of Songs*, though he insists that a "fleshy" understanding of the Song is "vicious," cannot finally avoid its proper implications: "This book seems to me an epithalamium, that is a wedding song, written by Solomon in the form of a play, which he recited in the character of a bride who was being married and burned with a heavenly love for her bridegroom, who is the Word of God. For whether she is the soul made after his image or the Church, she has fallen deeply in love with him."[67] The Mary of modern fiction, like the Mary of old, takes the priest as her lover and teaches him what, in his seeming perfection, he had forgotten. In each version of the story, she is profoundly present in her brown, naked body, wooing him by her absence and by her presence. But, we instinctively feel, such deep, ascetic, physical love cannot last forever, the body and spirit in perfect harmony, in perfect *askesis* or practice—or can it? Father Zozimus, it seems, has that puritan streak that is somehow bred into all of us. The modern narrative reflects, "You couldn't spend you entire life just enjoying yourself, could you? And yet he had enjoyed himself."[68] He ought to be getting back.

But that is not Mary's way. For her, there are no limits to the generosity of love—and so he stays on at *The Oasis*, running the bar with his Mary for the next twenty years. In the old story, Mary dies leaving her lover to tell her story in memory of her; she becomes the word though herself unlettered, too much in the body to have time to write like us poor scribblers who follow her so passionately. But there is always an alternative ending in literature—like the famous two endings of Charles Dickens' novel *Great Expectations*. Does it matter which we choose? Probably not, as Mary is there equally in each version. The modern Mary of *The Oasis* and her Father Zozimus die together, with Hollywood grandeur, hand in hand as they disappear into the desert, which, as is wholly proper, covers their grave (prepared by their old friend, the conveniently passing and courtly lion) and its place knows it no more.

Read either way, St. Mary of Egypt's story is a celebration of the spirit of generosity. In each case it is a spirit that is not won easily—finding out what you are best at can take a long time and a lot of effort. It lies at the heart of the ascetic way. The monks with whom Zossima stayed in the monastery were not bad at it in their Boy Scout sort of way, and the history of Western monasticism owes them much and remains more deeply engrained in us, both for good and ill, than we probably realize. But Mary was the best, an icon of repentance and a model for the good life. In her, metaphor and metonymy meet and kiss. Her cultured and countercultural life, in Newlands' words, "has nothing to do with violence or coercion. It will encourage a generous and pluriform manifestation of human community, unfettered by prescribed forms of religious conformity."[69] Paradoxically, such may grant us, as a gift, a vision of the transcendence of God, Mary's asceticism truly a way of love, a way of the gentle-woman.

We turn in the next chapter from asceticism as a way of love to asceticism imposed in further reflections on the two ways of Mary and Martha in the gospel story—the *vita contemplativa* and the *vita activa*. From the third century, when Origen first ascribed the model of the contemplative life to Mary of Bethany, her conflation with Mary Magdalene linked the ascetic life of contemplation to the repentant prostitutes whose stories we have visited in this chapter. But what of Martha—the kitchen drudge who is related in her turn, perhaps, to the scullery maid of the *Lausiac History*? To her we now turn in a different approach to the ascetic life found in the secularity of the domestic life in Western culture, and its version of the wilderness of poverty and toil—and perhaps salvation.

Excursus

The Sheltering Sky

The shift in this brief excursus from the ancient narratives of St. Mary of Egypt to Paul Bowles' twentieth-century existentialist fiction *The Sheltering Sky* (1949) is deliberately extreme and radical. And yet there are curious and haunting similarities between the two. Each narrative maps a retreat into the vastnesses and solitary world of the desert and its symbolic landscapes in contrast to the urban cultures of the ancient Near East or twentieth-century North America. Each addresses issues of sensuality and asceticism, insistent exteriority and utter interiority. Each narrates an approach to nothingness within the silence of an immense landscape. And yet they are, at the same time, utterly the opposite of one another. For if Mary's life and death are vital and creative, still present in the church's liturgical celebration, Bowles' novel is utterly without God, his characters living within the horror of an abysmal nothingness that precludes every apocalypse and every possibility of resurrection or beginning. As one critic has written, "The long decline of faith throughout the Christian west and the increasing secularization of life nearly everywhere have contributed to an intuition of exposure and nakedness that transcends politics. And it is this perception of ultimate homelessness that Paul Bowles, expatriate writer, most powerfully images in his fiction."[70] The sheltering sky, a phrase drawn from a favorite childhood song of Bowles, "Under the Sheltering Palms," becomes a deeply ironic theme throughout the novel, for if it is looked up to in the expanses of the Saharan wilderness as a kind of protection, it is also a paradoxically claustrophobic covering blocking out life and reason, and beyond it there is nothing at all, a blank nothing—an absolute negation that kills. The two central characters are a young American couple, Kit and Port Moresby, seeking to find meaning in their lives and a restoration of their marital relationship on which, despite its terrible fragility, they are utterly dependant. As they wander deeper into the desert, they become lost in an absolute isolation that ends, for Port, in death, and for Kit, in insanity. In the first of three pivotal conversations, they discuss the desert sky as shelter, the hollowness of the spoken word emerging, like Mary's, but with the quite the opposite effect, from a long silence.

> "You know," said Port, and his voice sounded unreal, as voices are likely to do after a long pause in an utterly silent spot, "the sky here's very strange. I often have the sensation when I look at it that it's a solid thing up there, protecting us from what's behind."
> Kit shuddered slightly as she said: "From what's behind?"
> "Yes."
> "But what *is* behind?" Her voice was very small.
> "Nothing, I suppose. Just darkness. Absolute night."[71]

Bowles once described himself as an existentialist; he translated Sartre's play *Huis Clos* (1944), and his fiction has been compared to that of Camus.[72] In *The Sheltering Sky*, his existentialism is radical, without moral absolutes, in complete isolation, his character without pasts or futures, and drawing deeply and personally on his own life and marriage.

Port Moresby claims to be a writer, but he cannot write, his life, in a sense, being a blank page in contrast to the desert saints whose lives entered into a total coinherence with the text of Scripture. In Port, word and flesh are wholly separate. Between Kit and Port there are few uttered truths: "She did not say the withering things that were on the tip of her tongue" (17). Words spoken or written are instruments of either torture or destruction, the very negation of the creative word and the necessary text. In consequence, there is no possibility of creating a world for themselves or of constructing a geographical sense of place. Rather, each is trapped in their isolation: Port, "unable to break out of the cage into which he had shut himself, the cage he has built long ago to save himself from love,"[73] and Kit, a prisoner of "her system of omens," little narrative shelters to give herself a sense of structure, but which become meaningless boxes unrelated to any possible narratives of being. Thus, there is no outside to their world, and yet they are lost in the immense and trackless vastnesses of the desert, both exterior and interior. If Mary and Zossima find their true selves in the *desert absolu* and eventually the community of the liturgical text, Kit and Port encounter only silence and idiotic people, exiled and surviving on the edge in conditions of utter depravity, or else an indifferent African culture that sees them as nothing. Early in the novel, Port reflects on the people of North Africa whom they encounter: "What do they think of me? Probably nothing."[74]

Port dies of typhoid, at "the earth's sharp edge," while St. Antony and St. Mary had traveled toward its very center. He has lost his passport (or rather, it has been stolen from him), his last connection with his Western identity and the "official proof of his identity." He ceases to be, his delirium dividing him from himself, literally freezing to death in the burning heat of the Sahara. All he can say to Kit in a world lashed by storm and the lowering sky is "No, no, no, no, no, no, no."[75] He cannot even "be dead," for to die is not to "be." For the true ascetic to die is to die into life and the completion of being. And this, for Port, is "the famous silence of the Sahara," where there is "no one in sight. There was nothing."[76] It is the nothing of pure vacuity, of total absence. If the desert geography is perceived as the externalization of human nature,[77] it also devours all that is human, both body and soul, and thus Port's body becomes one with the indifferent life of the desert. After his death, Kit wanders into soullessness and a forgetfulness of the body—"it would be she who would have ceased to exist."[78] Wandering further into the desert, she becomes as much one with it, and indistinguishable from it, as Port, becoming the sex slave of a passing caravan, acting without conscious awareness and delighted "not to be responsible—not to have to decide anything of what was to happen."[79] In the words of Gena Dagel Caponi, "Kit has pierced the fabric of the sky and passed beyond it into the absolute silence and night of the other side."[80] In the end, she even ceases to speak, just as Port had ceased to write. Words cease. When she finally begins to struggle back to her own culture, her first recovery is of language—a painful journey as it uncovers the lost identity that her silence had sheltered. "In another minute life would be painful. The words were coming back, and inside the wrappings of the words there would be thoughts lying there."[81] When she finally reaches a telegraph office, she simply signals, "CANNOT GET BACK." Indeed, her return to the West confirms her complete insanity, her idiocy—all that lies beyond the sheltering sky.

Bernado Bertolucci's brilliant 1990 film of *The Sheltering Sky*, which captures beautifully and weirdly the utter interiority of the novel within its desert geography, ends with words from Bowles himself, the expatriate writer himself lost and the only possible deity sitting in the bar of the hotel, offering a despairing footnote to a textless, trackless world. In a review of the novel, Orville Prescott of the *New York Times* described it as "unquestionably repellent in its subject matter" yet "unquestionably compelling in its manner,"[82] and the book remained a best seller for three months in 1950. Bertolucci's film, driven by the stark, compelling, and disturbing performances of Debra Winger and John Malkovich, returned it to public attention at the end of the millennium. And yet, if its dark vision resonated with the morbidity, repression, and alienation of the late twentieth-century West, few seem to have observed its violent refusal of and opposition to the deep countercultural move within Christian asceticism and its absolute reversal of the necessary apocalypse of the *via negativa* and its plenitude of silence and the realization of the true nothingness of God. Only the playwright Tennessee Williams suggested that many people might read the novel without any suspicion that it was a spiritual allegory, a "mirror of what is most terrifying and cryptic within the Sahara of moral nihilism, into which the race of man now seems to be wandering blindly."[83] Indeed, critics who have written on Bowles have fastidiously avoided such implications, preferring to concentrate on Bowles' critique of Western civilization from the perspective of an expatriate. Wayne Pounds has offered a psychological study through Sigmund Freud and R. D. Laing's *The Divided Self: A Study of Sanity and Madness* (1960), seeing Bowles as the portrait painter of the disintegrating modern psyche, while Richard F. Patteson explores the world of the fictional narrative through the concepts and themes of architecture. Perhaps his most thorough critic, Gena Dagel Caponi, sets Bowles within the context of his wide cultural circle as both a musician and as a writer, a circle that included Aaron Copland, Gertrude Stein, Tennessee Williams, Gore Vidal, William Burroughs, and many others.[84]

No one, however, has recognized that Bowles' greatest work, *The Shelter-ing Sky*, represents the darkest of laments for a journey into the sacred and an absolute repudiation of that darkness and abyss that is both the death of God and the only possible apocalypse of sacramental presence realized in the ascetic body in a celebration of the enfleshed and passionate Word. The journey of Port and Kit (and I have left out much of the novel and its cast of strange, lost characters) into the hidden interior of the Sahara and the emptiness that might have been their souls is the precise and utter opposite and denial of the same journey made by the saints and ascetics who journey in the body and in the spirit into the deep desert. It is opposite in three ways, and let us take St. Mary of Egypt as our example before we move on in our journey through other images, texts, and narratives. As she crossed the Jor-dan into the desert, Mary moved not out of the body but into a union with the sacramental within, the union of body and soul, which real presence she comes herself to instantiate in what Jean-Luc Marion calls the eucharistic site of theology.[85] This is a genuine realization not only of body but also of place, a place of abundance that conjoins the division of earth and heaven. Mary does not hide beneath a sheltering sky beyond which is absolutely nothing, but stands naked before the limitless nothingness of God, uncircumscribed by being in the true fullness of her being. Second, Mary enters into the Word without reserve so that she becomes one with it though herself unlettered. In her flesh she entertains fully the Word made flesh—as Port and Kit both abandon and are abandoned by language and speech, and thus their own embodiment. Finally, Mary's bodily transfiguration is a genuine narrative of the Christian insistence on the resurrection of the body, a movement into the body through word and sacrament. Thus, scandalously she moves even beyond theology itself. In Marion's words, "Christian theology speaks of Christ. But Christ calls himself the Word. He does not speak words inspired by God concerning God, but he abolishes in himself the gap between the speaker who states (prophet or scribe) and the sign (speech or text); he abol-ishes this first gap only in abolishing a second, more fundamental gap, in us, men: the gap between the sign and the referent."[86] It is precisely this gap that Port and Kit open in their different narratives, for they know not what they say, and it becomes a gap without any possible reconciliation, a descent into idiocy. Thus, as they move beyond the body, and in the disintegration of the body and the soul, so also does language cease in the abyss between sign and referent, and ushers in a total silence that is quite opposite to the fullness of language and Total Presence, but a total emptiness and an incapacity even to "be." It is the advent of death and madness. Shortly before his death, Bowles was described in his role as a writer. It is a tragic and isolated portrait:

The voice of these stories is one of a man removed and detached from the world, powerless over his own life and other people in it, compelled nevertheless to comment and report. It is as if, as he wrote about his adolescence, he were viewing rather than participating in his own existence; as if, as he wrote during his twenties, he were pretending to be living. Only a portion of this work takes the form of unanswered, yet in a sense, all his work is a one-sided correspondence with the world. "One day my words may comfort you," he wrote in "Next to Nothing," "as yours can never comfort me."[87]

He is detached from the world and lost, but without comfort, without that pure detachment, equanimity, and balance that is of true being.

Asceticism, Imposed and Recovered

Velázquez, Martha, and the Eyes of Faith

The troubling story of Thaïs has not left us in the long history of the Western imagination. Centuries after Hrotsvit of Gandersheim's drama, Anatole France's novel entitled *Thaïs*, which was first published in 1890 reveals the nineteenth century's horror at her story through the bullying, sadistic fanaticism of France's version of Abbot Paphnutius, whose obsession with Thaïs' beauty is a perversion of any possible vision of her salvation so that he is seen as nothing less than that modern monster, a vampire, and in the end "he had become so repulsive, that passing his hand over his face, he felt his own hideousness."[1] This fascination with the human cruelty of her story is taken to yet higher self-absorption in Jules Massenet's opera of 1894, which is based directly on France's reading of the legend. In the nineteenth century, the eyes to see its grace were closed, their gaze blind in the refusal of an impossible vision that is glimpsed for us now not in the words of theology or in literature, but only in the vision and art of Cézanne and, above all, Van Gogh. It is almost entirely forgotten in the tragic reversals of Christian theology and its closure on the apocalyptic Jesus who is met only in the narratives of asceticism, and yet more in that theology's obsession, as Thomas Altizer has put it, with a resurrection to

> the very evil and darkness that Jesus conquered by [its] exaltation of a solitary and transcendent God, a heteronomous and compulsive law, and a salvation history that is irrevocably past. Despite its great relevance to our situation, the faith of the radical Christian continues to remain largely unknown, and this is so both because that faith has never been able to speak in the established categories of Western thought and theology and because it has so seldom been given a visionary expression (or, at least, the theologian

has not been able to understand the radical vision, or even perhaps to identify its presence.[2]

The recovery of this visionary expression in a deeply immanent transcendence
within the body and at the very heart of asceticism will be the subject of this
chapter through the eyes of artists—Rembrandt, Velázquez, Van Gogh, and
Luca Signorelli.

In his book *Prolegomena to Charity* (1986), Jean-Luc Marion wrote on the
mystery of love in a manner reminiscent of St. Augustine on time: "We live
with love as if we knew what it was about. But as soon as we try to define it, or
at least approach it with concepts, it draws away from us. We conclude from
this that love ought not and cannot be conceived accurately, that it withdraws
from all intelligibility, and that every effort to thematize it belongs to soph-
istry or an unseemly abstraction."[3] The ascetic body is the home of love, its
baffling paradoxes of sacrality and profanity holding love's mystery before us
in its hiddenness and endless, unbearable fascinations. Thaïs has many sisters,
both sacred and profane, and none more alluring than the mythical Danaë,
the daughter of Acrisius, King of Argos. Warned in a prophecy that he would
die at the hands of his grandson, Acrisius sought to avoid this fate by incar-
cerating his only daughter in a "brazen" tower. Like Thaïs by Paphnutius,
Danaë is shut away in solitary confinement, but for her it is not to rescue her
from her sexual excesses but to preserve her from the dangers (for Acrisius) of
sex itself. Each girl, for quite different reasons, is destined for the ascetic life
at the hands of a domineering male. Each, however, is to find, through her
incarceration, a glorious bed: for Thaïs, it is the heavenly "bed adorned with
precious cloths" that St. Antony's disciple Paul saw in his vision—the true fulfillment of her life of love; for Danaë, it is the luxurious bed that Rembrandt
(1606–69) gives to her in her imprisonment in his glorious painting of her
that now hangs in the Hermitage in St. Petersburg.

Each sister also, we might say, is the recipient of grace—a divine gift—
linked to her bed as the resting place of her beauty. For Thaïs, it is the grace
of salvation, her body purified and perfected by her life of penance. For
Danaë, it is the visit of the impregnating god Jupiter, who descends on her
in her prison in the form of a downpour of gold, thus defeating the object
of Acrisius' exercise through the lust and opulence (*luxuria*) of the god. They
make curious and fascinating siblings, in more ways than one, each powerful
through their bodies. Typically, Rembrandt offers us a Danaë that is at once
alluring and utterly problematic to the gaze, a figure of sensuality and yet also,
like Thaïs, an emblem of the ascetic life in the body preserved and glorified.
The fact that in June 1985 a visitor to the Hermitage slashed and desecrated

the painting beyond proper repair, his motives unclear but almost certainly to deface and cast out the profanity of her gorgeous, naked body, is a violent witness to the continuing power of the body in all its beauty as at once both ascetic and provocatively sensual.[4]

Rembrandt's Danaë is a mass of contradictions. As she rests naked upon her bed, her right hand outstretched in a gesture that is either and equally one of welcome or prohibition, though Rembrandt later altered it to make it more of an inviting movement, she is surrounded by numerous odd and disturbing visual symbols that at once invite and prohibit the gaze. Her slippers on the floor seem to suggest her sex, while the weeping putto above her head has his hands tied, a "symbol" of forbidden sexuality.[5] The servant figure in the background looks away from her, perhaps toward the advancing deity, so that our gaze is simultaneously drawn toward her body and away from it—invited and forbidden. Mieke Bal, in her "reading" of the painting, which, like our imagined vision of Thaïs, moves between the verbal pretext and the immediate visual impression, typically focuses on the "textuality" of the painting.[6] Bal is, by training, a narratologist. She concentrates on the earthly Danaë and her at once available yet forbidden body. She reads the surface geometry and geography of the painting, her gaze rooted firmly in the complicated metaphors of its physicality and gender. Rembrandt, however, it seems to me, has a much larger and more complex vision of this lovely woman. Undeniably sexy, though without artistic idealization[7] (and perhaps, therefore, all the more troublingly erotic), she draws our gaze like the harlots of desert, Mary, Pelagia, and Thaïs, drew the admiring gaze of Zossima, Nonnus, and Paphnutius. But like her sister courtesans who became ascetics, she transfigures that gaze, without denying its eroticism, into a different level of bodily appreciation, a glimpse into the body that will be made perfect in resurrection. The story of the virginal Danaë, callously imprisoned by her father for his own protection and visited by a god, had become in Western art a moment to exploit the exposed and mercenary sexuality of the harlot—in paintings by Correggio, Titian, and Tintoretto. Rembrandt seems to follow the tradition. Accordingly, the nineteenth-century French art critic Louis Viardot, visiting St. Petersburg, noted that, quite rightly, this "indecent subject painted in a still more indecent manner" was "relegated far from the crowds of visitors," hidden away in the recesses of the royal palace.[8] But at the same time, Rembrandt, it might be said, added elements that suggest an earlier medieval tradition in which the virginal Danaë's visit from Jupiter prefigures the Annunication of the Virgin Mary from which results the miraculous birth of a son (in Danaë's case, Perseus—incidentally the accidental killer of his egregious grandfather Acrisius): the shackled cupid and the golden parrot, a bird sometimes associated with the Virgin Mary, on the foot of her bed. Thus, Simon Schama suggests (not, I think, entirely convinced himself) that "this is apparently another work from the hand of Rembrandt the Puritan *pretending* to celebrate the pleasures of the world when he was, in fact, scowling at them."[9]

But does this have to be an either/or? If Rembrandt is following the pattern outlined in the last chapter of asceticism as a way of love, may not his Danaë be another harlot/virgin, though her asceticism was imposed upon her, and her fulfillment was by a divine act of grace, a gift, that lacks the Christian dimension of her later sisters of the desert? But then, her glorious bed becomes the bed of Thaïs as envisioned in Paul's heavenly report to St. Antony. This is as seen through the eyes of Rembrandt (to which we shall shortly return)—that is, a seeing quite different from the gaze employed by Bal, the "gaze" that is returned to so insistently in cultural discussions of patriarchy, gender, and male dominance. In Rembrandt this is here taken up and transfigured in a longer and more steadfast gaze that sees the adored body as also and at once the body of the resurrection. Another sister harlot is the subject of Rembrandt's great painting of John 8:2–11, *Jesus and the Adulterous Woman*, now in the National Gallery of London. The artist here captures the two levels of seeing in the huge, imposing architecture of the temple, in the high background of which is a rich liturgical event, while in the foreground is a richly clad group of Pharisees (and one soldier in armor), static but for one black-clothed figure who gestures toward the kneeling woman as he tries to tempt Jesus into a discrediting of the law of Moses. The woman, dressed in white, is highlighted, her head bowed, while the standing figure of Jesus, head and shoulders taller than anyone else in the crowd, looks calmly down on her in motionless forgiveness. The light that holds them together reveals the higher vision, transforming the woman's beauty as it shines in the sea of harsh, accusing faces around her. "And Jesus said unto her, Neither do I condemn thee: go and sin no more" (John 8:11).[10]

* * *

We have seen in the previous chapter how Abbot Isaiah of Scetis emphasized the life of love as central in his *Ascetic Discourses*,[11] celebrating the active Martha equally with the contemplative Mary. The Western tradition has not been so generous toward the *vita activa*, perhaps taking to heart Jesus' warning against distractions and his statement that Mary had chosen the better part (Luke 10:41–42). For some, the *vita activa* might seem an alternative kind of asceticism as the imposed asceticism of a life of necessary labor and drudgery.

For these there is a different form of distinction between the sensual and the spiritual to the detriment of the former. Yet Meister Eckhart himself had preached from the story of Martha and Mary that all loving action arises from "the ground of contemplation," and that "thus too, in this activity we remain in a state of contemplation in God"[12]: asceticism imposed—and recovered?

And so we turn to another artist, Velázquez (1599–1660), and his early painting *Christ with Martha and Mary*, in the National Gallery of London. The origins of this part of my discussion lie in my involvement over a period of years with a recent publication, *Visuality and Biblical Text* (2004), a collaborative work by an artist, Jane Boyd, who works in light-based installations, and a biblical critic, Philip Esler of St. Andrews University, that concentrates almost entirely on this one painting. It presents a considerable hermeneutical challenge both in itself, to our present concerns, and to the biblical text on which it draws, Luke 10:38–42, which reads as follows:

> Now as they went on their way, he entered a certain village, where a woman named Martha welcomed him into her home. She had a sister named Mary, who sat at the Lord's feet and listened to what he was saying. But Martha was distracted by her many tasks; so she came to him and asked, "Lord, do you not care that my sister has left me to do all the work by myself? Tell her then to help me." But the Lord answered her, "Martha, Martha, you are worried and distracted by many things; there is need of only one thing. Mary has chosen the better part, which will not be taken away from her."

From at least the time of St. Augustine in the fifth century C.E., the episode was a favorite one with preachers and theologians in its contrasting of the contemplative with the active life, paralleled with a similar contrasting of the Old Testament figures of Rachel and Leah, Martha generally seen as a good-natured and reliable drudge beside Mary, who, from the fifteenth century at least, was frequently identified in devotional literature and religious art with Mary Magdalene, who, after her conversion, became both the patron and symbol of the contemplative life, a life of stillness lived freed from the physical concerns of the everyday. In a mid fifteenth-century painting of the Flanders artist Roger van der Weyden, also in the National Gallery in London, we see Mary Magdalene as Mary of Bethany, Martha's sister, quietly absorbed in the reading of a book and entirely oblivious to the world outside her window. By the sixteenth century, Mary as penitent and contemplative had become a common theme in art, not least in the many versions of the Spanish artist El Greco, painting in the last years of the century, or a few years later in the French painter Georges du Mesnil de La Tour's *Repentant Magdalen* (ca. 1640),[13] a perfect representation of the Mary described by the Pseudo-Bonaventura in his fourteenth-century *Meditations on the Life of Christ* as "searching for solitude of mind and attending only to God." She had become, it would seem, the perfect ascetic in her focus and solitude.

Velázquez' *Christ with Martha and Mary* probably dates from about 1617 to 1620—in other words, between the work of El Greco and de La Tour. It is a remarkably mature work from such a young artist, barely twenty years old, but still showing the influence of the Venetian School and Caravaggio, and insistently realistic rather than idealistic in its portraiture. Velázquez' early works are a mixture of deeply religious paintings—at the same time, he was producing magnificent pictures of *The Immaculate Conception* (1618–19, now in London) and *The Adoration of the Magi* (1619, in Madrid)—and paintings drawn from everyday life in Spain, his so-called *bodegónes*. Of fairly high birth himself, in these works he was yet a close observer of common and everyday scenes of life, as evidenced by his early paintings *The Old Woman Cooking Eggs* (1618; mentioned in chapter 5 of this volume as a reincarnation of St. Mary of Egypt), *The Kitchen Maid* (ca. 1618, Chicago), and *The Water-Seller of Seville* (1618–22, Apsley House), all of which relate immediately to the kitchen interior of *Christ with Martha and Mary*, with their images of pots, cooking, and domestic activity. All these works combine a dispassionate, homely realism and attention to detail with a profound sense of the dignity of the subject, even in the humblest of tasks. The old woman cooking eggs is a particularly fine example of the kind of nobility and beauty that Velázquez grants to such people, anticipating, perhaps, the portraits of Rembrandt later in the seventeenth century. In addition—and this will be of crucial importance as we consider *Christ with Martha and Mary* in detail—the young Velázquez was clearly intrigued by mirrors and the use of mirror reflection in his painting, a fascination that was to find its maturity in his late masterpiece *Las Meninas* (*The Maids of Honour*) of 1656 and the mirror's capacity both to heighten realism in the involvement of subjects as viewers, and to allow what is not actually present be seen. Indeed, it might be said that what we see in an image cannot be fully appreciated until we recognize what is not seen—the hidden life of the picture.[14] A small detail in another celebrated painting, *The Rokeby Venus* (its more formal title is *Venus at her Toilet*), will acquire a more theological significance in our discussion of *Christ with Martha and Mary*. Venus, her back turned to the viewer, becomes a viewer of herself as she regards herself in a mirror. She is leaning on her right arm—but in the mirror image, she appears to be leaning on her left arm. Could this be an artistic clue as to why Christ, in the earlier painting, raises his *left* hand to the two women in a curious gesture of blessing, against all tradition and convention? Boyd and Esler, noting this, go so far as to suggest that "it is surprising that such a depiction of Jesus did not fall foul of the Inquisition."[15]

We have already in this chapter referred to issue of the "gaze." Jacques Lacan has written, reminding us here, perhaps, of the almost hidden saints of the ascetic tradition, that "the world is all-seeing, but it is not exhibitionist, it does not provoke our gaze. [Yet] when it begins to provoke it, the feeling of strangeness begins too."[16] To look properly and seriously in any kind of way leads to complications and complexities of "seeing." Velázquez' painting of *Christ with Martha and Mary* certainly provokes our gaze and introduces a new sense of strangeness and uneasiness to our reading of the biblical pretext of Luke 10:38–42. Within the complex framing of the picture, we are prompted to ask new questions that simply do not arise in the act of the literary interpretation of the biblical pretext. Quite simply, and to begin with, for example, who exactly *are* the various characters that we are looking at, and how do they relate to one another? What do their expressions and gestures imply? To be true to Velázquez, the viewer of this painting must acknowledge his cultural context of seventeenth-century Seville, just as the biblical critic must establish the text of the gospel in its context of the first century of the Christian era. Thus, the various horizons of hermeneutical enquiry and judgement, and historical interleaving, become ever more complicated for the contemporary and universal viewer or reader. In what sense do we "read" as viewers and "see" as readers?

It is in the questions that it prompts and in the revealing of what cannot be seen that the painting and its characters enter into dialogue with the biblical text and its tradition, not as subservient to it, but with equal claims on our attention. We miss the point if we see Velázquez' work as simply a painting *of* an episode in St. Luke's Gospel. And so, what are we now interpreting—the gospel or the painting, or the one through the other, and if so, which way round, for the universality of art stands in defiance of the chronology of history? The answer, of course, is that we are interpreting *two* "texts"—one verbal and the other visual—each prompting a different kind of hermeneutical judgement, and each perfectly capable of existing independently of the other. Through two separate, yet at the same time intertwined, acts of interpretation, we confront the issue of intertextuality and thus the possibility of the radical redescription of the theological conclusions that readings of the biblical text have generally given rise to within the Christian tradition and the traditions of the church. To put this another way, the problems of "reading" that the painting of Velázquez prompts actually deconstruct models of church art that are based on the communicative reliability of words—that is, the models for which Martin Luther and the Protestant Reformation paved the way.[17] And it was precisely on this presupposition about the "word" that the new science of biblical criticism in Germany and England in the eighteenth century based itself. But in the image of the artist, such reading is reversed as the Word becomes flesh, not only in the body of Christ, but also in the claims made on us by the bodies of the women in the picture, and, above all, the young girl who gazes out from the center of the painting.

In the remainder of this discussion of this work, I want to try a practical exercise in "reading" it as a depiction, perhaps, of the tragedy of limited perspective that imposes an "ascetic" way of life without the vision that drives and justifies the ascetic tradition of the body. It builds on the fine work of Boyd and Esler (though behind it are the labors of many other scholars—Bal, Joseph Koerner, Jane Dillenberger, and John Drury, to name but a few). In taking Velázquez' picture "of" a biblical text seriously as a work of art in itself, and as a visual image that provokes questions and difficulties requiring different (though related) hermeneutical tools from those honed in the factory of biblical criticism, we can begin to situate the problems of biblical interpretation within the context of art interpretation (and this could easily be turned around the other way), so that we can only return to the text of St. Luke's Gospel and its history within the Christian tradition via a route that radically alters our response to the text in new understandings of and sympathies with its characters and the shape of its narrative. And in each case, between image and text, it is in the seeing what is not seen, and in the imagining what is not written, that a genuinely creative dialogue begins to take place. In contemplating the young woman of the picture, we move beyond words to a reflection on the flesh made Word, the body calling to our attention in silence, and thus an attention all too quickly missed by our busy, inquiring minds.[18]

No text, and no work of art, exists in isolation. The danger in the Christian tradition has always been that the Bible, by its very sacrality (and make no mistake, Veláquez was a very devout man and, within the Church of the Counter Reformation, took the Bible with the utmost seriousness), is often isolated from the larger community of literature and art that seeks conversation with it in acts of consuming and consummation. What Boyd and Esler call "the provocative bafflement which this painting induces in its viewers" connects it with not only its biblical pretext but also with all other art up to the present day that shares and explores this bafflement. We gaze, through windows, into mirrors, at pictures—we enter now into the marvels of three-dimensional cinema—exploring the mystery of "seeing," which provokes a renewed intellectual, emotional, and perhaps even spiritual response to Luke 10:38–42 itself. And so, before we too eagerly seek to resolve the "meaning" of the gospel narrative, we must pose the question, who is the young woman whose sad, almost tearful, gaze calls on our attention as she works at her humble but necessary task? She does indeed provoke our gaze, and in her provocation the feelings of strangeness and distance begin also in our sympathy and curiosity, and it is a strangeness that affects all other characters in the pictures and the roles given to them in the biblical story—including Our Lord himself.

Let us now turn in detail to the painting itself. We have been calling it *Christ with Martha and Mary*. In the National Gallery, its full title is *Kitchen Scene with Christ in the House of Martha and Mary*. What, then, is it a picture *of*? The focus is on the young girl engaged in an act of cooking, left of center as we view the painting. Technical analysis has suggested that the figure of the old woman looking over her right shoulder is a later addition, though this may or may not be significant for our understanding of the work. The inset at the top right shows us, we might say, the biblical scene, though it would appear that the girl herself is too absorbed, even self-absorbed, to look at it. Is the inset a window into the next room? Is it a painting on the wall—a painting within a painting? Is it a mirror reflecting another part of the room *behind*, so to speak, us, the viewers, so that the girl *is* actually looking at this scene, her gaze and expression a direct response to it? Is she Martha—or a latter-day Martha bewailing her humble lot as another forgotten scullery maid,[19] her short hair bound back as befits a servant as she looks despondently at the flowing golden locks of the contemplative figure of Mary? Some people, she might be thinking, have everything—the blessing of the Lord, no housework, *and* the blonde, free-flowing hair of the beauty!

But where do we situate the painting—what is its "setting-in-life," its *Sitz im Leben*? Let us first place it entirely within Velázquez' Spain, seeing it as one of his *bodegón* paintings of everyday life with a religious theme. The characters must then be interpreted in the context of the cultural expectations of early seventeenth-century Spain. The focus of the painting is clearly on the young servant girl, as herself an interpreter of the Bible. She looks, perhaps, at the scene reflected on the back wall, and looks back, with her mournful inward gaze, to the gospel narrative and its insistence that Mary has chosen the better part, reflecting, perhaps that this "better part," the contemplative life, is simply unavailable to her. It leaves her an outsider, a drudge, with the voice of age and experience looking over her shoulder wagging its finger as it tells her to get on with her work. The ingredients—perhaps for the master's supper as he sits and waits for his meal—are on the table, but all need to be prepared: the food is raw, the fish need to be gutted, the eggs broken and cooked, the spices and garlic crushed and mixed. There is work to be done, and food does not cook itself. The figure of the old woman is not looking at either the viewer or the inset scene (if that is what the girl is doing). Her eyes are black pits, looking at nothing. Her mouth is set and and her hair iron gray. She is, perhaps, an image of the young woman as she will be in later life, and all she can expect to be.

This interpretation, setting the time of the picture firmly in the Spain of Velázquez, is best explained if we consider the artist's fascination with mirrored reflection. I suggest, to begin with, that the whole painting is to be seen as a mirror image. Imagine that the painter is actually standing *behind* the young girl, and that therefore what we see is as in a mirror, the inset scene also actually facing in the same direction as both the artist and we the viewers, looking toward the mirror. If this is the case, a number of curious details can be explained. For example, the girl's jacket is folded left over right, which was the custom of men's dress, women's then being right over left (opposite to our own custom). But if this is a mirror image, this would explain the anomaly. Also, the left-hand edge of the table, as we see it, appears oddly distorted, as it might be if seen in a mirror. But most importantly, the figure of Christ appears with a raised *left* hand, in absolute contrast to proper custom, in breach of the decree of the Council of Trent on sacred images, in terms of which it would be regarded as *inordinatum* (disordered) and *praepostere* (irregular).[20] But if this is an image seen as in a mirror, then Christ is actually raising his *right* hand in the proper and acceptable manner of blessing.

More could be said about this proposal in terms of light and shadow in the painting, suggesting just such a reversal, but I would suggest that a more important issue arises if we regard the whole picture as in a mirror: for that then obliges the model for the young girl to participate in the act of viewing as we do. If she is standing in front of the artist, facing away from him and toward the mirror, then she is looking at exactly what we see—she sees not only herself but also the inset scene from the gospel. She then is obliged to see *herself* as Martha, toiling away, even while she looks at the golden-haired Mary sitting at the feet of Jesus, gazing at him adoringly and enjoying his blessing. It is, in fact, a prime example of having one's nose rubbed in it, and her tears almost well up as she is forced to look at herself in the mirror. Meanwhile, the characters in the "inset" await the meal that she is preparing. Furthermore, Christ himself has become a kind of present absence, not in the painting except as a reflection, the picture showing us, as it were, what cannot be seen, the one who comes to us as one unknown. The so-called biblical scene becomes, indeed, a sort of reflection in the mind of the young girl herself as she identifies with it in her own sad and forgotten circumstances.

But let us now shift our perspective, joining with the many commentators on the picture who have seen it as a depiction of Luke 10:38–42 in its entirety, its setting wholly biblical and within the world of the gospel. If this is so, then we might change our view of the inset (for this, and not the larger figure of the girl, is what the painting is actually "about"). Forget, then, the whole hypothesis about mirrors. The inset is not to be seen as a picture on the wall, but rather as a window, or even a kind of doorway into the next room. Now we might imagine a house with two rooms—Jesus is seated comfortably on a handsome chair in a well-lit room that would serve well to accommodate an honored guest. The girl and the old woman are in the next room, a darker and less attractive kitchen, at the very beginning of the preparation of a meal for the guest. How, then, might we identify the various characters in the picture? Perhaps significantly the woman standing behind the seated woman has her head covered with a shawl like the old woman at the far left of the picture. Can we suggest that there are, in fact, two servants, the old woman and the standing woman in the inset, neither of whom figure in the biblical narrative, perhaps because of their lowly status in society? This leaves us free to identify Mary with the seated female figure, and the young girl herself now actually is Martha, distracted from attending upon the Lord by her concern to get the meal ready (Luke 10:40). What, in fact, we are looking at is not actually a moment within the biblical narrative, but one just after its conclusion in verse 42 with Jesus' words, "Mary has chosen the better part, which will not be taken away from her," and we see Martha's *reaction* to this statement in her look of almost tearful resentment. Hard at work, hers cannot be the "better" part. She is too humble, forgotten. She has gone into the next room to prepare the meal, while Mary is left with *her* servant-figure, who is not pointing as if to encourage work to proceed, but also looking rapt in attention to Jesus' words. What, then of Mary? Her hair is free-flowing and her clothes loose and rich in their folds. Are these suggestive of her former profession, seeing her as Mary Magdalene, of harlot, though now she sits in submissive attention, her eyes dreamily fixed on Jesus? The room they occupy contains no signs of domestic bustle. The only equipment is a bowl and jug on the low table, perhaps for washing before the meal is brought in. Finally, there is the figure of Jesus himself. If we are looking at a direct image and not a mirror reflection, there are a number of difficulties that have no easy solution. It has frequently been noted that the biblical text presents a problem (as found variously elsewhere in the Gospels—in John 4, and Jesus' encounter with the Samaritan woman at the well, for example) of the impropriety in ancient, patriarchal culture of two women entertaining a single man in their home without male chaperons. The motives behind such a visit would have been, at the very least, questionable, though Isaiah of Scetis described them easily here as "free from anxiety, reclining at table with Jesus."[21]

And so, if it is possible to overcome such impropriety within the radical terms of the gospels and the traditions of asceticism, might it not also be that Velázquez is reintroducing a highly dangerously critical comment in his portrayal of Mary, and a Jesus who extends his *left* hand, not the hand of blessing, as he sits comfortably in the best, indeed, the only seat in the house? On the one hand, his attitude is that of the teacher, at whose feet the disciple sits, but on the other, it can be interpreted very differently. Why is he in the house at all? Mary seems to vacillate between her old role as prostitute and her new role as contemplative. Meanwhile, Martha remains crucially and diligently in the kitchen as she gets on with preparing the love feast. Is the meal a "Lenten fast," as suggested by the art historian Norbert Wolf,[22] or, as others have suggested, an anticipated meal full, even, of sexual symbolism? Now, if all this is certainly far-fetched as an interpretation of the gospel narrative by such a devout Catholic as Velázquez, nevertheless, might it not be suggested by the kind of thoughts that could be racing through the mind of the girl herself in her misery and perhaps jealousy over Mary's "better part"? Or is she another humble "sponge," the one who is nothing but who makes all things possible?

A third suggestion (actually not so far removed from the first) is that the painting is a deliberate mixture of the biblical and the contemporary cultures. In the inset the figures wear what Velázquez might have taken to be the dress of Jesus' time, while the larger figures are clearly dressed in the manner of the poor of seventeenth-century Spain. On this basis here is Wolf's reading of the picture:

> The sublimity of the main religious subject of Christ with the two sisters in Bethany is banished to a small area in the background, while the down-to-earth subsidiary theme of the kitchen scene occupies the foreground. Velázquez is not setting out to tell a Biblical story, but to establish connections between the religious parable and the everyday life of his own time: the food on the table is obviously part of a Lenten meal being prepared by the young maidservant, while the old woman's pointing hand is telling the girl that—as the Biblical scene behind them states—industry and work (the *vita activa*) are not enough in themselves for true piety, which also requires serious contemplation and the strength of faith (the *vita contemplativa*).[23]

Wolf then reads the picture rather simply as a religious parable, using the episode in the gospel to extol the quiet virtues of contemplation—and certainly in the medieval tradition the exaltation of Mary's choice tends, though, as we have seen, not always, to predominate, naturally following our Lord's words in verse 42 concerning the "better part." But, on the basis of what I have been suggesting, this seems just too simple, too assured. Velázquez is doing something much more complex than this straightforward interpretation allows for and, in doing so, recovers a truth too easily forgotten in the history of Christian spirituality. Certainly, there is a deliberate mingling of the biblical and the contemporary, but it is perhaps more clearly to be seen as a deliberate *mingling* in Velázquez' art of the *bodegón* painting of everyday life in Spain, drawing on the then-popular boisterous genre scenes in Flemish art, and his religious paintings from the Bible or theology, an image confusing time and thus beyond all time.

Before I begin to draw some conclusions from this discussion about the art of Velázquez and the Bible, we need to be quite clear that the artist was, although still youthful, by then already a notable citizen of Seville, a city at the zenith of its greatness as a gateway to the Americas, and by 1624 (only some four years after this painting was executed) he was elected to the court of Philip IV in Madrid, and at the end of his life, in 1659, was to receive the Red Cross of Santiago. This was within a society in the grip of a confident post–Tridentine Roman Catholicism, at the height of the Counter-Reformation and the power of the Holy Inquisition. In one day in 1625, the archbishop of Seville ordained five hundred men as priests, and these clergy have been described as "the very sinews and tendons of the body politic."[24] In other words, deliberately to paint a biblically doubtful picture that might catch the eagle eye of the church and risk its wrath, was, to put it mildly, hardly sensible, and certainly Velázquez was not the man to do such a thing. But, as an artist, he was doing something far more profound.

Am I, then, simply reading too much into this picture? Is Wolf right in his very simple interpretation, and perhaps you should just forget all I have said, and be satisfied with this parabolic reading to be placed alongside a venerable exaltation of the *vita contemplativa* in a tradition that includes St. Bernard of Clairvaux, William of St. Thierry, and the whole weight of Cistercian piety? Well, I remain unrepentant, my argument being grounded not in Velázquez' religious consciousness so much as in his undoubtedly precocious ambition and vision as an artist. It has more to do with the subtle and complex relationship between art and the biblical tradition, the deep wisdom in art, and the delicate place of images and image making within the life of faith rooted in the Bible and its consuming traditions. In *Christ with Martha and Mary*, the artist is certainly playing technically with levels of reality, "pictures within a picture," and the use of mirrors, such as might explain oddities like the raised left hand of Jesus, against all tradition. He is, above all, an artist (as perhaps were all true ascetics, though theirs was an art of their bodies and souls), not a theologian, and it is his art, within his context of piety, that drives his creativity and insight. He was certainly deeply influenced by the work of Caravaggio and his followers, and in this tradition, only some twenty years before Velázquez' picture, we have Caravaggio's magnificent *Martha and Mary Magdalene* of about 1598,[25] which portrays a rather plain Martha, in the shadows, looking up at a glorious Magdalene, resplendent in a low-cut dress, showing Martha her image in a glass—the painting is also known (with, perhaps, lack of insight) as *Martha Reproaching Mary for her Vanity.* At the same time, this Mary hovers between an image of sexuality and one of contemplation—an image caught in "the transition from the entirely non-secular to the growing tradition of genre-painting in Western art" that would shortly be taken up in the work of Velázquez himself.[26]

The artist, as artist, does have a crucial and creative role to play in the business of the reading and interpreting the Bible and religious tradition. Bal has described Rembrandt as perhaps Holland's greatest biblical critic. I have suggested that Velázquez also ushers us into a complex and challenging relationship with a narrative that is itself deeply embedded in a history of Christian interpretation, and thereby we return to the text carrying with us a burden of sympathies and questions that cannot be simply eradicated by "proper interpretation." "Mary has chosen the better part"—now we should look at this picture again. Are not these remote words baffled by the tragic, almost tearful, face of Martha, or every other drudge and scullery maid for whom the way of contemplation is, it seems, not even an option? Here, as elsewhere, in the scandal of art we see things that theology and the tradition can sometimes find it hard to get into focus. The art critic Leo Steinberg in his justly acclaimed work, *The Sexuality of Christ in Renaissance Art and in Modern Oblivion* (1996), has observed, "I have risked hypothetical interpre-tations chiefly to show that, whether one looks with the eye of faith or with a mythographer's cool, the full content of the icons discussed bears looking at without shying. And perhaps from one further motive: to remind the literate among us that there are moments, even in a wordy culture like ours, when images start from no preformed program to become primary texts. Treated as illustrations of what is already scripted, they withhold their secrets."[27] In Velázquez' painting, we see the face of asceticism "imposed" yet untransfig-ured by the vision that drives the human into worldly limitations and trans-forms the body of limitation into the glorious body that was Antony's as he emerges from his tomb, or Mary of Egypt adored by Zossima, or Thaïs on her heavenly couch—or Jesus after his resurrection. For Martha, the vision is but distant in a culture of drudgery, though Isaiah of Scetis grants even her both diligence and joy. We have, perhaps, culturally lost the possibility of true asceticism, schooled by a Christian tradition that has assigned it simply to bodily denial or the contemplative life that abandons all the glories of the created body (or prioritizes the solely contemplative above the practical and the celebratory). But in the eyes of the artist, there is now and then recovered for us the complexities and coincidence of opposites that our theologies have consigned to oblivion. Martha gazes in sorrow, but also into a distance that sees beyond all things and into the unity of all things, a wholly paradoxical sorrow that is almost forgotten but sees only a deep joy in the abyss. Thus, in the words of Meister Eckhart, "There were three things too which caused Martha to move about and serve her beloved Christ. The first was her maturity and the ground of her being which she had trained to the greatest extent and which, she believed, qualified her best of all to undertake these tasks. The second was wise understanding which knew how to perform those works perfectly that love commands. And third was the particular honour of her precious guest."[28]

From his numerous self-portraits, Rembrandt, too, gazes on us with eyes that see nothing and everything, perhaps above all in the sombre *Self-Portrait with Beret and Turned-Up Collar* of 1659, now in the National Gallery of Art in Washington, D.C., in which the eyes are a whole world, seeing inwardly with a sad stillness that accepts all and sees beyond into another world. The term "self-portrait" actually came into use only in the nineteenth century[29] in the wake of Romantic forms of self-reflection. For Rembrandt, the self-image emerged from a humanistic ethics grounded in classicism and "is directed more towards what unites him with the rest of mankind than what sets him apart."[30] And the only true successor to Rembrandt in such portraiture is Van Gogh, through whose eyes we ourselves begin to see, tragically, the lost ascetic body that Christianity has largely forgotten. Van Gogh's last self-portrait, now in the Louvre, was painted just two months before his death by suicide in July 1890. Like those of Rembrandt and of Velázquez' servant girl, Van Gogh's eyes draw our gaze as they stare sightlessly at eternity. But each look in their own way. If Rembrandt's eyes are full of a deep sadness, Van Gogh's eyes stare with an understated rage—each artist, near the end of their mortal lives, looking for us out of one world into the next. Is it rage, or defiance, or a moment of terrible recognition, as if Van Gogh *knew* something hidden, not cognitively but in the depths of his being? Thus, he stares with the eyes of Christ as in an icon, a form of art hitherto almost unknown in the West, in which "the image of Christ is empty of His presence and full of His absence,"[31] an image of absolute *kenosis*. Only in the icon is the possibility present of rendering visible the invisible in the moment of impossible recognition,[32] so that Van Gogh's eyes pierce the very barrier between life and death: embody death itself. In the words of Altizer,

> Then it is present as life itself, a life embodied in those eyes, and if these are the eyes of the face of death, those eyes thereby are dazzlingly present, and present not only as the centre of his vision, but as the periphery or horizon of a totality of death, but a totality thereby truly embodied, and embodied in these self-portraits. Such an embodiment could only be a *transfiguring embodiment*, now life and death are truly indistinguishable, for death in being truly embodied, thereby ceases to be death alone, ceases to be a sheer nothingness, but becomes instead an *embodied nothingness* or an embodied death, and thus a death actually occurring in these self-portraits.[33]

In Van Gogh's last painting, *Wheatfield with Crows* (1890), we encounter the reversal of the iconic as the darkness of the crows carry the eye from the brilliant light of the field to the blue-blackness of the sky above in a harmonious movement from light to darkness. The movement is perfectly expressed by Van Gogh himself when he wrote to his brother of the desire "to express sadness and extreme loneliness," and yet at the same time, "I am almost certain that I have expressed in these canvasses what I cannot put into words, namely how healthy and invigorating I find the countryside."[34] The deep spirituality of the artist's last letters, expressing his inspiration as "a ray from on high, things not in ourselves, in order to do beautiful things,"[35] links his vision of things unseen and eyes of faith with the deepest traditions of asceticism for they bring about his own mortal demise, beyond reason, in its very fulfillment. His last words to his brother are a pure expression of the "yes" of his self-portraits: "Well, my own work, I am risking my life for it and my reason has half-foundered owing to it—that's all right—but you are not among the dealers in men so far as I now, and you can choose your side, I think, acting with true humanity, but what's the use?"[36] Few words have ever been meant so seriously. They express the impossible sanctification of darkness seen in his last works, an unbearable transfiguration of embodiment that sees in utter darkness the beauty of the ascetic body, describable only in the myths of hagiography and its forbidden loves and in the eyes of the artist, which alone see into the abyss in which opposites meet in both the fullness and the finality of death. For the scullery maid, it lies in the menial task given to her; for Rembrandt, it is expressed in profound sadness; for Van Gogh, in a steadfast defiance—each recording the apocalyptic impossibility of the vision that the Christian narrative presents in the true fiction of the resurrection and in the lives of the saints in a final *imitatio Christi* that the church, with its model in

Fyodor Dostoevsky's Grand Inquisitor, a good though utterly deluded and godless man, has rarely been able to bear or honestly tolerate.

The eyes of Van Gogh gaze into the darkness that is the only truth of which the gorgeous beauty of the wheatfield is but the mirror. It is thus a darkness transfigured, and realized in the truly ascetic body only possible in the harlot turned saint, not the reversal of humanity's sinful embodiment but its transformation in the body of love seen only in the abyss that glorifies its utter profanity as total sacrality. Here is infinity thought in being, and perhaps its closest theological expression in the art of the West is to be found in Signorelli's (ca. 1441?–1523) paintings of resurrected bodies in the San Brizio Chapel in Orvieto. They deeply influenced Michelangelo in his painting of the Last Judgement in the Sistine Chapel some forty years later. Signorelli miraculously shows us the moment, perhaps the most authentic in Christian imagination, when the bodies struggle from their graves "in various stages of enfleshment"[37] and reassemble themselves in the resurrected flesh with eyes, as St. Augustine says in *De Civitate Dei*, now capable of seeing God.

The remarkable poem on Signorelli's painting by the American writer Jorie Graham explores the paradoxical energy of this rush to flesh:

> See how they hurry
>   to enter
> their bodies,
>   these spirits.
> Is it better, flesh,
>   that they
>
> should hurry so?
>   From above
> the green-winged angels
>   blare down
> trumpets and light. But
>   they don't care,
>
> they hurry to congregate,
>   they hurry
> into speech, until
>   it's a marketplace,
> it is humanity. But still
>   we wonder
>
> in the chancel
>   of the dark cathedral,
> is it better, back?[38]

These are the ascetic bodies made perfect. And we, who are below, stand in the dark chancel of the cathedral church, and we cannot understand how they are so eager to return to the miseries of the flesh: but there is the very paradox—that we who have been unwilling or unable to undertake the ascetic performance, to realize the "reversals of the flow of the body,"[39] cannot conceive of the body resurrected and glorified. For us, all too often, asceticism is seen merely as either deprivation or imposition.

Signorelli's vision begins in a personal tragedy. His son Antonio died shortly before he began to work in the Orvieto Chapel. Giorgio Vasari records that he actually painted the dead and naked body of his son, though the work has not survived: but to him, as an artist, is given the insight into a divine grieving as a dark passage to life. Vasari writes, "It is related of Luca Signorelli that he had a son killed in Cortona, a youth of singular beauty in face and person (*bellisimo di volto e di persona*) whom he tenderly loved. In his deep grief, the father had his [son's] body stripped naked and with great self control, without complaint or tears, he painted the portrait of his dead child so that he might still be able to meditate, by means of the work of his own hands, that which nature had given him but which an evil fortune had taken away."[40] The poet Graham is less prosaic in her description. In her poem, Signorelli actually dissects the body of his son, cutting into bone and sinew in the "cold light" of day—a hard, unbelievably demanding, ascetic, and utterly real exercise of fleshly exploration,

> until his mind
>   could climb into
> the open flesh and
>   mend itself.[41]

Through the flesh itself the mind can perform the physical act of enfleshment and become whole. It is this utterly seamless unity of mind and body, flesh and spirit, that the bodies of Signorelli's resurrection have come to know. The flesh into which they climb is superb, gorgeous, and yet untainted by the partial lusts of the flesh. They are not subject to the despotism of the "gaze" as limited by the feminist perspective of Bal. In Margaret Miles' words, "Signorelli's female nudes are not the standard erotic female body of the (male) 'period eye.' In the Renaissance, and until the seventeenth century, the erotic female body was characterized by small high breasts, a short waist, and a large belly. Signorelli's female nudes exhibit neither the small high breasts nor the exaggerated belly that was considered erotic. Moreover, male and female nudes touch each other with infinite tenderness but without lust. They enjoy one another's beauty for its own sake, as Augustine had described."[42] Indeed, by far, the best commentary on Signorelli's *Resurrection of the Flesh* is to be found in St. Augustine's *City of God*, book 22, with its descriptions of the bodies of the resurrection life, those entirely "shaped into the likeness of God's Son." In them sexual distinction is not eliminated, but as in those for whom asceticism has become a way of love, glorified and incorrupt. St. Augustine writes, "Thus while all defects will be removed from those bodies, their essential nature will be preserved. Now a woman's sex is not a defect; it is natural. And in the resurrection it will be free of the necessity of intercourse and childbirth. However, the female organs will not subserve their former use; they will be part of a new beauty, which will not excite the lust of the beholder—there will be no lust in that life—but will arouse the praises of God."[43] But yet Signorelli's resurrected bodies retain a physical tenderness perhaps more than St. Augustine (or Miles) would allow, as they seem to exchange a perfect harmony of mutual delight, a pure subsuming of the sacred into the profane and the profane into the sacred. Male and female have an equal sensuousness in size and power, freed from all gender socializations—an unprecedented moment in Western art born out of the personal tragedy of the artist.

In the eye of the artist, schooled in the tradition of Greek sculpture that had as early as six centuries before the Christian era known the human body as both unique and universal—above all in the Apollo of Piombino,[44] which touches both humanity and divinity in equal measure—two worlds meet in simultaneous and yet impossible celebration. It is a moment embracing both the deepest sorrow and uttermost rage, yet transfigured in the ascetic body as a sunlight landscape amid the night of nonbeing. It embodies a joy that Dante knew as the vision of Beatrice, but only through the darkness of hell and purgatory, and which Joyce knows in the deepest sacramental heresies of *Finnegans Wake*.[45] It embraces a wisdom that we constantly discover and immediately forget in our inevitable incapacity to entertain the asceticism of the body that all our social and political principles refuse, schooled by the dark vision of the church. In his essay "The Body/Body Problem," Arthur C. Danto traces something of its history and repeated oblivion: "It has sometimes happened in the history of thought that what appeared at a given time to be an ineradicable distinction of the utmost philosophical moment proved to be indexed to a certain stage of scientific understanding and did not interestingly survive into the next stage."[46] In each age the ragged ascetics and mystics who hold, for a moment, the mystery before us become either forgotten, or the heretics, or at best the absurd myths of the next age, persecuted or neglected because we cannot bear their reality. Thus, we flee them in our post-Enlightenment wisdom, the mental irreducibly differentiated from the physical, the spiritual from the bodily, in our seemingly inevitable fall into dualism—a fall that Christianity knows only too well (which therefore consigns a Milton to the devil's party and to be a heretic because he is indeed a true poet). Theology, it seems, usually cannot bear to affirm "the distinction between terrestrial and celestial as in the end of no great relevance to the deep partitions of the universe—if there are any deep partitions." Even science itself seems to belie the distinction from time to time, but the greater human project continually fails to embrace the implications, beyond, perhaps, those few ragged figures who dare to embody a unity by which the world is kept in being. "No distinction in its time could have been more fundamental than that between the earthly and the heavenly, but the discovery of sunspots damaged the contrast on the basis of presumed celestial immaculateness, and the discovery that planets moved in unedifying ellipses blunted any expectation of an invidious moral geometry."[47] Danto spends much of his essay reflecting on the implications for us of Descartes' *Meditations*—a definitive text for the modern mind and its understanding, imposing on our sense of reality the limitations of our boundaries of thought, and finally separating mind and body, flesh and spirit. Descartes almost gets to the point but finally refuses its radical possibilities, for, he says, "though the mind or soul of man is really distinct from the body," it is "nevertheless so tightly bound up and united with it that it forms with it what is almost a single entity."[48] "Almost"—ah, there's the rub. Neither conjunction nor separation is easy or simple. Velázquez' Martha gazes, perhaps, with tragic recognition that her enslavement to a life of drudgery, which is yet her maturity and the ground of her being, is still imposed on her by a religion that celebrates only the unearthly and removed beauty of her contemplative sister—the profane (in its tragedy) and the sacred separated by a huge gulf, in two frames of being.

But if the artist has seen the tragedy, then the artist perhaps alone has also touched on the celebration of the body as spirit in the ascetic body, has known the unity of its being, just as the true mystic falls back into ordinary human language to capture what is beyond the power of words in words so that "the mystical text gropes, gestures, bears witness to something beyond itself."[49] At the end of his essay, Danto returns to perhaps the most contradictory of the sisterhood that embraces Thaïs, Danaë, and St. Mary of Egypt: Molly Bloom in whom "the body is finally the text made flesh."[50] "And first I put my arms around him yes and drew him down on me so he could feel my breasts all perfume yes and his heart was going like mad and yes I said yes I will Yes."[51] Is Molly, then, the last of the great ascetics, after whom there is only *Finnegans Wake* in literature? Has she embraced that moment, from within, which the exteriorities of both religion and science have carefully avoided in their distinctions that seek to guarantee our systems, the ethical and the material? But unseen in their distinctions lurks the apocalyptic moment that we fail to see, the moment realized above all in the death of Jesus, which is the acceptance of an absolute darkness that is alone the moment of absolute joy and light? Thus Danto concludes—and his final, critical sentence is an implied and sublime celebration of every body that has embraced the fullness of being in time and in the at once sacred and profane unity that is of eternity: "How singular, even so, that what appears to be an ineradicable distinction, of the utmost moment to scientific thought, should be indexed, for once, to a certain stage of philosophical analysis, most especially if it should be a consequence of that analysis that there is no further stage of thought into which it need worry about survival. *The future has been the present for thousands and thousands of years.*"[52]

THE EUCHARISTIC BODY IN LITERATURE AND MODERN EXPERIENCE

George Herbert and Simone Weil

The Eucharistic Body

The liturgy and the Eucharist have never been far from our thoughts in our meditations on asceticism and the body. At each new celebration of the Eucharist, and in obedience to the divine command, the body is displayed, eaten, and consumed. The words in Scripture are unequivocal—*this* is my body, *this* is my blood in the species of bread and wine, though there is a clear reference to the physical body of Jesus present before his disciples at their last supper together, now to be ingested by them as an act of remembrance. It is a performance and a display, the materials shockingly held up for all to see. Tertullian's sarcasm against the naivity of pagan critics cannot reduce the appalling fact: "No doubt [the Christian] would say, 'You must get a child still very young who does not know what it means to die, and can smile under your knife; and bread to collect the gushing blood. . . . Come, plunge your knife into the infant. . . . Or, if that is someone else's job, simply stand before a human being dying before it has really lived. . . . Take the fresh young blood, saturate your bread with it, and eat freely.'"[1] At the heart of the mystery there is an irreduceable violence and a necessary scandal of the flesh, an insistent reminder that the body cannot be removed from thought, and that human history, red in tooth and claw, swims in the river of blood from its torn and shredded victims, torn by hatred and torn by desire. In *The Ideology of the Aesthetic*, Terry Eagleton remarks that "few literary texts are likely to make it nowadays into the new-historicist canon unless they contain at least one mutilated body. A recovery of the importance of the body has been one of the most precious achievements of recent radical thought."[2] But there has to be more to mutilation than that, perhaps especially in our age of bodily dismemberment which has progressed from the singular to the genocidal. To move from the Passion to the eucharistic is to enact a transfer of the broken body from the meaningless to the mythic, the ritualized and the liturgical—no less scandalous or terrible but at least, and at the very least, a gesture toward a wholeness of being, a brokenness endured and restored in its consumption.

Christianity, perhaps inevitably, given its focus on the cross, has always been ambivalent in its attitude toward the body. As Fyodor Dostoevsky's character demanded,[3] could even Christ himself have born to look on the cadaver that had been his living flesh, let alone asked this of his disciples? From the body, which suffers such corruption in death, there is the temptation to flee to the bliss of the disembodied soul, but there is yet always and ever a return to that deep, elusive claim that "in my flesh shall I see God" and an insistence on the scandalous physicality, in all its aspects, of the Word made flesh. Even within the deepest recesses of the practice of contemplative prayer, the body is acknowledged, though tranquil and not on display, but held in balance and equilibrium, and ready to acknowledge its fleshly integrity with the soul. In George Eliot's *Adam Bede* (1859), the Methodist preacher, Dinah Morris, sits by her bedroom window as she prepares to leave the community to whom she has ministered. "And the pressure of this thought soon became too strong for her to enjoy the unresponding stillness of the moonlit fields. She closed her eyes, that she might feel more intensely the presence of a Love and Sympathy deeper and more tender than was breathed from the earth and sky. This was Dinah's mode of praying in solitude. Simply to close her eyes, and to feel herself enclosed by the Divine Presence; then gradually her fears, yearning anxieties for others, melted away like ice-crystals in a warm ocean."[4] This description of Dinah in contemplation is profoundly physical, albeit still and silent, a movement not away from the body, but rather into it and into a sense of feeling that remains responsive to the physical metaphors of warmth and cold. It involves a movement toward presence so that, within her flesh, Dinah comes to "see God," though never experiences what is merely a thought, never abstract or abstracted. If James Joyce's Mr. Duffy always "lived at a little distance from his body," the very opposite is true of Dinah and all true contemplatives. They live entirely within them, and their bodies are embraced by their souls.

Yet this deepest presence is always also an absence, the displayed body— *Corpus Domini nostri*—too much to bear, crossing the boundaries of body and spirit. Graham Greene catches this quixotic limit most movingly in the final pages of his novel *Monsignor Quixote* (1982), in which the holy fool of a priest, the priest who is no priest, a *Suspensión a Divinis* having been imposed on him by his bishop, and approaching death, celebrates the sacrament without physical bread or wine: "And with no hesitation at all he took from the invisible paten the invisible Host and his fingers laid the nothing on his tongue. Then he raised the invisible chalice and seemed to drink from it. The Mayor could see the movement of his throat as he swallowed."[5] Can we ever do more than this even with the fragment of bread and the drop of wine, touching for a moment the deepest interiority of the body—our bodies— with the divine absent presence in an act of pure remembrance? And Greene's crazy, dying priest passes on from this life, like Walter Pater's Marius in the peace of a "kind of candid discontent,"[6] with the mystic bread on his lips, the awful and necessary opposite being the suffering flesh of Holman Hunt's terribly visible *Scapegoat* (1854), hovering between life and death in the salt flats of the Dead Sea, the bedraggled image of the scandalous flesh that sees things to their bitter end. The scapegoat is the harsh reality, the reverse side, of the body removed, of what slips down the Monsignor Quixote's throat unseen, brings him to puzzlement, his candid discontent, and becomes both his end and his ultimate consummation.

The scandalous body removed and devoured—a body so terrible would Christ himself have asked us to endure the sight of it had he known—is also the body remembered in its "unaccountable darkness."[7] Thus, to remember is no passive thing but a recreation in the whole of, and at the most profound depths of, our being, a presencing as in Dinah and her body's call to prayer. Not only the liturgy of the Eucharist, or the Passover festival, but also all literature echoes with the hauntings of memory—of *anamnesis*, of the eternal presence of what is most deeply absent. The most deeply sensuous art is the most interior, almost nothing on the surface but that tingling to the touch, unforgettable and almost forgotten. Thus we read at the beginning of Michael Ondaatje's novel *The English Patient* (1992):

> Every four days she washes his black body, beginning at the destroyed feet. She wets a washcloth and holding it above his ankles squeezes the water onto him, looking up as he murmurs, seeing his smile. Above the shins the burns are worst. Beyond purple. Bone.
> She has nursed him for months and she knows the body well, the penis sleeping like a sea horse, the thin tight hips. The hipbones of Christ, she thinks. He is her despairing saint. He lies flat on his back, no pillow, looking up at the foliage painted onto the ceiling, its canopy of branches, and above that, blue sky.[8]

The body in *The English Patient*, unknown and unrecognizable, is half-brother to Hans Holbein's *Dead Christ* but for the smile. It is a body remembered and still known in its sexual potential as the woman, like those who washed the body of their dead Master, nurses her "despairing saint." But at the same time, it is a body now almost entirely interior. Is not sainthood a condition of despair? The man murmurs and smiles, and his weakness and its mystery, after he fell burning into the desert, is the still center of Ondaatje's narrative. He is one unknown—even he does not know who he is—but his weakness, like every genuine weakness, proves to be, above all, strength as he draws the woman's care on him.[9] Ondaatje's later novel, *Anil's Ghost* (2000), continues the theme of embodied haunting, the stretching out of the forgotten and the half-remembered, in our own lives and in the lives of others both known and unknown, and the insistence of "this sweet touch from the world."[10] And so the scandalous, exhibited body—*this is my body*—is interiorized, removed and remembered and always present. It is the very opposite of kitsch, whose objects and themes are instantly recognizable and identifiable,[11] and finally, the very opposite of the obscene (although it touches obscenity in a meeting of opposites)—for its terrible beauty, as in Mathias Grünewald's great image of the crucifixion, finally draws us to its deepest consolations. Even in its scandal, it effects a transfiguration that is the obverse of the transformation of the beautiful and debauched body of Emile Zola's prostitute Nana, finally a Venus decomposing and for whom there is no kind nurse and only utter, empty solitude: "'Ah, she's changed, she's changed,' murmured Rose Mignon, the last to leave."[12] But there is more than one way to change.

Why transfiguration—a world-changing, though often in the deepest deserts of space and interiority, in this show of fractured body and blood? It is precisely because at this most profound moment of embodied, human suffering, in absolute pain of body and spirit, it is possible to go no further, and this alone guarantees—something—within the utter despair uncontaminated by false hope or the consolation of illusions. Art and literature continue to touch upon a barely conscious depth that Christian consciousness, nursed by theology, can barely comprehend in its sequential narratives of resurrection and ascension, for it is only in a radical reversal of such consciousness, in an acknowledgment of the utter scandal of the body, that sacramental presence can truly begin.[13] Indeed, the celebration of the sacrament, and perhaps above all for the priest, is a descent into hell whose darkness cannot comprehend the light that shines in the flesh. The body displayed is a broken body, a mutilation that is at the same time a regaining in the mythic and the ritual. But it begins only in true despair and a necessary deconstruction of all that is dearly and most desperately preserved. Think only of the dismantling of the patterns of faith in the poetry of Wilfred Owen with its piercing slants of light shed on the bodies of young soldiers horribly mangled by war. Here is not the dismemberment that is celebrated in our consumerist entertainment culture, the easy body counts of popular cinema that dull to extinction our awful *anagnorisis*, our shock of recognition, our possibility of reversal.[14] On July 4, 1918, Owen wrote to Osbert Sitwell of his experience as an officer training young men to fight on the Western Front: "For 14 hours yesterday I was at work—teaching Christ to lift his cross by numbers, and how to adjust his crown; and not to imagine his thirst till after the last halt. I attended his Supper to see that there were not complaints; and inspected his feet that they should be worthy of the nails. I see to it that he is dumb, and stands at attention before his accusers. With a piece of silver I buy him every day, and with maps I make him familiar with the topography of Golgotha."[15] The effect of one narrative placed on another is almost unbearable—the Passion Narrative already overlaid by millennia of ritual and theology, its outcome celebrated in the guarantees of Easter symbolism: the narrative of the young troops, another story entirely conveyed through Owen's heavy irony in his role as Judas, a national hero. Or, are the narratives so very different? What makes these bodies of young men, separated by nearly two thousand years of bloodshed, and eucharistic celebration, so different? At least Owen takes us back to the shock of recognition and the insistent presence of the body, so that even in its absence, in the "mock" Eucharist celebrated by the fictional Monsignor Quixote, it makes his beating heart cease. Into every Eucharist we die. And the suffering of the mutilated body can never be justified. In Pat Barker's novel *Regeneration* (1991), the first of her trilogy of novels on World War I, army psychologist W. H. R. Rivers witnesses the total breakdown of a young man, of no particular virtue, who has come back utterly shell-shocked from the Front, his mind and body in a state of complete collapse.

> His body felt like a stone. Rivers got hold of him and held him, coaxing, rocking. He looked up at the tower that loomed squat and menacing above them, and thought, *Nothing justifies this. Nothing, nothing, nothing.* Burns' body remained rigid in his arms. Rivers was aware that if it came to a fight he might not win. Burns was terribly emaciated, but he was also thirty years younger. His surrender, when it came, was almost shocking. Suddenly his body had the rag-doll floppiness of the newborn. He collapsed against Rivers and started to shake, and from there it was possible to half lead, half push him out of the moat and up on to the relative safety of the path.[16]

This is another scene of nurturing, almost reminiscent of a *Pieta*, but yet a moment of utter, empty negativity. No great cause, no national security, *nothing* justifies the sufferings of this ordinary young man: what then of the sufferings of another young man who died at about the age of thirty in the most ghastly way imaginable? What justifies such mutilation of body and soul: the salvation of the world? Perhaps it is only at this meeting point of all realities where time and history cease and where alone true ritual is born and where every narrative is deconstructed, and only then, is any gesture of wholeness possible.

But every saint is a despairing soul. R. S. Thomas, in his poem "The Priest," picks his way, a crippled soul, through an uncaring, uncomprehending, superficial parish, yet—"'Let it be so,' I say. 'Amen and amen,'"[17] Thomas' poem is another pattern placed on the eucharistic narrative, a further realization of human identity with the broken, present body, unbearable save for the insight of St. Athanasius, developed in the theology of St. Maximus the Confessor, that God became like us so that we might become like him in the deified flesh.[18] But the suffering and the scandal remain—absolutely.

Perhaps there is a further scandal that we have barely touched on yet. For this scandalous body—so blatantly displayed in the insistent "this is my body," and in the "wildly counter-evidential, counter-cultural claim"[19] that "in my flesh I shall see God"—is also a gendered, decaying body, endlessly unsettled by its own eroticism and its aging processes and the differences between male and female. If excess and the exploitation of the differences offer endless possibilities to the darker elements in human nature, even sheer frankness can be hard to contemplate in *this* body in all its disturbing qualities. D. H. Lawrence's *Lady Chatterley's Lover* (1928), described by Richard Hoggart in the introduction to the Penguin edition as *not* a dirty book, but as "clean, serious and beautiful,"[20] may seem to us now almost unreadable and even turgid, but at least there is a certain honesty in its attempt to unravel the language of sex from its late Romantic and Edwardian pseudomysticism and to "represent sexuality as a cognitive activity."[21] Lawrence does not deflect our gaze. Much later, John Updike, in his novel *Seek My Face* (2002) offers an uncompromising image of aging flesh in the central character of Hope Chafetz, sitting alone in her underwear and wondering at the decay of her own body, hardly able to own it.[22] The contemplation of even our own bodies can be unbearable, because of what they signify, because of their reality. Or it might be simply the difficulty of deviation from a norm into which a gendered element has been introduced, a shift away from accepted cultural or social patterns. Thus, Eric Gill's 1922 woodcut, *The Nuptials of God*, shows

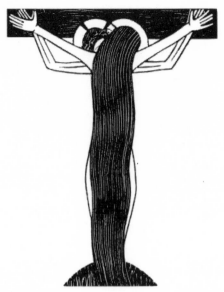

Eric Gill, *The Nuptials of God.* Courtesy of the Bridgeman Art Gallery.

what appears to be a haloed female form pressing herself on the crucified Christ, thereby herself crucified even as she appears to embrace and kiss the figure before her and hidden by her body. This suggestive and elusive image sets up countercurrents in its bodily display, its intrusion into our established patterns of response to the image of the cross. The confusion to such established patterns has been taken in a different direction by Margaret Miles in her essay "The Virgin's One Bare Breast: Female Nudity and Religious Meaning in Tuscan Early Renaissance Culture."[23] She studies a theme in fourteenth-century Tuscan paintings of the Virgin Mary with one breast exposed, feeding the infant Jesus, arguing that the messages conveyed by the image have a complex history beyond, but never wholly distinct from, bodily exposure. Clearly, the theme of the nurturing and sustaining Mother is predominant, though Miles argues that the image was not associated with eroticism in the mind of the medieval viewer.[24]

However, and with further reference to Leo Steinberg's now classic text *The Sexuality of Christ in Renaissance Art and Modern Oblivion,* it is clear that such images are actually rarely unambiguous or entirely innocent, as is suggested by the Renaissance convention of portraying the covered side of Mary as entirely flat and the exposed breast as a rather artificial cone that appears as an appendage rather than as part of the woman's actual body.[25] At best there seems to be a certain coyness here. The point is that, however much theology and its themes intervene (and one may add further curious images in Western art of a nurturing and lactating Jesus and paintings of Mary squirting life-giving milk from her breast into the mouths of St. Jerome and other skinny, isolated, and ascetic saints), images of the body are invariably complex and have the power to disturb in more ways than one and at the same time. However deeply removed, interiorized, and remembered, the displayed body remains insistently *there*, like the body of St. Mary of Egypt to Father Zossima, in all its fullness, its consumption in the Eucharist a scandal, albeit a necessary and even salvific one—in more ways than one.

Let us pursue Miles' theme a little further in the context of two disturbing though rather beautiful moments in modern fiction. At the end of John Steinbeck's novel *The Grapes of Wrath* (1939), Rose of Sharon, having given birth to a stillborn child, feeds a dying man with her milk, the man awed by what is offered to him. The final scene is another and complex *Pieta*.

> She moved slowly to the corner and stood looking down at the wasted face, into the wide, frightened eyes. Then slowly she lay down beside him. He shook his head slowly from side to side. Rose of Sharon loosened one side of the blanket and bared her breast. "You got to," she said. She squirmed closer and pulled his head close. "There!" she said. "There." Her hand moved behind his head and supported it. Her fingers moved gently in his hair. She looked up and across the barn, and her lips came together and smiled mysteriously.[26]

There are elements here of seduction as well as nurturing, reminiscent of George Herbert's great eucharistic poem "Love Bade me Welcome." Above all there is a showing and a feeding on the body of the girl—an eating and a drinking. The same image is explored more scandalously, but no less movingly, in Guy de Maupassant's short story "Idyll" in which a wet nurse, trapped on a train with breasts strained to the full with milk, feeds a poor peasant man in her carriage. She thanks him for the relief he has given her, but her gift to him is even greater, even life itself: "And he gratefully replied: 'It's me as has to thank you, Madame. I hadn't had a thing to eat for two days.'"[27] And yet there is something deliberately illicit in de Maupassant's telling of the story. The young man remarks, "That's put new life into me," and somehow this ingesting of forbidden yet freely offered nutrition has a knowing complexity that is at once deeply sacred and utterly scandalous, even blasphemous.

"This is my body . . . this is my blood." The words remain with us insistently, showing and inviting to the even deeper horror of consuming the elements, thus becoming one with the flesh incarnate, dismembered and resurrected. Some critical focus has been given in recent years on the eucharistic presence in the writings of poets within the English tradition from the writings of John Donne through Gerard Manley Hopkins and up to Geoffrey Hill and R. S. Thomas.[28] But the study remains resolutely *wordy*, forgetting the power of the image and the real presence of a body that is infinitely complex, incorporating and transgressing modes of discourse, offering itself as food to the eyes and to the mouth, and that remains present (as bodies do) even and perhaps especially troubling in its physical absence. In his now standard book, *The Power of Images* (1989), David Freedberg reviews both the history of idolatry and iconoclasm, examining the power of images to disturb so that we frantically embrace them and equally frantically destroy them before they destroy us. But at the heart of the Eucharist is more than an image. It is the Word made flesh, a shift toward an infinitely complex territory of embodiment, known only fully in the ascetic body, that we share with the incarnate Word. When Jesus showed his disciples his body in the simple forms of bread and wine, he showed them nothing less than everything, and the cost which was all. But turn the image around, into the notion of the flesh made Word.[29] Is that not what we more often do? And this is a move that is both more simple and ultimately infinitely more dangerous. For to trap the body in words, and to designate the flesh in a word, is to define and limit it, to circumscribe it and to hold it for our own purposes and within the limits of our own definitions: bodies become the slaves of the words ascribed to them—defining both our moral response and the roles expected of them. The body is clad in the voluminous folds of language, for good and usually for ill, and becomes the victim of its defining rhetoric. Bodies are granted stability —true—but are framed as metaphors of power and enslavement. But to show the body of the Word made flesh, however, and to invite its ingestion, is to enter a far more complex and liturgical world of presence and absence, of the unity of body and soul in a profound silence that is beyond the mere constructions of language, and still capable of utterance in a language that is strange and even violent beyond all collective intolerances and mysterious beyond all comprehension—but entirely familiar and inwardly known, yet always as if for the first time.

George Herbert

I have long thought that all true poetry seeks for and finds its end in silence, being not so much a matter of approaching some hidden meaning within the verse, but rather, as Martin Heidegger once put it, a "letting the unsayable be not said" in defiance of propositional logic.[30] This is that "something understood" of

George Herbert that constitutes the essential unspokenness of the language
and images of true prayer, and in poetry a conclusion in silence that is, in
the nice description of James Boyd White, "given meaning by the words that
have come before."[31] It is a profound and sacramental silence at the heart of
language, the silence of the Word itself.

The very impossibility of adequate speech that is paradoxically admitted
in the depths of Herbert's verse is also an eloquent recognition of the final
incapacity of all theological language to reflect the ineffable and the infinite.
"Now I am here, what thou wilt do with me / None of my books will show.
/ I reade, and sigh, and wish I were a tree; / or sure then I should grow / To
fruit or shade."[32] But such an admission of linguistic limitation by no means
confines sacred poetry to the narrow uses ascribed to it by, for example, Dr.
Samuel Johnson in the eighteenth century, which are, he says, "to help the
memory, and delight the ear. . . . but [yet] it supplies nothing to the mind.
[For] the *ideas* of Christian Theology are too simple for eloquence, too sacred
for fiction, and too majestick for ornament; to recommend them by tropes
and figures, is to magnify for a concave mirror the sidereal hemisphere."[33]
Rather, indeed, for Herbert, like St. Augustine before him, the mind is never
more theologically alive than in the energetic and vital language of the poet
as it seeks to bring to life the connection between what we say and the most
profound, even unknown, reality that we strive to express in our relationship
with it. In Herbert's verse, the language provokes us on competing, simultaneous levels, always profoundly aware of its limitations while yet opening up
a polyphony of meanings that can be heard and felt not separately but only in
the challenging grandeur of their harmony and dissonance. Thus, our experience of the literary in the text moves beyond and then returns to the claims
of religious doctrine and dogma, at once exploring them and also, at the same
time, rendering them silent in our devout and humble appropriation of them.
Like the language of the gospels themselves, Herbert's poems are cryptic and
often exploratory of the impossible.[34] But if his verse is not so much precisely
prayerful as exploring and living within the impossibility of prayer (though is
there a difference?), almost all of it is in the form of spiritual autobiography,[35]
its language crisp and almost clinically exact, indeed, likened recently by
David L. Edwards to the experimental science advocated by Bacon "(whether
or not [Herbert himself] was conscious of this)."[36]

In thus recording his own complex and profound relationship with God
and with Christ, Herbert takes his reader through his words inside the very
sanctuary of a life that, as Izaak Walton admitted in his own hagiographic
manner, defeats description in words, a life beyond common possibility

demanding nothing short of the golden tongue of St. John Chrysostom him-self: "I have now brought him [says Walton] to the parsonage of Bemerton and to the thirty-sixth year of his age, and must stop here, and bespeak the reader to prepare for an almost incredible story of the great sanctity of the short remainder of his holy life; a life so full of Charity, Humility and all Christian virtues that it deserves the eloquence of St. Chrysostom to com-mend and declare it."[37] In short, in Herbert's very life, we are brought within the space of literature and to that essential solitude, though yet a communal and liturgical one, which, in the words of the French literary and cultural critic Maurice Blanchot, though writing not of Herbert himself, of course, "excludes the complacent isolation of individualism; it has nothing to do with the quest for singularity."[38] In this solitary literary space, the writer is lost in the greater work, the delimited site of an endless task, defined only by the limits of a particular poetic structure, or theological conclusion, the momentary vision that casts its passing light on a whole human life and its specifics. In Herbert's words in "The Glimpse": "Thou cam'st but now; wilt thou so soon depart / And give me up to night?"[39]

In Blanchot's thinking, the solitude of the work has as its primary frame-work the absence of any defining criteria. As he suggests: "This absence makes it impossible ever to declare the work finished or unfinished. The work is without any proof, just as it is without any use. It can't be verified. Truth can appropriate it, renown draws attention to it, but the existence it thus acquires doesn't concern it . . . The work is solitary: this does not mean it remains uncommunicable, that it has no reader. But whoever reads it enters into the affirmation of the work's solitude, just as he who reads it belongs to the risk of this solitude."[40] We need to unpack this *literary* reflection in the reading of Herbert's poems. Within their complex linguistic structures, the reader, who is always the universal reader, enters a deeply solitary, interior place that is profoundly human, though one that entirely excludes any complacent indi-vidualism either of Christian believer or nonbeliever. At the same time, the reader cannot ignore Herbert's saturation in the language of the English Bible and the liturgy of the Church of England. Nor is this, for us, simply a herme-neutical issue between the horizons of the religious language of his time and the very different, more secular English of our own. For the reader, indeed, still familiar with the language of the *Book of Common Prayer* in the practice of worship and sacrament, it will have yet a resonance inaudible to those unfamil-iar with this particular music: but it is not even a question of belief or unbelief. Thus, I want to move beyond the question posed by White—that is, "How far is it possible to read Herbert's poetry, cast as it is in religious language, and with a theologically defined audience, without ourselves in some sense sharing in the beliefs that the language expresses?"[41] I do move beyond that question inasmuch as the authenticity of the verse both embraces and expands the particularity of its immediate resonances and the references that are its landscape, but a landscape into which we are *all* graciously invited, its beauties and complexities open to us in manifold ways, whether they are familiar or strange, comfortable or alien in time, space, or culture.

Before I return more specifically to Herbert's poetry, let me put my point into a somewhat broader context in Renaissance and more recent literature. This is to seek to establish, in the larger context of our reflections on text and body, the close relationship between *religious experience* (which, as Dominic Baker-Smith has said, "results from a willingness to adopt a particular frame of reference [that] . . . in turn, structures the content of perception"[42]) and *literary (textual) experience* that recognizes but does not necessarily adopt such a frame. Or does it, though perhaps in a different way? Erasmus encouraged his reader to make a library of Christ in his own breast. But that library or book then has a linguistic energy of its own. It is the universal energy with which we as universal readers respond to and ingest in the glorious description of Scripture given us in 1611 by the translators of the Authorized Version of the Bible as "a tree, or rather a whole paradise of trees of life, which brings forth fruits every month, and the fruit thereof is for meat, and the leaves for medicine. . . . Finally a fountain of most pure water springing up into everlasting life."[43] Thus we see that from the landscape of devotion emerges also a space of literature that is a place of universal solitude found also in Donne's finest literary achievements in which religion and its *particular* language "is treated as a repertory of roles to be enacted in a world demanding constant interpretation"[44] and constant expansion into the universal. So Donne writes in the *Devotions Upon Emergent Occasions* (and we might recall the Christ who is the library within our breasts): "The *stile* of thy *works*, the *phrase* of thin *Actions*, is *Metaphorical*. The *institution* of thy whole *worship* in the *old Law*, was a continuall *Allegory*; types & *figures* overspread all; and *figures* flowed unto *figures*, and powered themselves out into further figures."[45] Such extraordinary energy is also characteristic of Sir Philip Sidney's 1595 work, *An Apology for Poetry*, with its theologically colored and, at the same time, highly suggestive physical language (one might instance phrases such as "erected wit" or "infected will"), which leads the reader into a world of art in which the glories of the imagination and the poor stumblings of all humanity kiss and are found together. "So no doubt the philosopher with his learned definition [says Sidney—and we might add the theologian to his picture]—be it of virtue, vices, matters of public policy or private government—replenisheth the memory with many infallible grounds of wisdom, which, notwithstanding, lie dark before the imaginative and judging power, if they be not illuminated or figured by the speaking picture of Poesy."[46] In the inspired imagination and the continuances of literature, words, even those hallowed by the devotion that sanctifies language, are ever alert to the experience of the body and of the world. As Samuel Taylor Coleridge was to say to William Godwin in September 1800, "I would endeavour to destroy the old antithesis of *Words & Things*, elevating, as it were, Words into Things, & living Things too."[47] And in 1822, objecting to the sole assumption to itself by the Roman Church of the word "Catholic," Coleridge calls words *"Spirits* and *Living Agents* that are seldom misused without avenging themselves."[48] And, to sound one final note within the alchemy of language and its vicarious experience from a fellow poet in modern literature before returning to Herbert, there is a verse from D. J. Enright on the "History of World Languages" celebrating Word and flesh:

> They spoke the loveliest of languages.
> Their tongues entwined in Persian, ran
> And fused. Words kissed, a phrase embraced,
> Verbs conjugated sweetly. Verse began.
> So Eve and Adam lapped each other up
> The livelong day, the lyric night.[49]

And all this went on in innocence, before the fall, so Adam and Eve exercised their wits to conceive as love bade them welcome. Such is the space of literature, the space of the text.

In March 1615, Lancelot Andrewes, then bishop of Ely, was in attendance at the king's state visit to the University of Cambridge, where Herbert, then only twenty-three, was a Minor Fellow of Trinity College, his ordination to the priesthood still some ten years away. It is likely that on this occasion he was introduced to Bishop Andrewes, a meeting that led to a friendship and correspondence between the two men. Shortly afterward, Herbert sent Andrewes a letter (written in Greek) containing "some safe and useful aphorisms" on the subjects of predestination and sanctity of life, a letter, records Walton, "so remarkable for the language and reason of it, that, after reading it, the bishop put it into bosom, and did often show it to many scholars, both of his and foreign nations; but did always return it back to the place where he first lodged it and continued it so near his heart till the last day of his life."[50] Such was the fate of this learned letter written by a young man on the verge of worldly success, his courtly career, which he would later entirely eschew, seemingly assured. And it is precisely such success that would contribute to the textual confluence in his poetry of an utterly embodied spirituality that continues to address us directly, a union of body and soul such that no language of the body affronts the soul, but rather embellishes it in the space of literature as a truly aesthetic asceticism. In the most fragile, yet tenacious, of literary connections, we can link the ancient fathers and mothers of the desert tradition with the English priest Herbert, and then, in another unlikely leap of the imagination, to the twentieth-century thinker and mystic Simone Weil, who, in fact, read Herbert's poetry with remarkable insight and empathy. In the chapter of his prose work on the priestly ministry, *A Priest to the Temple* (1652), titled "The Parson's State of Life," Herbert writes of his subject, going even beyond the authority of the church:

> He therefore thinks it not enough for him to observe the fasting days of the Church and the daily prayers enjoined him by authority, which he observeth out of humble conformity and obedience; but adds to them, out of choice and devotion, some other days for fasting and hours for prayers; and by these he keeps his body tame, serviceable and healthful; and his soul fervent, active, young and lusty as an eagle. He often readeth the Lives of the Primitive Monks, Hermits and Virgins, and wondereth not so much at their patient suffering and cheerful dying under persecuting emperors. . . . as at their daily temperance, abstinence, watchings, and constant prayers and mortifications in times of peace and prosperity.[51]

Thus, in prayer and devotion, the parson mirrors the ancient ascetics, while the "taming" of his body flourishes gloriously in an extraordinarily "embodied" (and scriptural) description of the lusty soul rising like an eagle.

By far the best way to read Herbert's collection of poems *The Temple* (1633) is to take them as a whole in order to best appreciate their complex inner geography and the subtle interrelationships between texts and levels of reference. In the puns and riddles of language, words are continually slipping to different and ever more complex levels of activity and meaning, even learnedly across different languages in the macaronic tradition of verse, without losing touch with the simple initial level, so that language becomes a medium that simultaneously embraces different worlds, at once interior and exterior, bodily and spiritual. The poetry both sacralizes the profane and profanes the sacred in an endless *kenosis* of certainty, and is yet sustained by a profound and utterly real sense of presence in absence. Immersed as Herbert was in the Anglican *Book of Common Prayer*,[52] it was article 28 of the Thirty-Nine Articles of Religion of 1562 that was central to his poetry. "The Supper of the Lord is not only a sign of the love that Christians ought to have among themselves one

Mathias Grünewald, *Isenheim Altarpiece: The Crucifixion*. Courtesy of the Musée d'Unterlinden Colmar.

Diego Rodriguez de Silva Y Velázquez, *Christ in the House of Martha and Mary.* Courtesy of the National Gallery Picture Library, London.

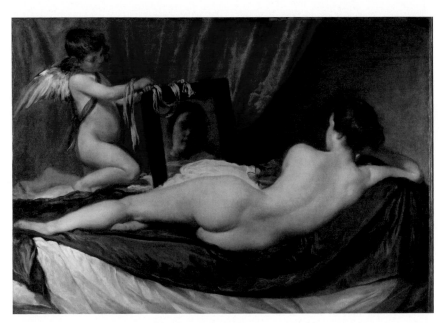

Diego Rodriguez de Silva Y Velázquez, *The Rokeby Venus*. Courtesy of the National Gallery Picture Library, London.

Georges du Mesnil de la Tour, *Repentant Magdalen*. Ailsa Mellon Bruce Fund. Courtesy of the Board of Trustees, National Gallery of Art, Washington, D.C.

Roger van der Weyden, *Mary Magdalene.* Courtesy of the National Gallery Picture Library, London.

Rembrandt, *Danaë*. Courtesy of the State Hermitage Museum, St. Petersburg, Russia.

Luca Signorelli, *The Resurrection of the Body* (Orvieto Cathedral). Courtesy of akg-images, Berlin, London, and Paris.

Caspar David Friedrich, *The Monk by the Sea*. Courtesy of bpk / Nationalgalerie, Staatliche Museen zu Berlin. Photo: Jörg P. Anders.

to another; but rather as a Sacrament of our Redemption by Christ's death: insomuch that to such as rightly, worthily, and with faith, receive the same, the Bread which we break is a partaking of the Body of Christ; and likewise the Cup of Blessing is a partaking of the Blood of Christ."[53] The nuanced language of the Articles is careful in what it avoids saying as much as in what it affirms: to "partake" (a word reaffirmed in the Archbishop Thomas Cranmer's eucharistic rite) skirts theological controversy while affirming a genuine sacramental presence. It allows Herbert to shift easily into a broad imagery that, in his most familiar poem, "Love (III)," permits the celebration of the sacrament to entertain also the language of wayside hospitality and even an overt eroticism. In the sacrament, all is transfigured—nothing is ever wasted.

The reader of Herbert's poems comes to know, in the exercise of reading itself, a sense of transformed embodiment and real presence. Entering into the world of the poem is a transfiguring experience, words becoming real presences in sensual embraces, collating and colliding terms of reference in a merging of body, mind, and spirit, requiring an impossible dwelling in iconoclastic ways of thinking about what it means to be a human being. (I shall shortly return again to the theme of "poetic dwelling" as I link Herbert further, in another unlikely connection, with the later thought of Heidegger.)[54] But Herbert's wit does more than pose puzzles or quibbles for the reader. Reversals of meaning, opaque endings, dialogues and conversations, words opening out into ever new depths of reference, sometimes across different languages, lay a heavy burden of interpretation (or perhaps better call it "response") on the reader. Herbert does not *tell* you, he *shows* you, and leaves you to accommodate yourself to violent intersections of being in words made flesh in the body and soul. As in the Song of Songs itself, moments of sexual exchange becomes places of profound ascetic spirituality (as St. Bernard of Clairvaux well knew), theology is discovered in practice in dramatically conceived exchanges, and familiar images from the Bible flood out in opposing voices and in new complexities of relationship with the everyday. Words stand physically on the page in shapes that propose and embody meaning and narrative progress, as in "Easter-Wings,"[55] or as biblical quotations hidden within a larger body of language, so that Scripture is found embedded in every verbal expression, giving new meaning to the verse from Colossians 3:3: "Your life is hidden with Christ in God." Christ speaks directly from the verse through the liturgical reproaches of Good Friday in "The Sacrifice."[56] And behind all is the enigmatic, priestly, courtly poet who engenders a world that is at once familiar and yet utterly strange, a world that acknowledges the flesh, but a flesh transfigured and disciplined by the spiritual.

Herbert's poetry both loses and finds itself in a language of opposites, a chiastic structure of verse that at once empties words and fills them with their contraries, in weakness stout. Words themselves are unreliable, like the impulse of the poet himself, sources of delusion, until, emptied of meaning, they find themselves afresh in a coincidence of opposites. Only in such verbal *kenosis* can the word of the poet find its true being and poetic dwelling become possible. Here, I am deliberately employing the language of Heidegger, a language that is born of Heidegger's engagement with another, later, poet who bears a deep, hidden, and mysterious relationship with Herbert—the German Romantic Friedrich Hölderlin—though Herbert is utterly removed from the world of Hölderlin's politics and, of course, from German idealism. But in Heidegger's reading of him, we focus on the crucial feature of the artwork—that is, its singularity.[57] The poetic work (*Dichtung*), Heidegger says, is a "self-sufficient presence,"[58] irreducible in our understanding. We rest in its texture and images, our interpretations "disappearing before the pure presence of the poem."[59] The poem becomes a world that embraces the reader, at once familiar and unfamiliar, but always finally unsusceptible to the grasping hand of "knowledge." There is, at its heart, an essential unthought, a mode of being that comes close, even in Herbert, to a religion without an object. In Timothy Clark's words, this is a poetry that enacts "the possibility of other non-appropriative ways of knowing,"[60] and only thus, I would wish to say, can we even begin to draw closer to the sacred or, what Heidegger calls, the "mystery of the reserving nearness."[61] The task of the poet is to turn poetic language back on its own foundations in the *kenosis* of language in which, in Herbert's words, "I am clean forgot."

It is precisely this that Heidegger calls "poetic dwelling," a being in the world in which words themselves dwell among us in their mystery and salvific potential. Such dwelling in Herbert's verse has many textual resonances, past and present, but above all those from Scripture. There is supremely the first chapter of St. John's Gospel (which has never actually been far from our thoughts), negative theology, the theology of the death of God, Heidegger, and Hölderlin. But do not misunderstand me. I am neither offering you a "positive" reading of Heidegger's interpretation of his poet, with the peculiar nationalisms and redemptive politics that that would require, nor am I doing that with Herbert either in any traditional sense of reading him as a Christian poet, or an Anglican of the early sixteenth century. My concern is much more to move within and behind the poetry as the *embodiment*, not the reflection or statement, of theological *possibilities*—no more than that. It is to seek for a place within the disturbing semantic shifts of the verse. Consider for a moment Herbert's poem "Christmas."[62] This is not a poem *about* Christmas. To start with, its setting is any time—"as I rid *one day*." Rather, the poem is an exploration, a calling into question even, of the earthly hospitality granted to the heavenly child when the scene is transported from Bethlehem to the soul of the poet. Here are the first fourteen lines:

All after pleasures as I rid one day,
    My horse and I, both tir'd, bodie and minde,
    With full crie of affections, quite astray;
I took up in the next inne I could finde

There when I came, whom found I but my deare,
    My dearest Lord, expecting till the grief
    Of pleasures brought me to him, readie there
To be all passengers most sweet relief?

O Thou, whose glorious, yet contracted light,
    Wrapt in a nights mantle, stole into a manger;
    Since my dark soul and brutish is thy right,
To Man of all beasts be not thou a stranger:

        Furnish & deck my soul, that thou mayst have
        A better lodging, then a rack, or grave.

Here, indeed, is a poetic dwelling, and a dwelling of the word in the poet, a theology instantiated *within* language itself, and our complex experience of words.[63] We begin after a journey, wearied from "pleasures," and setting down at the first inn at hand to rest, which becomes, in a sense, the Christmas inn, but immediately moves to the interiority of the poet's "dark soul" burdened with "the grief of pleasures," its sinfulness awaited by the "contracted light" of its dear Lord. Moving between the different levels of reference (in a manner reminiscent of the Cranmerian Collects of the *Book of Common Prayer*[64]), the reader is kept alert to shifts of place and inclusive slippages of language— theology, spiritual condition, the inn itself intertwining at every level, even to complexities in single words. In the next nineteen lines, which are almost a second and separate poem, a song to be sung in the conditions set up by the first lines (a device Herbert also uses in his poems on Good Friday and Easter), an extended play on the word "sun" concludes with an harmonious exchange—"Till ev'n his beams sing, and my musick shine."

"Christmas" then ends with a celebration, realized in defiance, almost, of all sophisticated hermeneutics. We know, as it were, "something understood"[65] though barely articulated even as the verse has simultaneously constructed and deconstructed the images and metaphors of the theological narrative in a new awareness of the possibility of presence of being in the clearing of the poem. And here, as we move from poetry to theology, I make perhaps my most shocking move from Herbert to the contemporary writings of the Italian philosopher Gianni Vattimo, who links the truth of Christianity with what he calls "postmodern nihilism" or "the end of metaphysics," "which is to say that Christianity's truth appears to be the dissolution of the (metaphysical) truth concept itself."[66] At the heart of Vattimo's post-Heideggerian deconstructed and reconstructed Christianity is a deeply poetic reading of *kenosis*, an understanding of the incarnation as God's renunciation of his own sovereign transcendence, after Philippians 2:6–8. In what Vattimo calls a "reduced faith" (perhaps something close, paradoxically, to the deep and hidden faith of the ascetic), he suggests that "the 'kenotic' interpretation of the articles of faith goes hand in hand with the life of every person, that is, with the commitment to transform them into concrete principles that are incarnate in one's own existence, and irreducible to a formula."[67] At the heart of this faith—its terms drawn from a century of existential thinking that includes Rudolf Bultmann, Heidegger, and Paul Tillich—is "the recognition that the commandment of charity is the sole content of the myths of Scripture, of the history of spirituality and Christian theology."[68]

Now I am not, of course, wishing in any way to attribute to Herbert anything like the radical post-postmodern theology of Vattimo. That would be absurd and indefensible. But I do think that there are similarities between where each of them actually is, each in their own time, in their search for the truth of Christianity. (The phrase is Vattimo's, not mine.) The contemporary postmetaphysical philosopher finds such truth in those processes of secularization that allow him to move away from the unacceptable constraints of a church that still attempts to impose rules that cannot be accepted, but still acknowledges a culture that is (for him) shaped by the biblical and specifically Christian message.[69] One thinks also of the deep countercultural move of the fathers and mothers of the desert away from the institutions of church and society. Reading the poetry of Herbert, I find it also in a space of literature that allows truth to be "understood" without the imposition of doctrine but realizes the profound authenticity of the Bible, the church and its beloved sacramental and liturgical discipline only through the appropriation of its impossible, living necessities. Herbert is a Renaissance Anglican clergyman: Vattimo is an Italian, Roman Catholic philosopher, openly gay and rediscovering something like a Christian faith in terms that would have been utterly incomprehensible to the poet. Strangely, however, I read them both and find myself responding to the contemporary resonances of Herbert's call to his reader in all its interior earthiness and, in the defined freedom and continuances of the resulting space, understand a little better Vattimo's claim to belief as a crucial feature of our own cultural and personal lives.

And with this odd combination in mind—though it is important to me as it is only through this mysterious yet broad literary space that I am now able to legitimate the philosophical and cultural demands of theology, which is why Herbert remains such a major figure in my own reading—let me conclude this section with a brief reflection on a sonnet that links Herbert *back* through the Christian tradition to those early saints of the desert whose lives became utterly one with Scripture such that reading finally becomes living. And to read Herbert is to become wholly one with the Scriptures that inhabit not only almost every image and metaphor but also every word of his verse. The words of the Bible, "this book of stars" for our salvation, are realized in the flesh of the verse, and to read is to participate, shockingly, in the sacrament of the Word made Flesh, a "mass of strange delights."

> Oh Book! Infinite sweetnesse! let my heart
>   Suck ev'ry leter, and a hony gain,
>   Precious for any grief in any part;
> To clear the breast, to mollifie all pain.
>
> Thou art all health, health thriving, till it make
>   A full eternitie: thou art a masse
>   Of strange delights, where we may wish & take.
> Ladies, look here; this is the thankfull glasse,
>
> That mends the lookers eyes: this is the well
>   That washes what it shows. Who can indeare
>   Thy praise too much? thou art heavens Lidger here,
> Working against the states of death and hell.
>
>   Thou art joyes handsell: heav'n lies flat in thee,
>   Subject to ev'ry mounters bended knee.[70]

The poem opens with a reference to Psalm 119:103, "How sweet are your words to my taste: sweeter than honey to my mouth." The heart of the Scripture reader is like a bee drawing honey from the flower, making for full health. The poet's address to the ladies daringly draws on a commonplace image from theater of the vanity of women who admire themselves in the mirror.[71] Here, however, is the true cosmetic that does not merely reveal imperfection but washes it away. Throughout the sonnet, images and individual words expand in reference across the spiritual and the physical realms. The Bible is "heaven's lidger here"—a pun that refers at once to "resident ambassador" and "register" (book)[72] and is politically continued in the reference in the next line to the "states" of death and hell. Indeed, heaven itself lies flat between the pages of the Bible, its very words active in our salvation. In this brief sonnet, Herbert ranges across an extraordinary geography of different worlds and societies— in nature, the courtly lady, the politician—drawing them all together in the words of Scripture.

In Herbert we find another impossible saint—the courtier turned country parson whose poetry remains utterly immersed in the world even while sustaining an ascetic vision that is grounded entirely in the living Word of Scripture and in the sacrament of the Eucharist, which permeates every aspect of life lived to the full. The poet of *The Temple* is full of a boundless energy, but it is an energy finally driven into an interiority within its language and its dramatic power that suffers endless reversals and negations: and the frequent violence of the images and metaphors is finally consumed in the still, insistent voice—the voice that calls silently from the wilderness without explanation and cannot be gainsaid. For, as something understood, it is the final negation of all language and its demands—and their complete fulfillment in the silence of the Total Presence of God.[73]

Simone Weil

To shift our attention rather abruptly from the English priest and poet George Herbert to the French mystical writer of the twentieth century Simone Weil, may appear to be one of the more bizarre shifts in the many modulations of this book. But there are times when a sharp change of key can demonstrate a deeper underlying unity, a surprising coherence that is indicative of profound truths in hidden narratives that are not always apparent on the surface of things. What Herbert and Weil have in common, and in continuity with others whom we have followed in text and narrative action, is a deep incorporation in sense of the sacramental as a driving quality of embodiment—that to be fully in the flesh is to participate at every level in the self-embodiment of God, even and perhaps inevitably at the final cost of life itself. Furthermore, Weil certainly read Herbert's poetry and was deeply affected by it, especially that most well known of all Herbert's verses, "Love (III)," "Love bade me welcome." Of this, she wrote, "I learnt it by heart. Often, at the culminating moment of a violent headache, I make myself say it over, concentrating all my attention on it and clinging with all my soul to the tenderness it enshrines. I used to think I was merely reciting it as a beautiful poem, but without my knowing it the recitation had the virtue of a prayer. It was during one of these recitations that. . . . Christ himself came down and took possession of me."[74] Weil is indubitably another impossible saint, difficult, perverse, treading a path that none can follow, reminding us also, perhaps, of another holy eccentric, Dame Julian of Norwich and her celebration of her illness sent by God so that, as far as she could tell, her "body was dead from the waist downwards."[75] Weil needs no hagiographer to make her yet more inaccessible to the common mortal. In her writing and in her spirituality, she is deeply Christian, though she was never baptized and elected to remain outside the church, on an edge that places her beyond reach and yet, as always, utterly central. She expresses a desire for, and yet imposes on herself a deliberate deprivation of the sacraments, and this, she suggests, "might constitute a contact which was more pure than actual participation."[76] Frequently, she insists that she feels "ordained" to be alone, and to be "a stranger and an exile in relation to every human circle without exception." And yet, as with almost every other subject of this book, her move away into an apparent negation, though it undoubtedly has in her a certain morbidity, is also, paradoxically, a move *into* the body, a self-emptying that is, at the same time, a full realization of being through nonbeing, a eucharistic participation that is at once, through the body, a descent into hell and true resurrection. Like every true ascetic and mystic, she sustains a profound sense of beauty and a necessary sense of the transfigured, deified body. She is, at once, the passionate body of utter God-forsakeness and the glorious, perfected body of St. Antony emerging from his tomb. In words that are at once appalling and extraordinary, Weil wrote, "The beauty of the world is the mouth of a labyrinth. The unwary individual who on entering takes a few steps, is soon unable to find the opening. . . . [But] if he does not lose courage, if he goes on walking, it is absolutely certain that he will finally arrive at the centre of the labyrinth. And there God is waiting to eat him. Later he will go out again, but he will be changed, he will have become different, after being eaten and digested by God."[77] Weil spent the last months of her life after December 1942 in England working for the Free French organization. Despite her earlier belief in pacifism, she became convinced of the need to oppose the savagery of Hitler's progress, and her contribution to the recovery and spiritual regeneration of her country France was her proposal for a "project for a formation of frontline nurses,"[78] a body of women, including herself, who would dedicate themselves, at the almost certain cost of their own lives, to the care of soldiers wounded in the frontline of battle. Their purpose was not only simply practical, but they would also constitute powerful symbols, and yet more than that. She asked for everything of her to be stripped away, "devoured by God, transformed into Christ's substance, and given for food to afflicted men whose body and soul lacked every kind of nourishment."[79] She prayed for herself to become Eucharist, utterly at one with the Word made flesh in the *incarnatio continua*.

In her project document, and in a more domestic image, she asks, "what could be better" than to have French and allied soldiers "accompanied under enemy fire, amid scenes of the greatest brutality, by something that constitutes a living evocation of the homes they have had to leave behind: not a saddening evocation, but an exalting one?. . . . This female corps would constitute precisely that concrete and exalting evocation."[80] This unfulfilled project was Weil's concretization, in the context of war an occupied France, of the actual and symbolic offering of the body in the deep desert—a move at once utterly sacrificial and a realization of the mystical, deified body. Her proposal was entirely consistent with her deepening move into a mystical theology that was at once Christian and also nurtured by her immersion in both the *Bhagavad Gita* and the literature of classical Greece. It was a genuine realization of the Word made flesh of the Fourth Gospel in its absolute conjoining of the utter particularity of the body and the totally universal soul in a given historical moment to be redeemed only by a death. It was her moment to instantiate in the particularity that was given to her, her observation, which draws on Pascal and the Fourth Gospel, that "an historical anecdote whose central character is God cannot be refracted into eternity."[81] Now it was her moment in history in the intersection of time and eternity. Like all her predecessors in the mystical tradition, Weil was totally practical, locked into a full realization of the necessary sacramental grounding of being in the body. Despite her bizarre, sometimes seemingly perverse, face on the world, she rejects neither the material world nor the human body. Indeed, in her reversals, she aspires to quite the reverse. She sought a moment when pure matter and pure spirit "exchange their secrets"[82] in an instant of perfection, a surrender of identity to God that can only be made in death.

Weil saw the moment of France's despair in 1942 as a true moment of possible redemption beyond Europe's idolatrous obsession with nationhood and power. Suffering and death itself offered an opportunity for a genuine apocalypse, a moment of genuine incarnation that Weil and her nurses would embody and symbolize in a sacramental energy that was fighting, at the most universal level, the evil of Nazism and the threat of nonbeing. It was also perceived by Weil in deeply Romantic terms (and to Romanticism we will return more fully in chapter 9), as a possible recovery of France's "genius," an authenticity only incarnated historically in figures like Joan of Arc. And, like Christ's action on the cross, it was an "act of war": "The unique source of salvation and greatness for France is to re-establish contact with her genius in the depths of her affliction. This must be done now, immediately, while the affliction is still crushing, while France still has before her, in the future, the possibility to realize the first glimmer of the consciousness of her rediscovered genius, by expressing it through an act of war. . . . *War must be the teacher who develops and nourishes this inspiration; for that, a deep, authentic inspiration, a true light, must surge up in the very midst of war.*"[83] Weil's extraordinary proposal, almost certainly suicidal and offered as "symbolic," can easily be dismissed as pathological, linked to her self-hatred and what has been termed her profound misogyny. It can also be seen as her deep insight into the absolute and present power and virtue of the real metaphor, one of those instants in which an extreme act of the body and spirit effects a reconciliation and a fragile moment by which the world is kept in being. It was what the desert ascetics, together with Meister Eckhart, Angelus Silesius, and others, were seeking in a perfect identity with Christ that can only be at once a moment of extinction and a moment of transfiguration. It was not to be, for Weil's plan was never accepted—it was, of course, too mad, too impossible. And so she remained in England, compulsively writing in the final months of her life, putting her being necessarily into a text that finally consumed her. In the words of Alexander Irwin, "That life was relentless hunger for the impossible: a kind of madness, surely. But Weil's madness was also a metaphor: a poetic figure, a sacred ceremony, an effort of communication. Her mad life, the 'real metaphor,' had to be written."[84] The final months of Weil's life have been seen as a realization of the Eucharist in her own body, her version of the extraordinary ascetic feats of the saints of the desert in a literal feeding on her own flesh even to death. She knew in herself the truth proposed by Helen Oppenheimer that resurrection "is the fulfillment in which the pattern of each person shall again become presence, our own real presence of which we may each say (perhaps in surprised delight) 'This is my body.'"[85] There are, of course, other interpretations of her pathological condition—undoubtedly, she was anorexic, impossible. Desiring to share absolutely in the sufferings of those she had left behind in occupied France, she refused to eat more than the meager rations that she believed (probably wrongly) were their portion. By the late summer of 1943, she was transferred to a sanatorium in Ashford, Kent, where she died on August 24.

In her unrealized project for frontline nurses, and in her absolute need to participate in her own frail and failing body in the war effort, Weil, perhaps uniquely, was articulating the realization that it is in the exchange of real symbols that human existence is determined at its deepest, and that those symbols are the most profound conjoining of soul and body. Although never carried out, the very writing of the project had its effect on how the war was "read." One of the great texts to which Weil returned consistently was Homer's *Iliad*, and from this she recognized that war was as much in the influencing of minds as in the physical encounter of bodies. In her remarkable essay "The *Iliad*, Poem of Might,"[86] whose spirit she sees as directly transmitted to the gospels, she concludes of its readers, knowing its impossibility: "Perhaps they will rediscover that epic genius when they learn how to accept the fact that nothing is sheltered from fate, how never to admire might, or hate the enemy, or to despise sufferers. It is doubtful if this will happen soon."[87]

Throughout her writings, Weil returns to the dark night of the soul of St. John of the Cross, and in her brief life she embraced that night more than almost any other being in the twentieth century. She returns also to the theme of God's quest for humanity—the religious life not so much a search for God, but a waiting on God's search for us. But yet we persevere, and it is only in utter negation, in the despair of the negativity of God—our terrible acknowledgment of the cry from the cross, "My God, my God, why have you forsaken me?"[88]—that God speaks. "Just when the soul is spent and has ceased to wait for God, when the external affliction or the interior aridity forces it to believe that God is not a reality, if then nevertheless the soul still loves, and holds in horror those worldly riches which would take his place, then it is that God comes to the soul, reveals Himself, speaks to it, touches it. This is what St. John of the Cross names the dark night of the soul."[89] Like the saints of old, Weil deliberately deprives herself of the sacraments, stands outside, for it is only there, paradoxically, that the sacrament can finally and fully be realized—just as to be a priest, one must learn to be a false priest.[90]

Weil is by no means immune to beauty, but for her it can be found not in any religious or artistic pressing forward, but rather in a waiting on God in his search for us. Beauty is, and her argument is reminiscent of the aesthetics of Kant's *Third Critique*, without purpose or intention. To ask why a particular word is right in a poem is to prompt no reasonable response. As she puts it, "In the case of a really beautiful poem the only answer is that the word is there because it is suitable that it should be." Beauty in the world, and any imitation of it, is found only in "the absence of finality, intention and discrimination,"[91] just as the rain and the sun fall and shine indiscriminately on the just and the unjust. Clearly, Weil is echoing the ancient ascetic practice of indifference or "passionlessness." She would resonate to the words of St. Simeon the New Theologian in the *Philokalia*: "For if a man has not first renounced himself and has not exhausted his blood for the sake of this truly blessed life, how can he imagine that anyone else has done this, to acquire passionlessness?"[92] Thus, the love of true beauty is an ascent on St. John Climacus' ladder of divine ascent to what is always beyond. Nowhere is this more apparent than in the real presence of the sacrament, and it is to this real presence that Weil aspires in her deepest and most bodily being. In her words,

> The virtue of the dogma of the real presence lies in its very absurdity. Except for the infinitely touching symbolism of food, there is nothing in a morsel of bread which can be associated with our thought of God. Thus the conventional character of the divine presence is evident. Christ can only be present in such an object by convention. For this very reason he can be perfectly present in it. God can only be present in a secret here below. His presence in the Eucharist is truly secret since no part of our thought can reach the secret. Thus it is total.[93]

The secret presence in the Eucharist is the poetic silence that Herbert finally comes to rest in.

In her exercises in inutility, Weil has been compared to her fellow Frenchman and contemporary Georges Bataille.[94] Each aspired to a sense of sainthood that was ever new, ever appallingly radical. Looking back to Jacques Maritain, Weil asserted that "we must have the saintliness demanded by the present moment, a new saintliness, itself also without precedent."[95] Each, in their different ways, realized the sacrificial necessity of the body—to be celebrated and offered, fully realized in its very absurdity. Its presence is utterly conventional, and therefore only in its consummation, its consuming and utter appropriation, can the secret of the divine presence there be realized as a total absence, because it is utterly beyond all thought and reason and even experience. Such presence is the fullness of the Word in silence, the presence of God without being, possible only in total negation. In the reversals of her life, her offering finally refused as absurd in the war effort against Hitler's regime, Weil sought to instantiate the sacred—to be one with Christ in his descent into hell, which is the only possible moment of redemption. Her life becomes her text, another eucharistic site of theology in the abolition of the gap between sign and reference—an impossible conjunction.[96] Again, in her, the excess of sainthood provides no pattern to be reenacted in our lives but a eucharistic consummation: a Total Presence.

8

Holiness and
the Resurrection Body

Meister Eckhart and James Joyce

From the unlikely pairing of George Herbert and Simone Weil in the theme of the eucharistic body, this chapter will again focus on to two very different writers on the theme that has haunted almost every page of this book, that of the resurrection body. I can find no evidence that James Joyce studied the writings of Meister Eckhart. There are no obvious or immediate comparisons to be made between them. Parallels will once again be largely left to grow in the mind of the reader, who, in Jean-Michel Rabaté's term, may thus become an "authorized reader"[1]—that is, one who participates in the texts to the point at which, with Eckhart (who consumes and is consumed by the text of Scripture) and Joyce (who takes texts entirely seriously), one understands nothing and everything. The "authorized reader" begins to realize what Friedrich Nietzsche in *The Genealogy of Morals* calls "the ascetic ideal man" prior to whose emergence "the animal *man* had no meaning at all upon this earth" and who "would sooner have the void for his purpose than be void of purpose."[2]

Meister Eckhart

How could anyone by means of those things which we grasp by perception alone come to know that which is the altogether invisible, the formless, the sizeless, as far as bodily perception goes? And yet one should not, for this reason, despair of his desire simply because these things seem to be beyond his grasp.

—Gregory of Nyssa, *On Virginity*

The following few pages form an exchange between some of my reflections
in my earlier book titled *The Sacred Desert*, exploring themes from the Bible
to contemporary literature, film, and memoirs, in the context of the mystical
theology of the fourteenth-century Dominican priest, teacher, and mystic,
Meister Eckhart. I have moved on since that book was published, as one
always must, though yet in the stillness of the desert, now, as in Eckhart, more
interior than exterior, reflecting more recently on the nature of the ascetic tradition in Christianity that begins in the wilderness and its experience of the
body: but to move is always, at the same time, to return to the same ground,
to move from and enter once again the mysticism of the ground (in German,
grunt/grund[3]) and unity that lies at the heart of Eckhart's thought. I do not
intend to give a scholarly exposition of his theology, though there must be
learning on the way, but I begin as one who seems always to be following
the man of the desert once encountered by that irascible modern traveler in
distant lands, Wilfred Thesiger, who set out purposefully with an Arab companion from the beaten track, following a hidden path into the wilderness, a
mere trace invisible to the eye, but yet a highroad utterly easy to miss, into an
interior that is at once an absolute emptiness and the place that we seek with
every fiber of heart, mind, and body: utterly real, utterly nonexistent. At the
same time, I will suggest links between the writings and sermons of Eckhart
and the work of Joyce as we pursue the theme of holiness and the divination
of the body, which, for Eckhart, is attained in an *incarnatio continua*, "an ever
present hominification of God and deification of humanity."[4]

It is the case that, on the whole, we are not well trained to read either
Eckhart's sermons and writings of consolation and instruction, or Joyce's
masterwork *Finnegans Wake* (1939). Educationally, we are taught to read effi-
ciently and purposefully, and in the academic sphere this literary efficiency is
honed to a high degree under the rule of hermeneutical strategies that seek
a clear understanding and the identification of ideas and processes of argument. Thus, we quickly find Joyce's extraordinary linguistic virtuosity to be
"difficult," or even impenetrable, and unsusceptible to the speed-reading that
we hold dear—simply too much is going on at once and at different levels in
his text. The same is true of Eckhart's work, in which the rhetorical strategies
of "accumulation, antithesis, parallelism, and hyperbole"[5] provoke the reader
or listener to a response that is finally beyond the intellectual and conclusive.[6]
As Margaret Miles, in her brief review of Eckhart, expresses it, "Readers inter-
ested in a text's assumptions, its claims to authority, its imagery, metaphors,
and its rhetorical strategies, are not the ideal readers of mystical literature. . . .
the anonymous English *Cloud of Unknowing* begins by saying that no one

should read the book unless s/he is committed to 'perfection;' otherwise the book will seem nonsense."[7] The reader of the *Cloud* is drawn, by the reading of the text, through stages until reaching the third stage—the Solitary: "It is in this state that you will learn to take your first loving steps to the life of Perfection, the last stage of all."[8]

The text is consuming of the reader, and, finally, consumed in the journey from outer to inner self, a liturgical forgetting of the body, which is also its finding in a new perfection and an attunement to the silence in which God speaks into being a new creation, a silence that is the realization of the darkness of the desert and its glory in the Word incarnate.[9] Thus, the solitary reader becomes one with all things—an utter antithesis to the solitary idiocy of the satanic.[10]

Eckhart returns to the desert motif some dozen times in his works, referring thereby to the uncreated spark in the soul of the human being and to the inner ground of God. The wilderness theme in Christian mysticism begins in the Bible, with Moses' journey to Sinai, dramatically rehearsed in Gregory of Nyssa's *Life of Moses*, which anticipates a work beloved of Eckhart, the Pseudo-Dionysius' *Mystical Theology*, which describes Moses as he breaks "away from what sees and is seen, and. . . . plunges into the truly mysterious darkness of unknowing."[11] The other great biblical moment in the desert tradition, in Hosea, is revisited by Eckhart at the very end of his sermon *On the Noble Man* where, with a characteristic emphasis on unity, he refers to Hosea 2:14 where God affirms that he will allure the "noble soul" into the wilderness and speak tenderly to her.[12] The love with which God speaks to the noble soul is, Eckhart insists in his German sermons, different from our love, and this difference actually lies at the heart of our concerns here, at the heart of the deification of humanity in Christ. For if *we* love nothing but goodness, *God* loves to the extent that he is good and "loves us in so far as we are in him and in his love."[13] This takes us immediately to the body in the ascetic tradition (which Eckhart follows through a journey in the interior desert of the soul), wherein the body is not abandoned, but rather utterly fulfilled and divinized. What is here realized is that harmonious state of soul and body that Maximus the Confessor describes as the "Sabbath"—"that is, the immutable condition which is tranquil in virtue and peaceful,"[14] and the purest physical description of this peaceful equilibrium of the body and soul is to be found in St. Antony's glorious emergence from his years in his desert tomb as described by St. Athanasius.[15]

The body in Eckhart's mysticism is the body, like Antony's, maintained in equilibrium, in accord with nature and steadfast in "reason," already transfigured by the birth of God in the soul, yet remaining in the here and now. At the heart of such a transfiguration is Eckhart's great term (though he uses it himself but sparingly) *Gelassenheit*—"detachment"—picked up and used by many thinkers in the twentieth century from Ernst Bloch to Martin Heidegger and Jacques Derrida. It is a delicate word, conveying the sense of not only "releasement" but also relaxation, serenity, and even nonchalance—an ability to move gracefully through life's fortunes, vicissitudes, and accidents, and it is precisely what Athanasius means by "equilibrium." It is at the very core of the desert tradition, rendered in the writings of the *Philokalia* as "passionlessness," but found again most beautifully by Thomas Merton in the Latin term *quies*, or "rest," which is described by him as "simply the sanity and poise of a being that no longer has to look at itself because it is carried away by the perfection of freedom that is within it."[16] In other words, that is a being who has found entirely within itself the love of God, and the ground of unity of all being in both singularity and communality, and yet, like Eckhart, realizes the presence of the Word made flesh here and now, the flesh embraced by the soul, which is, on the one hand, the source of Eckhart's capacity to communicate through such lively, even practical, metaphors in his sermons and, on the other, the ancient fathers' presence in the stories of *Apophthegmata Patrum* as so delightfully homely, sane, everyday, and often even humorous.

At the same time, Eckhart shares with the desert tradition a common philosophical ground in Neoplatonism, but much more, perhaps, he actually shares with them a manner of living in a profound sense of the presence and "now" of eternity in the eternal birth of the Word in the soul,[17] an abandonment of the rags and vicissitudes of time in the immensity of the desert of God's love as "negation of negation" whereby interiority exchanges with exteriority in a perfect nonchalance, the inner life wholly lived in the flesh and the flesh wholly taken up in the reality of the soul. For a while in these pages we must remain in such language, struggling to understand it literally (for both Eckhart and the fathers were actually great literalists, which is why they are at once so immensely difficult and yet so simple, like all life in the desert), though later we shall visit more concretely the desert geography, which provides, for St. Antony and those who followed him in the unity of living on this earth as true citizens of heaven, the true and actual map of the soul.[18]

But before we step once more on the desert terrain itself, we must begin to think again within the *apophatic* tradition, rooted in Clement of Alexandria and Origen, as a way of talking about God by looking beyond all created categories of sensation and thought to the God who can in no way be conceptualized, unknowable as "nothingness" in a nonfoundational theology that echoes profoundly in Eckhart's radical words in his great sermon *Qui audit me*: "Man's last and highest parting occurs, when, for God's sake, he takes leave of God."[19] Only then, in the utter remoteness of the deepest desert, both and at once interior and exterior, can we dare to begin to whisper the greatest glory of Jesus' final words from the cross in the gospels of Mark and Matthew: "My God, my God, why hast thou forsaken me?" It was the Pseudo-Dionysius, that shadowy but influential figure from the fifth or sixth century, who distinguished the apophatic from *cataphatic* theology, which involves contemplation of God as he is in relation to the world, whereby we are able to describe God as, for example, "the Good" or even as "Life," though apophatic theology sees these terms as only provisional, moving instead to a union with God in the divine darkness that lies beyond all concept. It is precisely such "nothingness" that the fathers and mothers of the desert sought in their retreat into the absolute emptiness of the *desert absolu*. After Eckhart, the clearest and deepest reflection on the apophatic in Western theology is to be found in the work of Nicholas of Cusa titled *De Docta Ignorantia* (*On Learned Ignorance*; 1440), which celebrates the great principle of the *coincidentia oppositorum*, that it is only by intuition that we can discover God wherein all contradictions meet, and this is the highest stage of intellectual apprehension since Truth, which is unified and infinitely simple, is beyond any possible human comprehension, while mere knowledge, by contrast, is always only relative, complex, and incomplete.[20] Now it is this uniting of opposites in coincidence, in Nicholas' terms, that renders infinite concepts understandable and describable without violating their incomprehensibility or illimitability, and it is precisely this infinite simplicity that the fathers sought in their lives of desert stillness wherein opposites meet: the hermit in his cell in the limitless sands, the place of death wherein is paradise, the extremes of heat and cold, the horizontal plane of the landscape bringing the highest heaven to earth.

When Eckhart reads Galatians 4:4, in which St. Paul says that "in the fullness of time (*plenitudo temporis*) God sent his Son," he does not interpret it, as was customary in biblical hermeneutics, in relation to the course of history, but rather as referring to the "now" of eternity ever present in human time, Christ's synchronicity. Eckhart actually says very little of the past event of Jesus' earthly life or the historical moment of Christ on earth, but celebrates rather an *incarnatio continua*, the incarnation of the Word made flesh in the eternal present, all one in Christ. Like his teacher St. Augustine of Hippo in book 11 of his *Confessions*, Eckhart speaks much of time yet, as St. Augustine confesses, "I still do not know what time is."[21] For Eckhart seeks to live in the eternity that is always now and to realize in our own poor, but already divinized, flesh the incarnation of the Word. Thus, almost shockingly, the great Antony can even claim that he is wholly one with Christ, his flesh absorbed entirely in word and sacrament in a *coincidentia oppositorum* of utter detachment and utter coinherence. Through unbecoming, the birth of the Word in the soul takes place in a movement that is totally inimical to the Enlightenment obsession with subjectivity that we in our time have inherited. In the desert we are nothing and everything, and chronological time, the time of history and of the clock, is away—as in the deepest love.[22] And thus we find, quaintly to our ears, reports of their latest actual meeting with St. Antony by the contemporary monks of the monastery of St. Antony in Egypt.[23] In Christ, *all* is one. In the writings of the seventeenth-century disciple of Eckhart, Angelus Silesius, there is the verse,

> Eternity is time,
> Time, eternity.
> To see the two as opposites
> Is mind's perversity.
>
> Man has two eyes.
> One only sees what moves in fleeting time,
> The other
> What is eternal and divine.[24]

Every true poet and writer, the purveyor of texts, of course, is entirely at home within such synchronicity, though generally perhaps in a more domestic setting. In his review of the English novel, *Aspects of the Novel* (1927), E. M. Forster begins, with a hymnic reference resolved in the cosy warmth of English academia, by advising his reader that "time, all the way through, is to be our enemy. We are to visualize the English novelists not as floating down that stream that bears all its sons away unless they are careful, but as seated together in a room, a circular room, a sort of British Museum reading-room—all writing their novels simultaneously."[25] More portentously, Aristotle (in a warning too often forgotten in the more recent preoccupations of historical biblical criticism) contrasts the poet and the historian, the latter concerned merely with facts and the particular, but the former with the general and the universal, likely impossibilities always preferable to unconvincing possibilities. As Raman Selden has put it, "The writer does not merely imitate particular objects or events, but reveals *the logical coherence underlying events in human life*."[26] The ascetic tradition goes even further, seeking the possibility of what Jean-Luc Marion defines as "*the impossibility of impossibility*."[27]

The greatest modern writings on the timelessness of the desert, the cradle of Christian asceticism, in which the heat of one hour at noon or the cold of one hour at midnight can decide between life and death, are to be found in T. E. Lawrence's *Seven Pillars of Wisdom*, the account of his desert campaign in 1917. His descriptions of the Bedouin ring true to the spirituality of the fathers and Eckhart himself: "His [the Bedouin's] desert was a spiritual ice-house, in which was preserved intact but unimproved for all ages a vision of the unity of God. . . . The faith of the desert was impossible in the towns. It was at once too strange, too simple, too impalpable for export and common use. . . . The prophets returned from the desert with their glimpse of God, and through their stained medium (as through a dark glass) showed something of the majesty and brilliance whose full vision would blind, deafen, silence us."[28] In the *Historia Monachorum*, we find the same unbearable extremes among the men and women who, in the most radical countercultural move possible, left the cities for the desert, the place of death. Ancient tourists who visited them often found it too much and went home before venturing too far into the depths of the wilderness. Yet, at the same time, they encountered the deep truth that, through these wild people, "the world is kept in being and. . . . through them too human life is preserved and honoured by God."[29]

We have touched briefly on Eckhart's radical, even shocking Christology, wholly lacking in the Jesus of the nativity or even the bloody Christ on the cross. In a profound sense, the journey into the self, which is both a going out and, at the same time and more purely, a journey inward (the inner mountain is finally within), is toward a pure becoming one with God—the Word becomes flesh so that, in Eckhart's words, "I too might be God's son"— wholly and without reserve. Quoting St. Augustine's *On the Epistle of John to the Parthians* (tr. 2, n. 14), Eckhart preaches,

> "We are what we love. If we love a stone, then we are a stone, if we love a person, then we are that person, if we love God—I hesitate to go on, for if I said that we would then be God, you might want to stone me. But let me refer to the Scriptures." And so when someone wholly conforms themselves to God through love, they are stripped of images and are in-formed and transformed into the divine uniformity in which they are one with God. All this they possess by remaining within. Now observe the fruit which this produces. That is, if such a person is one with God, then they bring forth all creatures with God and, in so far as they are one with him, they bestow blessedness on all creatures.[30]

Yet the detachment, which is a being one with God, is at the same time a moving beyond the seeking for God, to that "Godhead" that is beyond "something," that is the "nothing," and the longing for nothing that is pure detachment. We are not only close here to central concerns of those at the papal court in Avignon who, at the end of Eckhart's life, accused him of heresy (though he died before the conclusion of the trial), but also close to the still heart of his thought, discerned clearly by Silesius at the beginning of his poetic work *The Cherubinic Wanderer* (1657):

> Where is my dwelling place? Where I can never stand,
> Where is my final goal, toward which I should ascend?
> It is beyond all place. What should my quest then be?
> I must, transcending God, into a desert flee.[31]

And yet such detachment is not, in Eckhart, to move beyond the virtues and practicalities of the Christian life. Denys Turner has put it most succinctly: "Detachment and interiority are, for Eckhart, not so much the names of experiences as *practices for the transformation of experience*; or, we can say, they are the critical practices of an apophatic theology in their application to human desire. 'Detachment,' in short, is the ascetical practice of the apophatic."[32] There are practical examples of exactly what Eckhart is referring to all through the writings on the desert fathers—often in disarmingly naïve, strange, and open-ended little stories that leave one wondering but yet somehow wiser. For instance, there is Abba Bes, in the *Historia Monachorum*, who "lived a life of the utmost stillness, and his manner was serene, since he had attained the angelic state. He was extremely humble and held himself of no account. We pressed him strongly to speak a word of encouragement to us, but he only consented to say a little about meekness and was reluctant to do even that." But when a hippopotamus ravages the surrounding country, Abba Bes speaks to it gently and the beast "as if driven away by an angel" leaves the district. On another occasion, he sent away a crocodile in the same manner.[33]

Always in Eckhart's self-forgetting there is a profound practicality, an acknowledgment of the suffering, glorious, gendered body even to the extraordinary abandonment of the other-worldliness of many previous Christian mystics. In one of his greatest of German sermons on the Lukan story of Martha and Mary,[34] Eckhart reverses the priority given to the *vita contemplativa* in a celebration of the way of Martha such that the "spirituality of the active life becomes visible."[35] In a supreme paradox, the entry into the depths of the ascetic body is an abandonment also of the tension between the active and the passive, a realization that "the contemplation of God is realized in fruitful action, that the only *way to proper engagement with the temporal world is through total detachment from it*."[36] Furthermore, we will see later in this chapter how the Martha of Eckhart's sermon anticipates and confirms the creative feminine (which Christian theology has actually systematically denied and eliminated) gloriously resurrected in Anna Livia Plurabelle, and before her, Molly Bloom. Daringly, even against the narrative flow of the gospel in which we hear that Mary has chosen the better part, Eckhart preaches, "But Martha was securely established in mature virtue and had an unencumbered mind, free of any impediment. Accordingly she wishes that her sister might be in the same state for she saw that she, her sister, was not yet *essentially* there."[37] It is Martha, in her true, practical detachment, who anticipates her later textual sisters and can say to Mary, "Yes, yes."

In a very real sense, the saints wholly forget themselves and are forgotten, except by the wisdom of the beasts, in Christ. In the desert, the fictive and the imaginative become utterly entwined with the real—at one level, perhaps, delusional, miragelike, but at another, constructive of a sense of transformed reality in which the desert becomes the paradise garden itself, a transformation to be found also in Hosea, *The Arabian Nights*, and the Qur'an in which the desert, in a manner reminiscent of the heavenly city in Revelation, becomes "a paradise made of gold and silver, where the rivers, trees and fruits are made of precious stones." This poetry of the desert can make its citizens seem, to our eyes, strange and often quite mad. They make connections and live in extremes, which strike us as beyond reason (though their life has a deep reason, known as something like, perhaps, Blaise Pascal's reasons of the heart of which reason knows nothing)—and their seeming perversity is repeated in Eckhart's readings of Scripture, which are exchanges with the text that, to modern ears, sound "made up," utterly ahistorical, intertextually chaotic, following the principle of reading from a sense of the "now" of eternity, all seen as one in the eternal Word.[38] As we shall see later in the textuality of *Finnegans Wake*, the demands of such reading are at once careless of narrative and perceive all things at once and as one, a total consumption of and by the Word. Just as we find it hard to take seriously the idea that we can now still converse, out there on his mountain, with St. Antony, we also want to say to Eckhart, "But that isn't there in the Bible, she didn't say that—you are making it up!" in his abandonment of the sequence of the temporal and its narrative coherences. But Eckhart's profound and congenial readings of Scripture are firmly in the tradition of those marvelous hagiographical stories of the desert that are some of the forgotten wonders of world literature—and spirituality: the stories of St. Mary of Egypt and Thaïs, John Moschos' *The Spiritual Meadow*, and the little tales of the *Lausiac History*. They read at a level of perversity and removal from what we call common sense that makes it easy to miss their delicacy, beauty, and spiritual profundity, for common sense has finally found it hard, in the end, to discredit even such perversity.[39] Sometimes, like Anatole France in his reading of the legend of Thaïs, we are simply too sternly moral, too poor as readers, and certainly too politically correct to hear the delightful, flagrant multiplicity of these ancient love stories of the desert, which resonate with a deep festivity that Eckhart knew as the presence of the nothingness of God, and Joyce knows in the mazes of *Finnegans Wake*.

Let us pursue this desert festivity a bit further. I suspect that many theologians, fearful of accusations of literalism, still might say of Genesis 1–11 that these stories are myths, and we do not actually believe the myths, though the doctrines or theology underlying them remain somehow important. Whether we know it or not, we have long been trained to be "demythologizers." For the alternative, for most of us, is quite unacceptable—that is, the kind of fundamentalism that takes everything as literally, even "historically" true—and God really did make the world in six days. But there is another way of reading, the way of Eckhart, and a way which the ancient desert fathers knew intimately—that is, to dive into the stories and the text, to embrace them and instantiate them in yourself; that is, in the language of my old friend, the late Robert Detweiler, to "read religiously." In the sociability of this term, Detweiler specifically draws on two terms that have never been far from our meditations on Eckhart: *Gelassenheit* and *Geselligkeit*—the latter best understood as "sociability" or perhaps "communality." Thus, Detweiler concludes, "Religious readings might be *gelassen* and *gesellig*, balancing our dogged insistence on interpretation with a pleasurable interchange made valuable precisely by a refusal to simplify and manipulate the text into something else, another statement."[40] Such reading, which is also a being read by the text, might constitute the beginning of a recovery of Christian origins and a conjoining of them with our own experience in an "imagined immediacy of lived experience"[41] that has its origin and its end in the deepest unknown of the ascetic tradition, in a figure beyond knowing and without a name who yet reveals himself "in the peace, the labours, the conflicts and the suffering that [people] may experience in his fellowship, and as an ineffable mystery they will learn who he is."[42]

Now in such acts of religious reading we are actually not too far from the way in which we sometimes read novels. For there, too, in an immediacy of lived experience, we can become "lost" in the text, consuming and consumed by it to the point (almost to the point) of oneness, like the Dubliner who cried of *Ulysses* (1922), "We're all in the bloody book!" Thus, we have found in the desert that, oddly, at a certain point, the fathers actually merge their religious reading with their lives and give their Bibles away, for, as Abbot Theodore says, "better than all else is to possess nothing." Rather, the good abbot enters wholly into Scripture to become absolutely one with it, to engage his entire being with it in a riotous exchange, and finally, daringly and sacramentally, becomes one with Christ—becomes Christ.

Now at this point the deepest *coincidentia oppositorum* is entered into. For is not this the deepest blasphemy, outstripped only by Jesus' own "blasphemy" at his trial? Thus it is that in the desert there is an endless warfare with the demons, a deep madness perhaps, as the self encounters the self and knows not whether what he or she sees is the devil—or God. In the desert, stripped of all our clothing of ecclesiology and doctrine, opposites meet, struggle, and finally become one. Then the greatest denial becomes at once also the greatest affirmation, and all our hierarchies are reversed, and to find is to lose everything utterly and become nothing, to be nothing, to own nothing. Eckhart, in a sermon, puts it this way: "We should not take God as he is good or just, but should take him in the pure and clear substance in which he possesses himself. For goodness and justice are a garment of God, since they enfold him. Strip away from God therefore everything which clothes him and take him in his dressing room where he is naked and bare in himself. Thus you will remain in him."[43] One of the best illustrations of this in modern film is Wim Wenders' *Paris Texas* (1984). At the beginning of the film, a solitary man walks out of the desert where he has wandered to the point where he has lost everything, even his name. He does not speak. In a former life, he has been married with a child, but he was a poor husband who, perhaps, has loved too much. In the film it is only when, at the very end, he becomes again nothing, finally disappearing again in the desert, that he is able to reunite his wife and child and restore them to each other, though at the cost of himself. This stripping away is repeated again and again in the literature of the desert—the becoming nothing both external and internal. It has its roots, for us, perhaps, in the farewell discourses in the Fourth Gospel, when Jesus says to his disciples, "If I do not go away, the Advocate will not come to you; but if I go, I will send him to you" (John 16:7). And it is present in one of the most moving of modern narratives of departure and loss that is only resolved in C. S. Lewis' final words of *A Grief Observed* (1961), when he can finally let go of the soul of his beloved departed wife: "She smiled, but not at me. *Poi si tornò all' eterna fontana.*"[44]

In the deep mystery of *Gelassenheit*—abandonment—the final self-embodiment of God is found. In the deep desert, it is entered into, where death and life become one. This self-embodiment is one with God's self-abandonment on the cross, where finally we realize the truth of the truly glorious body—here in the broken figure of Christ. "The Word became flesh, and we beheld his glory." Nowhere in Western art, as we have seen,[45] is this glory of the body more celebrated than in the crucified Christ of Mathias Grünewald's *Isenheim Altarpiece*, for here the Word enters most deeply into the condition of the flesh. As the patients in the Antonine lazar-house, from the agonizing deserts of their own wrecked bodies, gazed on the Christ whose body suffered with the same wounds and suppurations, they see the profound truth proclaimed by St. Athanasius that he became like us so that we might become like him, so often echoed in the writings of Eckhart and his insistence on the deification of the human in Christ. And that moment of our salving and salvation is the deepest moment of letting go and *kenosis*, or emptying—God's utter self-embodiment in his own self-abandonment in death, the most profound of all *concidentiae oppositorum*. Thus, in the ruined bodies of the patients of the lazar-house is known again the glory of the Lord.

The Greek Fathers called the incarnation a *kenosis*, an emptying. But in the origins of the term in Philippians 2:6–11, there is a reference also to the passage in Isaiah 52–53 that concerns the Suffering Servant—who is, after all, the King. Yet,

> so marred was his appearance beyond human semblance,
> and his form beyond that of mortals.[46]

In the desert, to enter into nothingness is to follow the royal way: the desert icon a gaze into the uncircumscribability of the Word made flesh—its nothingness and insignificance. For in the desert, above all, we know our insignificance in the limitlessness of its interior.

In the preface to this book, I referred to a beautiful and ancient Algerian saying, with its echoes of the Lord's last peaceful walk in Eden before the fall in Genesis 3:8: "The desert is the Garden of Allah, from which the Lord of the faithful removed all superfluous human and animal life, so that there might be a place where he can walk in peace."[47] It was on his walk in Eden that the Lord God enjoyed the evening breeze. That breeze, or spirit, is the desert wind that is also the still small voice of Elijah's theophany, and it is still heard by Lawrence in the *Seven Pillars of Wisdom* as "the effortless, empty, eddyless wind of the desert" that comes to us as a slow breath without hindrance across empty space. "This," the Arabs tell Lawrence, "is the best: it has no taste."[48] And I have mentioned already in this chapter Thesiger's Arab traveller who sets out purposefully into the seemingly trackless desert, led by traces in the physical fabric of the wilderness that we are too impatient and too blind to even notice—a displacement of a few grains of sand, a tiny stone overturned, a blade of grass ever so slightly flattened by the foot of God as he takes his walk. But we, in our time, have trampled the desert with machines of war and aggression, and the silent meditation of the desert fathers, like the slow, stretched interior contemplations of Meister Eckhart, are forgotten and remain unheard in the din. Our seeing is habitually partial but in the desert one sees only the vastness, and also the vastness in a grain of sand—within God and God within us. And so I concluded *The Sacred Desert* with these words: "I imagine that there may be one or perhaps two gentle folk [we think now of Eckhart's noble man] of common sense left, who matter so little that they have been forgotten by the world, to the point that they are entirely other than all its concerns, and for that very reason. . . . human life will be preserved and honoured by God—for then he or she, too, will have a garden where he can walk in peace, and all opposites will be reconciled in Total Presence."[49] And what is this Total Presence? It is beyond all knowing and unknowing. It is what St. Antony describes as living as people dying,[50] which is living in the eternity of the present moment, without intelligible history, future, and without past, though all is future and all is past. It is to know entirely, which is beyond all knowing and beyond all experiencing. Thus Eckhart, who was the man from whom God hid nothing—that is, hid in his nothingness (truly the Cloud of Unknowing)—in one of his greatest sermons on Galatians 3:16–22, *Deus unus est*, said, recalling the breath of the desert breeze: "God is infinite in his simplicity and simple in his infinity. Therefore he is everywhere and is everywhere complete. He is everywhere on account of his infinity, and is everywhere complete on account of his simplicity. Only God flows into all things, their very essences. Nothing else flows into something else. God is in the innermost part of each and every thing, only in its innermost part, and he alone is *one*."[51] There is one simple paradox among the many paradoxes that lie at the heart of the mystical tradition that endlessly fascinates me. As we read the stories and the sayings of the desert fathers and mothers, they endlessly speak, sometimes almost chatter, with a disarming conviviality—and yet they celebrate the infinite silence. (We will shortly turn our attention to another chatterer in the silence—Joyce.) In the words of the *Philokalia*, "Silence of the lips is better and more wonderful than any edifying conversation. Our Fathers embraced it with reverence and were glorified through it." Yet the silence of the desert is not the absence of speech, but the presence of the absence of the fullness of all words in the Word. It is when speech is completed in the silence, which is the Total Presence, that ends all disembodiment, when speech is impossible because all being is fulfilled in the Word. This is to know the resurrection body known only in the deepest desert of the Interior Mountain. Like Moses before him, and like St. Mary of Egypt, according to St. Athanasius, Antony was buried in an unknown grave—for the desert, to cultured folk, is the place of the dead—and fully entered into it without reserve. Thus, he became utterly one with the unity that is at the heart of all Eckhart's life, the unity that is nothing, and therefore everything.

James Joyce

Full fathom five thy father lies;
Of his bones are coral made:
Those are pearls that were his eyes:
Nothing of him that doth fade,
But doth suffer a sea-change
Into something rich and strange.
Sea-nymphs hourly bring his knell:
Ding-dong.
Hark! now I hear them—ding-dong, bell.

—William Shakespeare, *The Tempest*, 1.2.400–408

And best of all, week by week and month by month, on a hundred thousand successive Sundays, faithfully, unfailingly, across all the parishes of Christendom, the pastors have done this just to *make* the *plebs sancta Dei*—the holy common people of God.

—Dom Gregory Dix, *The Shape of the Liturgy*

Like the texts, ancient and modern, with which it sports and plays, these pages on James Joyce are perhaps more to be devoured and consumed than precisely understood. They refuse the role of abstract commentary but dare to dally with the Word in Scripture, but above all, in Joyce's *Finnegans Wake*. Its words demand conversation with one another, echoing across the spaces of the text and demanding attention. As a kind of metanarrative, it even presumes and dares to claim equality with those with whom it converses, as the poets with the prophets and Milton with Genesis, daring even and necessarily to the ruin of sacred truths[52] in seeking to propose a theology in the very language itself and in the act of reading that it prompts and requires. In the read word is life.

The poet William Blake once remarked, rather casually, in "A Memorable Fancy," "The prophets Isaiah and Ezekiel dined with me and I asked them how they dared so roundly assert that God spake to them; and whether they did not think at the time that they would be misunderstood, and so be the cause of imposition."[53] In his time, Blake was not alone in his poetic presumption. His fellow Romantic poet Samuel Taylor Coleridge sought in his poetry the very language of heaven, words as living things, most deeply to be found in the Scriptures as "consubstantial with the truths, of which they are the conductors."[54] Such words, indeed, are, in Coleridge's description of them, the very wheels of the chariot that Ezekiel beheld "when the hand of the Lord was upon him"—the actual vehicles that bear up, for us, the very throne of the divine. Throughout his life, Coleridge was absorbed in the mystery of the Logos, the Word of the first chapter of the Fourth Gospel, and he proposed a major (and never written) work on "the Power and Use of Words"—the *Logosophia*,[55] and was certainly familiar with the deeply Anglican tradition,[56] learned from Archbishop Thomas Cranmer, and before him Erasmus, inscribed in the liturgies of the 1549 and 1552 Prayer Books, of Christ the Logos as the human form of divine speech, and the understanding of Logos not as a singular word, but as copious discourse, as "sermo," literally to be consumed and ingested in the participation in the Eucharist and the reading of Scripture. Thus, in Cranmer's Collect for the Second Sunday in Advent, we take the word of Scripture to "read, mark, learn and *inwardly digest*" in order to "embrace and ever hold fast the blessed hope of everlasting life."[57]

Both Blake and Coleridge took and embraced as poets the creative speech and Word of God, realizing fully that words are living, active, and deeply humanizing. But why should Blake, in all his prophetic oddity perhaps the most Christocentric of all Christian visionaries, give such reverence to the name of *Jesus*, though not to the Jesus of the church or of Christendom? It is because, for him, Jesus, in another *incarnatio continua, is,* and always is, the vocabulary of creation and creativity, the utterance and enactment of an actual descent into hell that is an absolute blasphemy and that is alone salvation and is finally only realized in a poetics of silence and Total Presence, an absolute inwardness so that, in Christ alone, as Thomas Altizer expresses it, "the real ending of speech is the dawning of resurrection, and the final ending of speech is the dawning of a totally present actuality."[58] Language then simply and impossibly *is*—that is, without referential distractions. Language, in the true poet, truly begins only when conversation and speech are truly impossible, an end that is the true beginning, as in Jesus' final word from the cross in the Fourth Gospel—τετέλεσται, "It is finished."

Thus, the reader of *Finnegans Wake* must become truly the ascetic in the text, reading ever new and thereby daring to be released from all repressions and into all memory, for, as Seamus Deane has observed, "the book is a titanic exercise in remembering everything at the level of the unconscious because at the conscious level so much has been repressed that amnesia is the abiding condition."[59] One reads always as if for the first time and only in this particularity of reading can be contained the universal, whereby amnesia is overwhelmed by the remembrance of what is ever new, the *anamnesis* that is the very heart of the liturgical act. Thus, the text both consumes and is consumed so that text is realized in its anti-text, meaning emptied and absorbed into its endless reversals. In daring to read *Finnegans Wake*, the reader risks a new illiteracy as "the total violence of the primordial sacrifice passes into the very act of writing."[60] At the same time, the writer risks the fraction that is the sole precondition of the wholly new, which is simultaneously, as Nietzsche knew supremely, a return to primordial origins "in the Nichtian glossery which purveys aprioric roots for the aposteriorious tongues this is nat language at any sinse of the world."[61] Joyce, like Milton at the outset of *Paradise Lost*, is consciously entering into the deep, deserted mystery of a text that is wholly new, "things unattempted yet in prose or rhyme."[62] Such originality lies only within the truly liturgical, in shocking repetitions of the ever wholly new that are necessary inversions or reversals of what is known only in the (deeply repressed) consciousness, when the plenitude of our understanding empties into the deep desert known only in the body, but wholly known as the summation of everything. D. G. Leahy precisely describes this in his appendix to *Novitas Mundi* on "Missa Jubilaea: The Celebration of the Infinite Passover": "The essence of the new transcendental involves the conception in essence of everything, the absolute nullification of the possible. Everything now comes to exist actually in the form of the body itself."[63] Thus, the reader, like every true ascetic, entertains that possibility of being that is shocking to common sense, a possibility known most deeply in the bodies of the saints or those who recognize its movements in the reversals of the liturgy, which even they can barely acknowledge. John Henry Newman in his *Apologia Pro Vita Sua* (1864) knows it in the *excess* of the saints and fathers of the Early Church, which is shocking to the common sense of those who have never read their writings,[64] in a "tradition of piety that common sense has found it had to discredit."[65] Equally shocking, though not generally recognized as such, and as we have seen in chapter 7, is the Anglican poet Herbert for whom the eucharistic feast, in his best loved poem "Love (III)," is necessarily also a gloriously profane celebration of the erotic body. And so, as such readers we dare to approach the text of *Finnegans Wake*.

   In Joyce's two great epics, *Ulysses* and *Finnegans Wake*, there is an epiphany of Satan, albeit silent and impassive, a Satan who is actually one with Christ, and a Christ who is one with Satan in the creative moment of the fall (known also to Blake)—that is, a collapse into the necessary original sin of language acknowledged as the fortunate fall or *felix culpa*. In Joyce's words at the beginning of *Finnegans Wake*, "The fall. . . . of a once wallstrait oldparr is retaled early in bed and later on life down through all christian minstrelsy."[66] But it is actually creatively "retaled"—endlessly retold—not in Christendom, but rather in the human act of copulation (understood by St. Augustine as the first sinful act after the fall), and spoken, later in life, in the words of the poets and minstrels. This deeply creative original sin is, for Joyce, God's creation of the world,[67] where, in the words of Rabaté, "There is no devouring of the host, no communion, in a word, that is not prey to the convoluted circuit of the father's bowels." In the dialectics of mystical fatherhood in *Finnegans Wake*, the father's sin, the original sin of the divine "Loud" of creation who thunders among the clouds, is anal—this Lord is like the God of Moses who showed his "back parts" to him instead of his face. And in his turn, as Rabaté puts it, "Moses, too, is a father who founds paternity upon the void, upon a cloud of incertitude that hides his own God, upon the living doubt which abhors material or maternal representations."[68]

To forbid the adoration of visible forms in the spirit of iconoclasm is a way of barring the way back to the mother, and in Joyce's epic the original sin of creation by the Father is finally only realized in the death in which, in Stephen Dedalus' words in *Ulysses* (episode 9), Father and Son are "sundered by a bodily shame so steadfast that the criminal annals of the world, stained with all other incests and bestialities, hardly records its breach."[69] This creative enormity is the subject of some of the most complex pages of *Finnegans Wake*, the very first to be written, and eventually the conclusion of book 2, chapter 3, most deeply sacramental and eucharistic (Joyce's word is "euchrerisk") and drawing deeply on the Roman Catholic liturgy for Holy Saturday. It was in March 1923 that Joyce wrote these central two pages describing King Roderick O'Conor, who was "anything you say yourself between fiftyodd and fiftyeven years of age at the time after the socalled last supper" and "the auspicious waterproof monarch of all Ireland,"[70] seen as a publican cleaning up his empty barroom. The language is a glorious interlacing of the language of the Eucharist with that of Irish myth and Dublin pub, taking place on "the anniversary of his finst homy commulion." The language of these pages lives, like all deeply liturgical language, finally in the physical reading, the text devoured and devouring, proclaimed and deepening in endless repetition in reflexivities that simultaneously (in the Irish tradition of Jonathan Swift and Laurence Sterne, both Dubliners, and incidentally both clergymen) undermine coherence—a fraction of language—and reestablish it in shocking

celebrations of the necessary evil of writing, a fall into sanctity in the sanctuary of all the bars in all the world. It is a text not to be read, but devoured,
delighted in until the reader realizes with keen dismayed delight the ingestion
of the sacrifice anew.[71] Through transgression is reached for a prior unity, a
union of all opposites in the ultimate sacrifice. "What did he go and do at all,
His Most Exuberant Majesty King Roderick O'Conor but, arrah bedamnbut,
he finalised by lowering his woolly throat with the wonderful midnight was
on him, as keen as mustard, he could not tell what he did ale."[72] Image follows
image unpicking the constraints of our linguistic habits, and we become, with
a joy hitherto unknown, what Nietzsche identifies as "the ascetic ideal man"
who "would sooner have the void for his purpose than be void of purpose."
And this can begin in *The Genealogy of Morals* only when, says Nietzsche,
"fortunately I learned in good time to divorce the theological prejudice from
the moral and no longer to seek the origin of evil *behind* the world."[73]

In the dark monotheism of divine creation is a divine acceptance of
death—*I've a terrible errible lot todue todie todue tootorribleday*—a death
realized in the language of *Finnegans Wake*, and constantly repeated, but
from which arises out of the sleeping Godhead ("Grant sleep in hour's time,
Loud") the "original sun," indeed a *felix culpa* and a "felicitous culpability." In
the dazzling wordplay of *Finnegans Wake* is a creation out of the very bodily
shame of the Father, which is a true negation or *kenosis*, a self-emptying that is
only finally consummated in the last page of the book, in the resurrection of
Anna Livia Plurabelle, a resurrection that absorbs the power of the Godhead
and finally recovers the feminine with a creative sensuality that Christian theology itself has actually systematically denied and eliminated in the insistent
cult of perpetual virginity. "So. Avelaval. My leaves have drifted from me. All.
But one clings still. I'll bear it on me. To remind me of. Lff! So soft this morning ours. Yes."[74] The final "yes" of *Finnegans Wake* then takes us back again
to the final triumphant shout of Molly Bloom in *Ulysses*: "And then he asked
me would I yes to say yes my mountain flower and first I put my arms around
him yes and drew him down to me so he could feel my breasts all perfume yes
and his heart was going like mad and yes I said yes I will Yes."[75] The moment
of creation, the moment of sexual consummation, is only realized fully in
the very language of *Finnegans Wake* (of which more later) and which, in its
final anamnesis, is fulfilled and completed only when it is realized that the
end is simply the beginning, the last page of the book only making possible
the reading, though not for the first time, of the first page, at the beginning,
in Dublin. To read the book you must first read the book—the birth of the

reader in the death of the author[76]—but, as Joyce asks gruffly, who wrote the durn thing anyhow?

> [End] Finn, again! Take. Bussoftlhee, mememormee! Till thousendsthee. Lps. The keys to. Given! A way a lone a last a loved a long the. . . .
> [Beginning] riverrun, past Eve and Adam's, from the swerve of shore to bend of bay, brings us by a commodius vicus of recirculation back to Howth Castle and Environs.[77]

In our end is our beginning—and how to *read* this? As Samuel Beckett once said, Joyce's words are alive, living powers and words themselves made flesh, not to be taken simply with the mind, but ingested, chewed slowly and lovingly until they partake of being. So to speak is to create, is to be, as the book dies (everything to be done backward) in a cosmic crucifixion, which alone enables a cosmic resurrection.

The hidden reference in Joyce is to Hegel ("hallhagal")—Derrida calls Joyce "the most Hegelian of writers" and Altizer has written, "If Hegel was the first and last thinker who could truly know history as theodicy, that providential totality has passed into its very opposite in our world."[78] Heidegger, meanwhile, never far from the conversation, remarks that "the one Western thinker who has enacted a thinking experience of thought is Hegel." The wary reader will understand the goodly company of those for whom words become not merely (in fact, not at *all*) instruments of reference, but themselves before all reference (how could anyone—for no one was there, for nothing and no one was as yet created—understand the first words in creation uttered from the mouth of God, yet without them not one thing came into being?). Joyce can only be read as an author who is also an *auctor*, one who augments or adds to our notion of literary totality and thereby to the world's being. To read Joyce, it might be said then, is only possible beyond reading and when his absolute unreadability is confessed, when reading passes into a kind of mysticism. This takes us back to Joyce's acknowledgment of Giambattista Vico, the inventor of Western aesthetics, who compared artistic creators to God the Creator in their production of imaginative universals. A lengthy excerpt from Rabaté, interpolated by myself, will illustrate the point well.

> Joyce agreed that Vico provided a valid philosophy of language, even if he was mistaken at times in his etymologies and historical surveys: ["In the beginning," how valid were etymologies and historical surveys anyway?] it is a philosophy of language one can *use* for the pleasure it offers, without having to believe all of its theses. [In what Coleridge called, in *Biographia Literaria*, "that willing suspension of disbelief for the moment, which constitutes poetic faith." Unlike the words themselves, it will pass away.] Thus,

for Joyce, it is the language of *Finnegans Wake* which takes Vico as a model, with its stress on playful circularity and the constant interaction of life and death and regeneration, not only because Vico brings the dynamics of language lacking in Aquinas and Hegel, but, more specifically, because Vico's philosophy carries out the aesthetic Hegel ought to have written.[79]

The language of the Wake simply *is*—of and in itself in its endless playfulness and circularities. To read it is to participate in the divine joy and delight that was God's in the act of creating (Genesis 1, "And God saw that it was good")—and no doubt Molly Bloom's also, in her own way.[80] In Vico's words in *The New Science* (1725), truly to read "should give thee a divine pleasure, since in God knowledge and creation are one and the same thing."[81] The ideal reader of *Finnegans Wake*, therefore, alive with an ideal insomnia or "wake," actually participates in the divine delight and enjoyment of creating a hitherto unknown world by speech and word, recreating language and history. Words are inwardly digested in a true memorial ("mememormee") that is a death which realizes at the same time the divinization of the reader—the reader then becomes authorized, though with the humility of the scullery maid, but only in the death of the author (who wrote the durn thing anyway?)—"*I sink I'd die down over his feet, humbly dumbly, only to washup.*"[82]

Joyce's great biographer, Richard Ellmann (who was forbidden to write T. S. Eliot's biography because he was Jewish and Leopold Bloom was once defined as a "perverted Jew" by Martin Cunningham), has written, "If we ask Joyce to bestride literature like a colossus, he will disappoint us. No generals paid him visits of homage, no one called him the sage of Dublin. As he makes clear enough himself, in the world's eyes he began as a bad boy and ended as an old codger. . . . Yet we have to ask with Parsifal the question that Joyce also asked, 'Who is good?'. . . . His passion for truth, however unpalatable, is a contagion which he would have his readers and his admirers share."[83] The passage has odd resonances. He was no Shakespearian Julius Caesar or Mark Antony bestriding the world.[84] He did not emulate in old the age the shuffling sage of Highgate—Samuel Taylor Coleridge. Why Parsifal—why not the other figure who eschewed goodness—"Call no-one good, except . . ."? As with his heroes, Joyce camouflages his greatness with frailties, but only thereby may the frailties of his readers aspire to greatness in the sacrifice of the author—"*He finalized by lowering his woolly throat with the wonderful midnight thirst was on him.*"[85]

In *Finnegans Wake* we participate in a world of contraries in which oppositions coincide. It is writing hinged between life and art, masculinity and femininity, subjectivity and objectivity, jewgreek and greekjew. In it we are deeply asleep and yet we "wake." The beginning is the end and the end is but a beginning. In the theme of death there is fullness of life, and in darkness light. As in Blake, Christ only becomes fully himself when he finally becomes Satan, his descent into hell alone a true resurrection, a truly fortunate fall. In it reading becomes truly theological as its extraordinary language "dissolves, diffuses, dissipates, in order to re-create"[86] and is essentially vital, not in its referentiality, but in its capacity to enact a Total Presence—in its being as the word creative. A character in John Steinbeck's novel *East of Eden* (1952) remarks that the purpose of reading the Bible is not to understand but to participate in its mystery, to take that into ourselves as readers and thereby, in some sense, to refashion the world. If that is so, then Joyce is the most deeply biblical of our writers, and *Finnegans Wake* the closest in modern literature to the very language of heaven. Reading Joyce's extraordinary book is, indeed, a strange and rare privilege, which few can tolerate, for it is to encounter language at its very furthest stretch, self-sufficient, a world unto itself and yet deeply creative, celebratory, and utterly sociable. From the very beginning, from the very first line, it plays with the text of Genesis, truly its closest predecessor, though filtered perversely through the narrative of the passion in the sacrament of the Word, and with the mysteries and perversions of parentage (inevitably odd in a religious tradition that celebrates virginal mothers and solitary fathers). In the patrilineal, anal perversities of *Finnegans Wake* (Earwicker, like Moses, is a stammerer, for both have alien fathers—Egyptian and Norse—and are forced to speak a foreign language), the mother is the "only true thing in life," the Liffey flowing to her "bitter ending": yet it is the father in being constantly denied, dethroned, negated, who generates the fall, the *felix culpa*, in the fictional field of the novel. And it is the mother, too often submerged in the tradition, the "riverrun," who is finally resurrected in the beginning. . . .

. . . . was the Word. As in one of Altizer's later books *Godhead and the Nothing*, Joyce's language is hardly comprehensible because it is utterly reflexive, like the Word made flesh utterly absorbed in making all things new. As in the phenomenal first words of God in Genesis, it is not meant to be heard or understood by *anyone*—it simply brings into being. It does not seek to *mean*—it hardly claims reference in its purpose. It makes a world, though the world barely comprehends it—and its desire is solely to lose itself in the act of creation itself, to be one with itself. This apocalypse Altizer describes as "thinking and vision for which an absolute No-saying and an absolute Yes-saying are not only inseparable, but finally identical, an identity which is finally the identity of 'Heaven' and 'Hell.'"[87] *Finnegans Wake* ends in silence (the silence that also falls after the great, triumphant cry of Molly Bloom that concludes *Ulysses*—truly an end and a new beginning), the reader finally authorized by the Total Presence of the Word, which is in its realization silence. Only then we too may dine with the prophets like Blake, or more, for "then speech is truly impossible, and as we hear and enact that impossibility, then even we can say: 'It is finished.'"[88] "Isn't it great he is swaying above us for his good and ours. Fly your balloons, dannies and dennises!"[89] At the center of *Finnegans Wake*, we are returned to *The Tempest*, and to the reference to it toward the end of the Proteus episode at the beginning of *Ulysses*. "Five fathoms out there. Full fathom five thy father lies. At one he said. Found drowned. High water at Dublin bar. Driving before it a loose drift of rubble, fanshoals of fishes, silly shells. A corpse rising saltwhite from the undertow, bobbing landward, a pace a pace a porpoise. . . . A seachange this, brown eyes saltblue. Seadeath, mildest of all deaths known to man. . . . Come. I thirst. Clouding over. No black clouds anywhere, are there? Thunderstorm. Allbright he falls, proud lightning of the intellect, *Lucifer, dico, qui nescit occasum*."[90] "He said to them, 'I have watched Satan fall from heaven like a flash of lightning'" (Luke 10:18). But in this fall, which is coterminous with the passion, Christ is the purely ritual victim, the fish, ἰχθύς, dying in a seadeath, the mildest of all deaths known to man, Christ becoming one with Satan, utterly anonymous and therefore one with all flesh, which therefore becomes one with him in an infinite Eucharist. Then we can truly say, "No longer are the elements on the table seen to be other than what they are in essence, namely, the flesh and blood of God in the form of man."[91]

9

ROMANTICISM AND THE RECOVERY
OF THE SACRED IN LANGUAGE

This, the penultimate chapter of the book, will act as both a conclusion to a theme (and a figure) that has been pervasive, that is the centrality of the word and language in the ascetic mystery of the Word made flesh, and especially in the Romantic thought of Samuel Taylor Coleridge, and also a prelude to the final chapter as a final exercise in the profoundly difficult and arcane arts of reading. Although its concerns are specifically with Romantic literature and art, its stance is firmly contemporary, inquiring into the very possibility of "holiness," the sacred and theology in our own age, and in the light of the profound theological crisis, still too often barely acknowledged—that is, foreshadowed in European Romanticism. *The Oxford English Dictionary* defines the "holy" as "specially belonging to, or devoted to God." But if traditional theism is replaced, not by atheism or unbelief, but by a nonfoundational, nonappropriative theology found not *through* but *in* language, in what sense can "holiness" be represented at all? This chapter forms, perhaps, the beginning of a response to that question.

The philosopher Richard Kearney believes that we are now present at the wake of imagination, a once glorious faculty now sadly trampled under the heavy heel of postmodernism.[1] My contention is that this is by no means the case, but not because I think we can turn the clock back, but rather because we have now moved beyond postmodernism to a time of the post-postmodern (a time, in a sense, outside the time of history, or at least in which history has become unintelligible) in which a genuinely imaginative theology (though not necessarily a specifically Christian theology) has again become possible, and we see it foreshadowed in remarkable ways in both the German and English Romanticism of the early nineteenth century. This will be a theology that is genuine precisely because it is not a language "about God," but is instantiated *within* language itself, and a language that is both its embodiment and vehicle. It is, we might say, a properly sacramental theology of real presence, and as the self-embodiment of God is a Total Presence as it finds its culmination and conclusion in that silence that is the fulfilment of all poetics and which is theological at both its deepest and highest point.

In 1840, J. S. Mill rightly said of Coleridge on the imagination that he "was anticipated in all the essentials of his doctrine by the great Germans of the latter half of the last century."[2] The link between Coleridge and German philosophy and idealist thinking is certainly crucial for my argument here, but it is only half the story, for it forgets that Coleridge's first tutor was not German intellectual life, but the Bible, and especially the Fourth Gospel. The great and even seminal definition of the Primary Imagination in chapter 13 of the *Biographia Literaria* (1817) as a "repetition in the finite mind of the eternal act of creation in the infinite I AM" refers back not only to the great theophany to Moses in the burning bush and the divine words in Exodus 3:14, but also to Jesus' saying in John 8:58, "Before Abraham was, I am." At the beginning of all things, God *speaks* the creation that arises, therefore, solely out of the Word of God. It is this living and dynamic word, most truly and actually a creative theology, that is repeated in the imagination of the finite human mind of the poet and artist. And if we go back a year before the publication of the *Biographia Literaria* to Coleridge's lay sermon titled *The Statesman's Manual*, we find another extraordinary discussion of the "living educts of the Imagination" that extends my point further. It is a familiar passage, but worth quoting again in full, describing the imagination as a "system of symbols" and as

> that reconciling and mediatory power, which incorporating the Reason in Images of the Sense, and organizing (as it were) the flux of the senses by the permanence and self-circling energies of the Reason, gives birth to a system of symbols, harmonious in themselves, and consubstantial with the truths, of which they are the *conductors*. These are the Wheels which Ezekiel beheld, when the hand of the Lord was upon him, and he saw visions of God as he sate among the captives by the river of Chebar. *Whithersoever the Spirit was to go, the wheels went, and thither was their spirit to go: for the spirit of the living creature was in the wheels also.* The truths and the symbols that represent them move in conjunction and form the living chariot that bears up (for *us*) the throne of the Divine Humanity. Hence, by a derivative, indeed, but not a divided, influence, and though in a secondary yet in more than a metaphorical sense, the Sacred Book is worthily intitled *the* WORD OF GOD.[3]

We move from Word to symbol and truth, bound by a consubstantiality that allows no division. Humanity, itself divine, is borne by the chariot that moves on the wheels of poetry, a system of symbols that both is and carries a sacramental presence. For Coleridge, the imagination inescapably requires and provokes the terms of Christian theology, as a *reconciling and mediatory* power, a creative energy that speaks, and in speaking gives birth to language and thence all that is. In his "Essay, Supplementary to the Preface to *The Lyrical Ballads*" (1802), William Wordsworth, less delicately and less self-consciously than Coleridge, also links poetry and religion, the former "ethereal and transcendent, yet incapable to sustain her existence without sensuous incarnation."[4] The point is almost Christological (with all the edginess that that implies), and returns us again to the first chapter of the Fourth Gospel and the Word made flesh. It also connects the living chariot of language, as we shall see shortly, to the preface to Hegel's *Phenomenology of Spirit* (1807) with its dialectical and kenotic mode of vision that reflects a ceaseless movement of negation that is yet the source of all life and movement.[5] But before we are carried too far and too fast, let us pause a moment and recollect ourselves.

Many years ago, the critic Eleanor Shaffer summed up the religious anxiety of Herder, Eichhorn, and Coleridge as the sense of a "need for a modern mythology," plagued as they were by the disintegrative effects of their own Enlightenment critical thinking.[6] Their dilemma was expressed in an observation by G. H. Lewes in his 1858 study of Goethe: "Herder had something of the Hebrew Prophet in him, but the Hebrew Prophet fallen upon Deistical times, with Spinoza and Lessing for teachers."[7] The problem with this, however, is that it is again only half the story, portraying the Romantics as some kind of protopostmoderns floundering in the consequences of their inescapable Enlightenment modes of thought. (Though it is true that Jacques Derrida and others, we should never forget, are themselves also genuine, if deeply ironic, children of the Enlightenment.) Coleridge, however, thought from *within* the chariot of language and the active and living powers of words as symbols, and more than symbols, inevitably fragmentary yet as shadows and types and as real presences of the great silent text of all creation as spoken by God in the beginning.[8] Avoiding system as mere "abstraction from the objects of the senses," he returned repeatedly in his reflections to words as the essence of thinking, and in his two-volume manuscript *Logic*, written during the 1820s, Coleridge embarked on a philosophical and "etymological history of the term *Logos* itself as the name of the science that treats of 'Words in relation to connected Thoughts.'" Here, Coleridge emphasizes, as Alice D. Snyder puts it, the "difference between λόγοι, or deliberate, carefully selected words, and *ῥήματα*, or the words of casual conversation."[9] While writing this, he was contemplating a detailed commentary on the Fourth Gospel and, in particular, its opening chapter, built around its primary statement, "In the beginning was the Word." In short, Coleridge was sketching out the possibility of a theological language, of a theology *within* language itself, by linking words as "living powers" with the divine Logos in a continuum that recognized an ultimately seamless connection between poor human speech and divine creativity. And if we have grown accustomed, in our post-Saussurean age, to the idea of words as merely arbitrary signs, Coleridge anticipated our dilemma, writing to William Godwin in 1800, "Is *thinking* impossible without arbitrary signs? & - how far is the word 'arbitrary' a misnomer?"[10] His search was not so much, I think, for a modern mythology, but for the recovery of a linguistic universe, a poetics, in which words are truly acknowledged as symbols and real presences, and as the wheels of the chariot, moving in glorious harmony and (as he put it), "characterized by a translucence of the Special in the Individual or of the General in the Especial or of the Universal in the General. Above all by the translucence of the Eternal through and in the Temporal. It [the Symbol] always partakes of the Reality which it renders intelligible; and while it enunciates the whole, abides itself as a living part in that Unity, of which it is the representative."[11] Words, powerfully alive, in short, are true sacraments.

Switch now to another familiar passage in literature. In Goethe's *Faust, Part I*, completed in 1801 and published in 1808, Faust, like Coleridge, meditates in his study on the first chapter of the Fourth Gospel.

> 'Tis writ, "In the beginning was the Word."
> I pause, to wonder what is here inferred.
> The Word I cannot set supremely high:
> A new translation I will try.
> I read, if by the Spirit I am taught,
> This sense: "In the beginning was the Thought."
> This opening I need to weigh again,
> Or sense may suffer from a hasty pen.
> Does Thought create, and work, and rule the hour?
> 'Twere best: "In the beginning was the Power."
> Yet, while the pen is urged with willing fingers,
> A sense of doubt and hesitancy lingers.
> The spirit comes to guide me in my need,
> I write, "In the beginning was the Deed."[12]

From this fateful decision emerged two centuries of bloodshed in Europe and the world. Coleridge's careful, faithful reading of that one verse of Scripture is set aside, and Christian theology is doomed to become the handmaid of violence in its celebration of a solitary deity who has disappeared, to be replaced by compulsion, a salvation known only in the history of the past and the glorification of the deed above the word. But even as Faust was pursuing his insatiable desire for real knowledge, a young poet and fellow student of Hegel at Tübingen, Friedrich Hölderlin, was discovering a different sense of the sacred in a poetry whose language is absolutely one with its origins and the instantiation of a new creation that is truly a repetition in the finite mind of the poet of the infinite I AM. Hölderlin's greatest reader, Martin Heidegger, writes that "the poet speaks by virtue of a tone (*Stimmung*) which sets (*bestimmt*) the ground and base and stakes out (*durchstimmt*) the space from and in which the *poetic saying established a mode of being.* This tone we name the fundamental tone of the poetry."[13]

I have already made brief reference to Heidegger's readings of Hölderlin's poetry in the discussion of George Herbert's verse in chapter 7 of this book. It is now time to expand on that in this chapter on Romanticism. The critic Timothy Clark has suggested that "Hölderlin turns poetic language back upon its own founding power—his mission is to disclose, or to bring the power of language itself to word."[14] We will need to examine this claim carefully, reading with the eyes of Heidegger, and then relate it to the visual art of Caspar David Friedrich, the philosophy of Hegel, and finally, again, the writing of Coleridge. Above all, Hölderlin is the poet of longing and spiritual crisis, his oft-repeated phrase "the gods" is indicative of an absence, an empty space without an object. His poem "Germania" opens with the following lines:

Not them, the blessed, who once appeared,
Those images of gods in the ancient land,
Them, it is true, I may not now invoke.[15]

And yet it is precisely this lack, this gap or space, that the poet is called to mediate in words that contain no meaning beyond the pure presence of the poem that celebrates, in Heidegger's commentary, the "letting the unsayable be not said. . . . in and through its own speech act." It is indeed a postmetaphysical religion without an object in which, in Maurice Blanchot's powerful observation on Hölderlin, "the poet's destiny is to expose himself to the force of the undetermined and to the pure violence of being from which nothing can be made, and to endure this force courageously, but also to contain it by imposing upon it restraint and the perfection of a form. This is a requirement full of risk."[16] Yet the risk lies at the heart of creation itself, the form the living chariot of language that bears up and enacts (for us) the possibility of a new and nonappropriative way of knowing.[17] In his poem "Homecoming"

(*Heimkunft*), Hölderlin celebrates the familiarity of place, family, and friends as something that is paradoxically wholly new and distinctive on his return, and celebrated, therefore, in its very strangeness and estrangement. It is a knowing that abides in what Heidegger calls the "mystery of the reserving nearness," or elsewhere simply the "sacred," and rests in the deep polarities of presence and absence, knowing and unknowing. To read Hölderlin is to accept that words cannot be reduced or even properly translated, but remain in their being as present, and to acknowledge that the task of the poet is the hardest of all:

> Whether he like it not, and often, a singer must harbour
> Cares like these in his soul; not, though, the wrong sort of cares.[18]

Hölderlin's poetry calls forth new modes of being and thinking beyond the metaphysical, and requires us to live in the language not with abstract notions or detached consciousness, but with an acknowledgment of the absolute singularity of the poem, which is *therefore* a true homecoming, a return to what it is truly to be. Thinking then actually becomes a form of unknowing and a return to beginnings in the pure presence of the poetry "as on a holiday" (*Wie wenn am Feiertage*), the "word," whether it be nature or God, wholly recast in the form of the ode, just as in the beginning God's word spoke a new creation out of chaos:

> According to the fixed law, begotten, as in the past, on holy Chaos,
> Delight, the all-creative,
> Delights in self-renewal.[19]

Infinity is thus repeated in the finite. Hölderlin's poetry cannot properly be understood for at its heart is an essential unthought on the surface of the words themselves. (Thus to reread Hölderlin is to deconstruct the whole misguided project of historical criticism in biblical studies as they veered away from the idealist project of the poet and of Hegel and Schelling, his fellow students.) He embraces nihilism, but finds in its space and the absence of God a mode of being that offers to the theologian a possibility that he has not dared to acknowledge in its transfigurative, nonfoundational demands.

In the opening lines of "Germania," Hölderlin renounces the "images of the gods in the ancient land," the gods who are fled, but this very renunciation opens up a space that only words can occupy, a disenchantment and a mourning that is sacred, and alone sacred.

> The priest is first to be struck, but lovingly
> The temple and the image and the cult
> Follow him down into darkness and none of them now may shine.[20]

The poem enacts an absolute sacrifice, a passion that is a descent into hell and that is, at the same time, a resurrection in the transformation of language, a pure *coincidentia oppositorum* that Heidegger was to term *Grundstimmung*, or the "ground tone" of things newly revealed in the poem: the revelation cannot be prior to the words themselves in their Total Presence.

> For almost as is the holy
> The Mother of all things, upholder of the abyss,
> Whom men at other times call the Concealed,
> Now full of loves and sorrows
> And full of presentiments
> And full of peace is your bosom.[21]

Thus, Clark summarizes Hölderlin's poetry: "The sacred is at work already in the poetic act as a kind of paradoxical knowing other than that of metaphysical thinking. This is a non-exploitative mode of knowledge that addresses but does not negate the otherness of what it touches. It lets 'the unsayable be not said,' and makes truly clear by leaving a reserve of mystery."[22] Hölderlin's great poem "Patmos" (1803) returns the reader to the island of St. John's vision and, like Coleridge's "Kubla Khan" (1798), creates a psychic geography that is a fearful space of literature, existing nowhere but in the poem, but which alone returns the reader to the no-place, the utopia of the insistent, half-forgotten dream of all Holy Writ, the alpha and omega:

> For he on honey-dew hath fed,
> And drunk the milk of Paradise.[23]

Hölderlin, of course, was mad—or at least feigned madness—while Coleridge's life was wrecked and broken. Or were they simply living the absolute, sacrificial demands of their art as poets—a necessary self-emptying or *kenosis* that was the risk of all who bear the burden of mediation, lights whom human darkness cannot or will not comprehend? In his prophetic calling, Hölderlin laments, like every false priest, his necessary descent into hell:

> And let me say at once
>
> That I approached to see the Heavenly,
> And they themselves cast me down, deep down
> Below the living, into the dark cast down
> The false priest that I am, to sing,
> For those who have ears to hear, the warning song.
> There[24]

And there were the others whom we have visited—the painters and artists—in whose self-sacrificing vision the Word was made in color.[25] Were not, after all, the first words ever given utterance, even before there was human language or human ears to hear, "Let there be light"? In 1810, Friedrich's painting *The Monk by the Sea* was exhibited in Berlin, earning a comment from the writer Heinrich von Kleist, who claimed not to understand the work: "Since in its uniformity and boundlessness it has no other foreground than the frame, when one looks at it, it is as if one's eyelids had been cut away."[26] In other words, it is a painting to which one literally cannot close one's eyes, for it has no frame outside the self. It forces one to look. The monk stands on the shore gazing at an empty sea and lowering sky. But what is so disturbing about this picture? There is something odd in the relationship between shore, sea, and sky, something abstract almost as in Mark Rothko's paintings (which Friedrich's work clearly anticipates), or more nearly the great *Colour Beginning* (1819) of J. M. W. Turner in the Tate Gallery, London. Each painting defies and displaces any possible interpretation so that the more one attempts to comprehend, the more the paintings become incomprehensible. How is this so? In Friedrich's picture, the land and sea meet in a jagged line that cannot be a beach so that somehow the sea must delve under it, while on the horizon the sea is drawn up into the sky: each boundary is unclear and strange. Rules of linear perspective are either ignored or transgressed in the three horizontal blocks of land, sea, and sky by the elimination of a connective midground and the use of asymmetry to draw the eye to the converging points of land and sky that yet do not fully or finally converge to fashion the X of perspectival composition.[27] The viewer's eye is then simultaneously drawn and discomforted by a landscape that allows no point of entry for composition and interpretation. We literally wander as if lost through this elemental space. Joanna Schopenhauer, writing in the *Journal of Luxury and Fashion* in 1810, notes that Friedrich omits "midground and background. . . . He likes to paint unfathomable expanses."[28] As in Hölderlin's poetry, or the paintings of the Abstract Expressionists, there is here no depth, only an abysmal surface, nothing but language and nothing but the paint itself. And in the midst of this elemental, unforegrounded nonplace stands the solitary monk as if lost in the space of the picture. *Where*, then, is he? Not in a place, but the painting itself, and its colors become his only sphere of existence, the lonely figure left to contemplate the nature of being without recourse to the consolations of any prevailing philosophy or theology. The monk, who is, of course, Friedrich himself, as well as me and you—the universal viewer viewing the self—stands at the point of an almost intersection between land and sky, the almost vanishing point, at the place of invitation and disruption, the fault lines of the painting revealing and concealing a "translucence of the Eternal through and in the Temporal" (the words again are Coleridge's from *The Statesman's Manual*). The companion of the painting (still hanging with it in Berlin), is Friedrich's *Abbey in the Oak Forest*, portraying a scene of desolation and an abbey graveyard. Is the monk by the sea contemplating the death of his fellow monk prior to the burial scene in the oak forest? He stands at a moment of disruption, between time and eternity, between life and death, a citizen already, almost of heaven itself.

Much the same may be disturbingly said of the viewer of Friedrich's most celebrated painting, *The Cross on the Mountains* (1808), originally conceived as an altarpiece (we might think back to Mathias Grünewald's *Isenheim Altarpiece*), but a picture in which the Christian tradition is interiorized in human feeling and experience, in a religion, we might almost say, of humanity. The point is that Friedrich is not concerned historically with the passion or crucifixion, and thus the painting's most celebrated contemporary critic, Freiherr von Ramdohr, is correct when he asserts that it would be a "veritable presumption, if landscape painting were to sneak into the church and creep onto the altar."[29] The painting portrays a landscape with a wayside crucifixion such as was common throughout the mountains of central Europe. In criticizing its failure to work as Christian allegory, Ramdohr was—rightly, as it happens—criticizing Friedrich's work as religious art, at least in the Christian sense. But what offended Ramdohr was the painting's *romanticism*—in the critic's own words, "that mysticism that is now insinuating itself everywhere and that comes wafting towards us from art and science, from philosophy and religion, like a narcotic vapour."[30] He specifically objected to the ambiguities of perspective in the picture that turn the concavity of a formal Claudian landscape into a convexity that disrupts and resists the gaze. Where does the viewer stand? We seem to be oddly at once below and above the cross, and thus, paradoxically, nowhere: the rays of the sun shine from beneath in contradiction to the logic of space and light. And so the critic Joseph Koerner concludes, "With neither firm ground on which to stand, nor a stable horizon on which to fix our gaze, we thus encounter Friedrich's crucifix within an anxious state of visual disequilibrium."[31] At the same time, this anxiety is born of the sense of what one of the painting's contemporary defenders, Gerhard von Kügelgen, called its "peculiarity" (*Eigentümlichkeit*), or, perhaps better, its "strangeness." The German term is also foundational to Friedrich Schleiermacher's philosophy of religion: Schleiermacher wrote in 1800, "It became clear to me that every man must represent humanity in his own way, in a particular [*eigen*] mix of its elements."[32] The point is that each work of art, whether it be a poem by Hölderlin or Coleridge, or a painting by Friedrich, has its own uniqueness in its universality, and is therefore untranslatable into any terms but its own, and in its language and symbolism is alone and absolutely the ground of any theological possibility, being, at the same time, ἄει ταυτγόρικον, "always tautegorical"—expressing the same subject but always with a difference, always new.[33] Each work is a living chariot, one might even say a liturgy, that bears up (for *us*) the throne of the Divine Humanity.

What Ramdohr calls "mysticism" is found everywhere in the writings of Wordsworth and Goethe as what the latter describes as "the common extraordinary. . . . the extraordinary common." In art and poetry it is the placing of reader or viewer, of you and me, in a place that exists only in the text of word or paint and is alone the space for theological beginning, the place to gaze on an eternally deferred transcendence. Coleridge wrote of it in his late poem "Limbo" (1817) as the place of both despair and the only possible hope; a place of necessary contradiction.

> 'Tis a strange place, this Limbo!—not a Place,
> Yet name it so;—where Time and weary Space
> Fettered from flight, with night-mare sense of fleeing,
> Strive for their last crepuscular half-being;
> . . .
> But that is lovely—looks like Human Time,—
> An Old Man with a steady look sublime,
> That stops his earthly task to watch the skies;
> But he is blind—a Statue hath such eyes.[34]

There could hardly be a better commentary on Friedrich's *Monk by the Sea*, and for Friedrich, too, like the poets, art involved a sacrifice as the prophetic language of his works became increasingly misunderstood and he withdrew into lonely solitude in later life.

This insinuation of the mystical finds its truest dialectical, and therefore kenotic, instantiation in Hegel's *Phenomenology of Spirit*, a work that is closely linked with the idealism of Hölderlin and the art of Friedrich and which will take us inevitably back to the Johannine insistences on the Logos of Coleridge, a connection articulated in the claim from the preface to the *Phenomenology* that "the task nowadays consists not so much in the purging of the individual of an immediate, sensuous mode of apprehension, and making him into a substance that is an object of thought and that thinks, but rather in just the opposite, in freeing determinate thoughts from their fixity so as to give actuality to the universal, and impart to it spiritual life."[35] But the road to such freedom must involve a continual movement of negation, which alone is the source of life, so that true conceptual understanding

(*Vernunft*) is identical, for Hegel, with religion in its negating of the given, only possible in the language and symbols of art, "for [says Hegel], religion equally with philosophy refuses to recognize in finitude a veritable being, or something ultimate and absolute, or nonposited, uncreated and eternal." Further in the preface to the *Phenomenology*, Hegel spells out the full kenotic meaning of Spirit that "is alone Reality." Spirit must both realize itself as object and at the same time empty itself of objective form in order to realize itself fully. In Hegel's own words, "It is in this element [of consciousness] that Spirit develops itself and explicates its moments, [and] these moments contain that antithesis, and they all appear as shapes of consciousness. . . . consciousness knows and comprehends only what falls within its experience; for what is contained in this is nothing but spiritual substance, and this, too, as *object* of the self. But the Spirit becomes object because it is just this movement of becoming an *other to itself*, i.e. becoming an *object to itself*, and of suspending this otherness."[36] Thus, Spirit must be its own object in which it finds itself reflected. Later in the *Phenomenology*, Hegel becomes even more explicit when he speaks of "the *kenosis* of the eternal Being," whereby it enters the sphere of actuality, becoming at once sensuous and uncomprehended.[37] This deeply Christian move, known to the disciples on the road to Emmaus, is only possible, for us, in and through the vehicle of the poetics for which the Romantic poets sacrificed themselves, in words and symbols that refuse to allow any movement *through* meaning but eliminate the trickery and illusions of perspective and hold us absolutely within the demands of their resistant, self-sufficient presence.[38]

Thus, the ground of true being is possible only in a self-emptying that is ultimately nothing other than the death of God—that, is a contentment to let the unsayable be not said, beyond both metaphysics and religious transcendence. What Romantic poetry made possible, though theologians refused to admit it, was the recovery of a genuine incarnation of the Word, which, in Hegelian thinking, is a self-negation of absolute Spirit that is the source of all life, and a self-negation or active *kenosis*, an obedience unto death by which alone the Godhead is raised up and recognized as pure absence. It was this impossibility that Hölderlin eagerly and tragically grasped:

> But, my friend, we have come too late! The gods are still alive,
> But up there, above our heads, in a different world.

It is this world that we glimpse as we gaze with Friedrich's monk by the sea if we can bear the impossible vision and do not attempt to interpret it away. Only then can we understand the final pages of the *Phenomenology of Spirit*, where Hegel writes,

This last shape of the Spirit—the Spirit which at the same time gives its complete and true content the form of the Self and hereby realizes its Notion as remaining in its Notion in this realization—this is absolute knowing; it is Spirit that knows itself in the shape of Spirit, or a *comprehensive knowing* [in terms of the Notion]. Truth is not only *in itself* completely identical with certainty, but it also has the shape of self-certainty, or it is in its existence in the form of self-knowledge. Truth is the *content*, which in religion is still not identical with its certainty. But this identity is now a fact, in that the content has received the shape of the Self.[39]

This identity is now a fact—if we will stand with the monk on the impossible shore, or with Hölderlin in the absolute self-enclosure of his poetry, or with Coleridge in the chariot in whose wheels is the spirit of the living creature. Yet our purgatory curse must still be endured, theology emerging only *in* language and the dullness of our striving for meaning. In Coleridge's words,

> Yet that is but a Purgatory curse;
> Hell knows a fear far worse,
> A fear—a future state; 'tis positive Negation![40]

And here alone is recovered the silence that is at the same time the recovery of true speech in the infinite I AM. Thus, the prophet Isaiah says to Blake in his "Memorable Fancy" when asked how he dared so roundly to assert that God spoke to him, "I saw no God, nor heard any, in a finite organical perception; but my senses discovered the infinite in everything, and as I was then persuaded, and remain confirmed, that the voice of honest indignation is the voice of God, I cared not for consequences but wrote."[41]

And so we return finally to Coleridge's chariot of language, and his fear that, in the present age, faith is buried in the dead letter "or its name and honors usurped by a counterfeit product of the mechanical understanding"[42] with all its blindness and self-complacency. It is a cry that has gone largely unheard by theologians for its demands are considerable, unbearable even. Toward the end of his life, Friedrich wrote a fragment titled "On Art and the Spirit of Art," published posthumously, in which he speaks of the "Temple of *Eigentümlichkeit*," that particularity and strangeness that is necessary for all greatness.[43] This principle of individuation, recognized also in German Romanticism by Ludwig Tieck, Novalis, Friedrich Schlegel, and others, locates the truth foreshadowed in Kant's *Third Critique* and of which Hegel speaks in the unique, particular, and the radically autonomous Self. It is found in the daring in the finite mind of the eternal act of creation in the infinite I AM, and its aspiration to repeat the creating Word, with all its consequences, in which alone is life and the light of people. It is found in its daring to abandon the Western logic of identity that resists polyvalent or multiple interpretations of texts[44] and discover in and not through the word itself the life of creation. In some respects it is to rediscover, though by another route, the ancient understanding of the words of Torah as the "shining garment of the text," but a garment that holds the mystery within itself. As Susan Handelman has said of the text of Torah: "Hence the written text is not only the enclothing of the fiery preexistent letters in which are contained the secrets of creation, but with the proper methods of interpretation one can unlock the mysteries of all being."[45] The technical hermeneutical consequences of such an understanding of text and "the proper methods of interpretation" are not specifically my concern here, but the results of the theological refusal to acknowledge its truth have been dire, and all I have tried to do in this chapter is clear something of the space that Romanticism began to open up for us. In effect, the last two centuries have seen a reversal of the biblical move from Word to flesh, to an obsession with the flesh made Word, and the metaphorizing of the body and the world with the consequence, in Coleridge's words in *The Statesman's Manual*, that "a hunger-bitten and idea-less philosophy naturally produces a starveling and comfortless religion."[46] The unknowable has become for us, as a result, a construct in language and the relationship between form and content, signifier and signified confused with the result that modern semiotics, "whether implicit or explicit, can imagine neither pure content, unsupported by the materiality of a signifier, nor pure form, i.e. the non-reference of a sign totally cleansed of its commerce with the symbolic order."[47] The result of this has been the theological failure to acknowledge the paradoxical possibility of a real presence of what is utterly and absolutely absent, or the possibility of a dialogue, on the edge of impossibility, between the eternal and the temporal, the particular and the universal. Hölderlin as poet is the great mediator, the false priest who sings his warning song to those who will hear. In the singularity of his texts, words gain new inflexions within the determinations of the verse alone in wholly new creations. Nothing and no meaning can be assumed. Blanchot sums up the poet's vocation in his essay "Hölderlin's Itinerary":

> The young Hölderlin, the author of *Hyperion*, yearns to take leave of his form, escape his limits, and be united with nature. "To be one with all that lives, and to return in blessed self-forgetfulness into the All of Nature—that is man's heaven." This aspiration to return into life's unity, into its eternal ardour, unreserved and immeasurable, seems to be the joyful movement which we are tempted to associate with inspiration. This movement is also

desire for death. Diotima dies through the very impulse that makes her live in familiarity with all. But, she says, "we will part only to live more closely united, in a holier peace with all things with ourselves."[48]

In nature and beyond it, after Romanticism, we, too, may become riders in the chariot, knowing in Scripture the living educts of the imagination.

10

THE POSSIBILITY OF A
CONTEMPORARY THEOLOGY

To recognize that part of what we cannot help think is that such thinking is
always a beseeching, is always a matter of measuring ourselves against something that exacts an absolute discipline of truthfulness and yet refuses the
consolation of an absolute achievement of truth: to recognize that is to be
who *we* are.

—James C. Edwards, *The Plain Sense of Things*

Although I ended the previous chapter with a deliberate avoidance of the
"technical hermeneutical consequences" of these many reflections on textuality, the consumed and consuming text, this final chapter will be, to a large
extend, a meditation, in the light of all that has been said, on the peculiar art
of reading, which begins in hermeneutics, implied in this study of the ascetic
and sacred body: a reading by an "authorized reader," which is ultimately an
act of liturgical living and a being in the body that offers just the possibility
of a contemporary theology—though perhaps it is older even than time itself.

I begin with a familiar apothegm of St. Francis of Assisi, given to us
through the medium of a story found in a fourteenth-century manuscript:

What then is true joy?
I return from Perugia and arrive here in the dead of night; and it is winter
time, muddy and so cold that icicles have formed on the edges of my habit
and keep striking my legs, and blood flows from such wounds. And all covered with mud and cold, I come to the gate and after I have knocked and
called for some time, a brother comes and asks: "Who are you?" I answer:
"Brother Francis." And he says: "Go away; this is not a proper hour for

171

going about; you may not come in." And when I insist, he answers: "Go away, you are a simple and stupid person; we are so many and we have no need of you. You are certainly not coming to us at this hour!" And I stand again at the door and say: "For the love of God, take me in tonight." And he answers: "I will not. Go to the Crosiers' place and ask there." I tell you this: If I had patience and did not become upset, there would be true joy in this and true virtue and the salvation of the soul.[1]

"If I had patience and did not become upset." Ostensibly, this is a story of humiliation through patience to an anticipated joy, a narrative of anticipation and "being-toward-death," of a paradoxical joy born of acute bodily suffering and an existence in *kenosis*, the emptying or denial of the demands of the body even while recognizing them, and the absolute refusal to be upset. The body waits between Good Friday and Easter Day in the patience of suffering, living in anticipation and in spite of the suffering felt in coldness and bloody wounds. Theologically and socially, of course, the story does not make sense, and so the first challenge to the theologian must be, how do we now *read* such a narrative, another story of saintly excess? At the beginning of all theological sense, there is a literary moment whereby the author and the reader together literally instantiate in the text the joyful anticipatory suffering of the body: a recognition born of hiddenness—the author, like the subject, seeking anonymity and obscurity in elision in order to reveal the work of the Lord, like St. Athanasius in his *Life of Antony*, the author himself hiding behind the text to effect God's call. As Derek Krueger in his book *Writing and Holiness* has suggested, "By eliding himself. . . . Athanasius has begun to conform to the model of humility. Moreover, the act of composition becomes an analogue for Antony's asceticism, which in Athanasius' incarnational persepective involves Antony's 'complete domination by the Logos.' Athanasius' textual mimesis of the saint fashions the author also as God's instrument."[2]

And so, in order to begin again the work of theology, in perhaps another odd place, I wish to allude for a moment to perhaps the purest of all novelists and story tellers, Henry James, of whom the physical density of language, at least in his later novels, intricately realizes the particularity of every small experience, both exterior and interior, to the point at which to read it is barely tolerable, at once a deeply sensual and a profoundly ascetic experience that is enacted simultaneously entirely within the mind and with every fiber of feeling within the body in a meeting of interior and exterior.[3] Like the saints of the ascetic tradition, James deals first with the matter of everyday, our entrapment within it and our endless anticipations in time. Take a simple sentence from the beginning of *The Wings of the Dove* (1902), describing Kate Croy as she waits for her father: "She tried to be sad, so as not to be angry; but it made her angry that she couldn't be sad."[4] It captures beautifully the all-too-familiar imbalance of impatience, the opposite of St. Francis' extraordinary, impossible balance and "indifference" in his cold waiting. It is just that we never actually stop to analyze what is so familiar to us—while the ascetic, like the author, endlessly meditates on such minute, quotidian commonplaces, which alone may become the stuff of theological realization. In his preface to the New York Edition (volume 23) of his last novel *The Golden Bowl* (1904), James insists on his *detachment* as an author in the business of "seeing my story"—a detachment that is not uncaring but precisely the opposite, a profound carefulness in his task of making us (the readers) see things for all they are worth. His language then becomes the medium for a profound consciousness of the everyday givenness of life in its complexity, both its opportunities (which are too often missed) and its temptations (which are too often misinterpreted). Above all, we need to realize that James' often baffling prose is deeply ascetic (not to say ethical) in its insistent sense of responsibility to the particular (as is also James Joyce's in *Finnegans Wake*), and therefore it is the only possible medium in language for a genuinely meditative, theological beginning. "Anything," James writes, "that relieves responsible prose of *the duty of being*, while placed before us, *good enough*, interesting enough and, if the question be of picture, pictorial enough, above all *in itself*, does it the worst of services."[5] Such prose is very hard to read, a demanding medium that requires simultaneously an utterly sensual, an absolutely intellectual, and a relentlessly ascetic response—and all this a celebration of being long before Martin Heidegger's philosophical guidance was given to us in *Sein und Zeit* (1927). James concludes his preface with a celebration of the "one sovereign truth" art, "which decrees that, as art is nothing if not exemplary, care nothing if not active, finish nothing if not consistent, the proved error is the base apologetic deed, the helpless regret is the barren commentary, and 'connexions' are employable for finer purposes than mere gaping contrition."[6] Contrition, regret, error—this is the language of the ascetic who seeks to transcend all such for the one sovereign truth in purity of body, as James' fiction does in purity of language. Each searches for a consistency of form and attention that is found in the final balance and coincidence of opposites, a coherence of body and spirit in the true life of the soul as it embraces the body. *The Golden Bowl* begins in Hyde Park, London, its language both communicating and embodying the inconsistency and the lack of balance in a young man's attention as it is distracted by different varieties of the sensual. "The young man's movements, however, betrayed *no consistency of attention*—not even, for that matter, when one of his arrests had proceeded from possibilities in faces shaded, as they passed him on the pavement, by huge beribboned hats, or more delicately tinted still under the tense silk of parasols held at perverse angles in waiting victorias."[7] The sexuality of the final phrase vibrates through the medium of the words. But the final image of the book is quite the opposite—a triumph of attention and a total seeing of the other as pure presence, no less embodied, as the young man affirms, "his whole act enclosing her. . . . 'See'? I see nothing but *you*."[8]

This, however, must be only a beginning in the finally conventional story of literature, which concludes with a full, romantic realization of being good enough in art. But the more radical vision of the true ascetic reaches in body and soul for an always unrealized self-embodiment that is possible only in a finally kenotic existence, an utter self-emptying through the most painful, passionate, and self-consuming knowing of the body reaching in the total interiority of the transcendent. In modern poetry it is found most nearly in the passion of the poetry of James' near contemporary Gerard Manley Hopkins, which triumphs only in the ultimate realization of the truth that is expressed in the verse from Isaiah quoted by Hopkins as an epigraph to "Nondum": "Verily Thou art a God that hidest Thyself" (Isa 45:15). His following of Christ to the triumph of utter desolation on the cross is summed up in J. Hillis Miller's rewriting of the Cartesian *Cogito* in Hopkins: "I taste myself, therefore I am, and when I taste myself I find myself utterly different from everything else whatsoever."[9] It is a sacramental fulfillment known only in anticipation, in a coming into being or being-toward-death that is also the pure joy of St. Francis as he stands outside, freezing and waiting on God. It is a joy known too to Angelus Silesius and to Simone Weil. Thus, Hans Urs von Balthasar's noble reading of Hopkins through St. Ignatius Loyola and Duns Scotus in his great work *The Glory of the Lord*[10] finally bypasses the poet's aesthetic, ascetic theology by beginning at the wrong end in the theological tradition and reading only from the outside inward, a theology of surface only that can now be sustained simply through an intellectual concurrence. But Hopkins' theological radicalism is, for him, a necessary daring to move outside to a wilderness that is an utter reversal of the tradition in which von Balthasar stands (though it is born of it) and of which the pillar in the nineteenth century is John Henry Newman. This tradition is finally a mental or purely intellectual one, "its instruments," in Newman's words, "are mental acts, not the formulas and contrivances of language."[11] Hopkins, however, dares to live in the desert and "dead letters"[12] of words, tasting their bitterness beyond thinking to a primordial, absent Godhead "that is only actualized in the advent of apocalyptic Godhead."[13] True theology is now only possible in the inscape of speech, in tasting pure sound as opposed to meaning. Only thus can Hopkins "call off thoughts awhile" for he cannot "live this tormented mind / With this tormented mind tormenting thus"[14] in endless circularity. (Thus do theologians live, like Kate Croy, trying not to be sad so as not to be angry, but angry because they cannot bear to be sad.)

In the deep embodiment of his spoken sound, Hopkins lives in the beyond in a being-toward-death. Miller describes it thus: "Far from being that almost disembodied infinitesimal sigh Hopkins wanted man's work towards his salvation to be, Hopkins' poems are initiatory, autonomous, even anomalous. They bring something new into the world, something that *does*, that is a way of doing things with words, but in a way that is not wholly controlled beforehand by social conventions nor by the expectations and assumptions of its auditors. In that sense Hopkins' poems are not lawful. They make their own laws."[15] To encounter Hopkins' poetry, deeply learned though he was, is to know again the ancient ascetics, like St. Mary of Egypt, who, though illiterate, consumed and were consumed by the words of Scripture that they could not understand but yet embodied wholly, becoming one with the Logos that is known only in a deep unknowing. And only at the point of breaking, at the limit and in despair is that embodiment fully realized in a final consumption:

> Flesh fade, and mortal trash
> Fall to the residuary worm; world's wildfire, leave but ash:
>   In a flash, at a trumpet crash,
> I am all at once what Christ is, since he was what I am, and
> This Jack, joke, poor potsherd, patch, matchwood, immortal diamond,
>   Is immortal diamond.[16]

But is this the final temptation? Is this indeed that "dwelling poetically on the earth" in the space that is at once a desert, an oasis, and a space of literature, or is it that coinherence with Christ that is the ascetic's greatest triumph and deepest temptation based on the principle articulated by von Balthasar that all truth is grounded in Christ, and that this, a theological statement that is realized only as absolute nothingness, is our deepest lure? Thus, "struggling against particular ignorances and incapacities to bring forth truth,"[17] we do not reside in truth, but we struggle to bring it into being, just as, for Gregory of Nyssa, the spiritual life is regarded as an *"epektasis"*—that is, a relentless straining forward or growth toward what is yet to come. Hence the life of struggle with and in the body is itself the discipline of truthfulness, what, following Jean-Yves Lacoste, and moving even beyond poetic dwelling, I call *liturgical* dwelling or experience. Himself drawing upon Heidegger, Lacoste insists that the "topologic of existence" rests in neither being-at-home nor not-being-at-home, but "admits only that corporeality, which imprints itself on our being in its entirety."[18] Properly speaking, finding ourselves in a liturgical experience of place—that is, a dwelling that insists on the distinction between the "messengers" of the sacred and the Absolute—is to dwell in perpetual transgression, between being and nonbeing, and therefore to dwell in continual excess. Thus, the excesses of the ascetic tradition as found in the writings of their hagiographers, and to which I have continually referred, point precisely and actually to the liturgical.

And so, moving even beyond the poetic, let us now begin to "read," in the physical density of language, the life of liturgical dwelling, moving from the language of text to the reinstatement of the theological through a new sense of its vocabulary within the practice of existence.[19] Thus it is to begin theology, as every ascetic knows, absolutely afresh in always provisional discoveries of perfect joy.

Dwelling on the Edge

We begin to speak truly only in prayer and praise. All else is mere surface chatter. Only in praise does language become good enough. For thus to speak is to give utterance when language itself begins to come apart in a purity of reference that is in the process of moving beyond the referential. Language in praise is not about anything in its universal particularity, uttered in the space and on the edge between the world and the *eschaton*,[20] the universal and the particular, time and eternity, the real and the symbolic. The body that speaks knows itself inasmuch as it realizes in speech what is its utter negation in exposure to the hiddenness of God, and yet remains available for interpretation by its actual extension into the symbolic that is possible only within the world while yet acknowledging its being "as not."

Dwelling in Anticipation

The return to the theological through liturgical existence cannot but be unhappy, for it necessarily involves a retreat, adopting the life of the recluse, and therefore a parting from the obvious embracing of the social dynamics of the ethical and the economic. The anxiety that this induces can be seen in all pragmatic questioning of the ascetic or monastic traditions, their apparent lack of common sense (as in the story of St. Francis), and the dangers of irresponsibility. Thus, Judas Iscariot upbraids Jesus for the waste of the precious perfume, worth three hundred denarii that could have been given to help the poor and needy (John 12:3–6), as indeed was the case. And true prayer, which is uttered on the edge or even over the abyss, is already falling into meaninglessness except as anticipation of what is "not yet," and thus within an ever-present dilemma sustained only by the discipline of "indifference" or "passionlessness." The demon of conscience remains, but the obverse of this is the dark vision of Matthew Arnold in his "Stanzas from the Grande Chartreuse," where we are left "Wandering between two worlds, one dead, / The other powerless to be born."[21] For Arnold, too, though his vision seems utterly dark, there is neither past nor future.

Dwelling as Vigil

Liturgical existence is necessarily experienced in darkness—the night of waiting or vigil, as with the watchman who looks for the morning. In pure darkness there are no signposts to give comfort, and in pure silence within which alone the language of prayer gives utterance there is no comforting, guiding chatter, or surface small talk. Indeed, it might be better to dispense with the language of "experience," for in such dwelling as vigil both mind and body move beyond consciousness; that is when the soul (which is the whole being) waits in suspension, yet fully alive, beyond experience and inexperience, beyond knowledge and ignorance, for the utterly simple truth that, as Nicholas of Cusa taught, is absolute, singular, and unknowable.[22]

Dwelling with Contingency

To learn to live liturgically in prayer and praise is to acknowledge the paradox of the necessity of the contingent. Inasmuch as we keep watch in absolute night then anticipation is only born of the utter gratuitousness of revelation, for otherwise the unknowable would be known from a necessity. The ascetic life acknowledges the reality of the body only in reversals and a discipline that at once fully knows the corporeal at the very limits and faces the contingency of the wholly other, which is the nothing that defies and deconstructs every constructed possibility. Literature, too, in its own way, has always insisted on the contingent, intimating that absolute contingency that distinguishes between Being and our "being as." Quite simply, as a character in Iris Murdoch's first novel, *Under the Net* (1954), in a celebration of the contingent, puts it: "'I don't know why it is,' I said, 'It's just one of the wonders of the world.'"[23]

Dwelling at the End of History

Liturgical existence is always a celebration at the end of history, but if Hegel purports to offer a "system" that gives us the final word, the liturgical always knows its place at the edge both after and before, beyond all system. Avoiding Hegel's intellectual ironic detachment, it dares to advance without the least hint of epistemic totalitarianism in the flux of time but always already on the edge of eternity. Thus, the desert fathers dwelt on earth, and "yet [already] they live as true citizens of heaven."[24] In Hegel, the task is to work back toward an implicit theological approval. Liturgical existence, however, begins in a language that embodies the theological in endless becoming. In Hegel, the Absolute is always threatened with realization, as Søren Kierkegaard perceived in *Fear and Trembling*, so that our "eternal consciousness" is, in turn, threatened with despair.

Dwelling in Dispossession

To dwell ascetically with nonpossession is to subvert the "natural" tendency to acquire and, above all, to acquire power for the self. To exercise the freedom not to possess, whether it be of knowledge, of material assets, or even of the spiritual way, asserts a radical possibility for living absolutely in the present and therefore open to every possibility in the particularities of existence in the breaking down of determinacies so that things are seen and known simply as they *are* and not as they are appropriated. Thus, life may be celebrated as conditional, as metaphors merge into the stuff of existence and the unknown becomes an impossible possibility in its condition of utter darkness. To abandon all totalitarian tendencies is to find freedom in the most deeply human encounter with the Absolute.

Dwelling in Perfect Joy

And so we return to where we began, with St. Francis as he waits in patience though covered with mud and cold, outside. Lacoste catches precisely the paradox of the story: "Thus the paradoxical joy that is born of humiliation may be the *fundamental mood* of preeschatological experience. The reconciled man, despite what Hegel might say, is still at a distance from his absolute future."[25]

Following this brief narrative excursus into aspects of the liturgical living of the ascetic life on earth, knowing the liturgical as a way of being and speaking rather than a way of knowing, I want to return to the question with which I began this chapter, which is, how we can now read the texts of theology, a question of more importance than ever in the West, at least, when the traditional claims of Christian theology and the practice of the Church have surrendered the final vestiges of their genuine validity in the discourses of contemporary culture. On the one hand, I would claim, Western philosophical understandings of what it means to be human, or a human being, upon which the claims of Christian theology have been built, have now been eroded to the point at which they are unable to stem the despairing tide of what has been termed "the threat of normal nihilism"[26] in our culture and societies. On the other, the power structures that have been the institutions of the churches have now withered to the point of no return, although they continue to attempt to impose their lost authority, with ever decreasing degrees of success. Thus, I find myself among those Christians, and by no means necessarily all of a radical hue, who lament the Jesus who remains sealed by Christendom in his tomb and the celebration of the church of the Grand Inquisitor, who does not finally believe in God, who is yet solitary and transcendent, but only a salvation history located finally in the past of history.[27]

But there has always been an alternative tradition in the religious life of the Christian West, validated, as I tried to show in my previous book, *The Sacred Desert*, by its equally insistent presence in literature, art, and culture. In its mystical tendencies, it has always had a countercultural aspect, living on the edge ecclesially, philosophically, and socially. In this present book, I have taken a further step by concentrating on the nature of the body—that is, the true body of the resurrection, realized rather than denied through the traditions of asceticism—and now finally I have modulated this discussion so that it has become an enquiry into texts, the Word, and *how* we read; that is, the recovery of a possible theology after the final acknowledgment of Friedrich Nietzsche's "death of God" is not through any reassertion of systematic possibilities (for their foundations have crumbled beyond repair), but in a radically creative revisioning of where we begin afresh the theological task, and how we then might start to rearticulate that (thus, I have drawn attention to the most articulate of all modern writers, Joyce and James, and their challenges to us as readers and interpreters).

And so, finally, in these meditations on the sacred body in theology, I draw attention once again to a remarkable recent text, Jean-Luc Marion's *The Erotic Phenomenon* (2003) as an act of love that forms a prolegomenon to theological possibilities and ways of being. Ostensibly a philosophical essay on the act and experience of erotic love, *The Erotic Phenomenon* poses an initial and actually quite simple question to the reader. In its dismantling of conceptual hierarchies and its leveling of literary genre distinctions, *how do we actually read it*? I mean, at what level of response do we appropriate it or assume its referentiality? The initial question is simply one of hermeneutics—and hermeneutics (but also what lies beyond them) have always lain close to the heart of Christian theology and practice. Do we follow it at the immediate level of our own experience of what it is to love one another and have children, testing its sense against what we know ourselves, though quickly aware that there are levels of verbal sense that both enlarge and outstrip our capacities to know love and family and carry them into the realm of the theological? Or do we read it as a philosophical text, armed with our knowledge of all the philosophical and intellectual traditions behind it? Now actually, reading this dense and intensely personal text is very close to the experience of reading the later novels of James, in which no violence is externalized, yet every action and every object is deeply felt in a manner that is close to mystical texts of pure embodiment wherein words finally lead to a silence that is both felt and heard beyond experience and beyond sound and audible only in such profundities of the self where the only and greatest necessity is an utterly painful honesty. Perhaps this is what Heidegger, drawing on the poetry of Friedrich Hölderlin, calls "measuring oneself against the godhead,"[28] for here alone is encountered the presence of the merest possibility of the impossible. The turn to poetry is to begin to do full justice to "modes of being and thinking that are still not fully determined by productionist metaphysics."[29] The dangers always lie in distractions and unbalance, our always wanting texts to be about what *we* want.

Once I gave some undergraduate students a poem to read without telling them what it was: it was St. John of the Cross' *Song of the Ascent of Mount Carmel*, which begins: "In a dark night, inflamed by love's desires—oh, lucky chance!—I went out unnoticed, all being then quiet in my house."[30] Quite naturally, and in a way rightly, they read it as an erotic poem (which it most profoundly is), and were deeply puzzled as to why we were reading this as part of a theology class. What they were not used to was precisely what asceticism practices, which is the internalizing of the text in a perfect of union of body and spirit so that the one knows the other wholly and without any intellectual or cerebral distance. They were not accustomed to reading and realizing religious experience *on the page*—for it is much easier to externalize it and export it to the safety and distance of the intellectual realm in theology or philosophy. But on the page, in the here and now of the text to be digested, experience through the being of the human is liturgical and utterly connected to all modes of being. Marion's text is theologically powerful because it allows no detachment of consciousness and no reduction to what the reader already understands. It keeps you in the immediacy of the words and their claims on you, attentive to all levels of the self, the body both acknowledged and disciplined. Reading it is at least a good start.[31]

Let me try and give you an example of what I mean. The theologian, my colleague, Werner Jeanrond states that Marion's "approach to love affirms both the necessity of distance for any act of love as well as the impossibility of an unconditional self-love."[32] That is, indeed, a perfectly fair explanation of Marion's approach. Love begins always with the prior other who calls forth our response. In his own words, "In order for me to enter into the erotic reduction, it was necessary for another lover to have gone before me, a lover who, from there, calls me there in silence."[33] But the point is that it is not enough simply to be *told* that. As the ascetic tradition is both an embracing of and struggling with the body, so it is with Marion's text, which actually instantiates the statement that it makes, so that the act of interpretation is more than an act of understanding but an acknowledgment that only in our own imperfect experience can we begin to construct a response to the "other" who is calling, for always and even in our own poor experience of love we recognize, as Marion puts it, "the excess in it of intuition over signification." And it is at such moments of crucial recognition that Marion shifts his language into a different key, and invariably that key is the theological. Thus, we are carried by our own hard-won self-analysis (to the moment of struggling with the narrative of the text when we can say, "Yes, I see what you mean, it is meaningful *for me*.") into the theological, whose language is thus brought startlingly close to home. Here is Marion's full description of this moment: "Love demands eternity because it can never finish telling itself the excess within it of intuition over signification. I will only know whom I love in the final instance—by eschatological anticipation of eternity, the sole condition of its endless erotic anticipation."[34]

Here, as readers, we have reached the fully liturgical place in present expectancy. At such moments we are invited into a new intimacy with all poets of love who know perfectly well what this means as a moment outside time yet entirely within history without laboring the point, be it John Donne's dismissal of "the rags of time," or Louis MacNeice's "Time was away, and somewhere else."[35] Nor is it irrelevant for theology to entertain the poets (as William Blake once dined with Isaiah and Ezekiel), for Marion's, like every true theological text, is deeply poetic, its texture open to conversations by intuition, discussions not dragged in unceremoniously by pedantry, but with gentle hospitality and ever an openness to new guests. His book, like every truly liturgical body, is like an ever open symposium, conversing with all "according to the flesh." Without the indelicacy of direct allusion, he holds quiet conversations with other texts, from Augustine to Descartes and the Fourth Gospel to Nietzsche: a close companion is the poet Hölderlin in his great poem "Homecoming" (*Heimkunft*), which insists that though the singer must harbor cares (*Sorgen*) in his soul, they are not to be the wrong sort of cares,[36] the cares of the distracted. But the most important voice is that interior one, which is deep within the reader and can be the most difficult to hear and respond to. For the truly theological text can and indeed must play in different narrative registers simultaneously, like George Herbert's polyphonic poetry, and, on the whole, we are very good at dissecting one narrative at a time but generally very poor at listening to and concentratedly embracing a textual polyphony that can only actually be *heard* (though hardly heard at all) in harmonious univocality.

Much of the time we read, as we live, merely skimming the surface of the text with our minds moving upon silence, rather like the long-legged fly of which W. B. Yeats writes that skims along the surface of the water where alone it feels a whole world of vibrations. Here I part company absolutely with Don Cupitt in his book that draws on Yeats' poem[37] to seek to articulate a purely and "perfectly horizontal" theology that rejects all transcendence and therefore also the deepest sense of the immanence of the divine after the death of God. For what is it to dive into the depths, to risk the impossible vertical? It is only in the approach to this in the consumed and consuming text of eroticism that the familiar terms of theology take on a different meaning through my flesh in all its immanence and its unlikely erotic antics, and through which such experience as, for example, that of chronological time takes on a new, transfigurative complexity. Quite simply, I mean, my daring to be "in love" (literally "within love") alone shifts time into something else apart from that cursed element that drags me out of bed every morning to go to work, and conspires to ensure that sometimes I miss the last bus home. (Again, although we may find the language of theology on time useful here, the best tutors are likely to be Shakespeare or Donne, though St. Augustine's *Confessions* are, it must be admitted, uniquely qualified.)

What I begin to learn again from reading Marion's text, which must always be preliminary to the discussions of excess that precede this chapter, is that, although I am a deeply imperfect lover, we can only be lovers at all in the perfection of love itself, in the text of its consumed and consuming eroticism. *Faithfulness* thus "defines the temporality of the phenomenon of love and its unique future."[38] The status of the lover is granted only by faithfulness, even in abandonment, and so the actual lover is always, to a greater or lesser extent (like all believers), like the half-believer of St. Mark's Gospel, crying, "I love, help thou my failure to love."[39] Such an admission of failure grants a whole new and deeply hopeful meaning to that resonant verse in the Song of Songs: "Many waters cannot quench love, neither can floods drown it" (8:7). It is not *my* love that is unquenchable (as Meister Eckhart well knew), but it becomes so through the nature of love itself encountered within the textuality of the erotic, which is ultimately a divine textuality. And the erotic, for Marion, the very experience of the flesh itself (that is, the *sarx* of the fourth Gospel, the Word made flesh), continuously carries us into patterns of anticipation that alone respond finally to the narratives of theology in their anticipations. This is not least because it transforms biological or social narratives of the flesh into utterly different and transfigurative modes of requirement (as literature repeatedly shows us in tragedy from *Antigone* to the gospels and even, in its way, to *Romeo and Juliet*). But this is, in Marion's narrative (in its echoes of Trinitarian modes of thought, though oddly and I suspect not deliberately), above all, clear in the advent of the "third party."[40] The passage to the child explores dynamics that move beyond the immediate yet which are entirely testable, in the first instance at least, in experience, a presence that is present only in a familiar vocabulary (familiar also from John 14:18–29). "She [the child] projects into the future the present of the oath, if this oath no longer lives, the child, for as long as she lives, will *witness* to it against the lovers. Thus the child *consecrates in her flesh* the lovers' faithfulness or, in her flesh, lets jealousy speak and defends against them the lovers' honour."[41] In the third party, who is the child of our flesh, is realized in body what is yet other than the flesh of the lovers. Indeed, this third party actually precedes us and guarantees in spite of us the perfected end of the endless repetitions of love, pronouncing upon it a last judgment.

The narrative, and its very vocabulary, that emerges from Marion's portrait of the eschatological nature of love is actually, whatever he may say, a familiar and quite comprehensible rewriting of the Romantic pattern: "They married, had children, and lived happily ever after."[42] It is, in the end, also, dependent on social and gendered patterns of behavior as well as the narratives and models of Christian theology—the Trinity, Christology, judgment, and so on. Nevertheless, it still provokes us in its reading in the manner of many of the earlier texts that we have been considering from the Christian tradition, especially within mysticism, and their return to the erotic. Thus, it is not a bad place to start again. But the difference is that this earlier tradition emerges, unlike Marion, from a body that also deeply knows the ascetic way of the body and is already transfigured—resurrected if you will—and therefore allows a much more subtle and complex series of narratives to be traced upon it. Thus, from a *literary* point of view, a work like St. Sophronius' *Life of St. Mary of Egypt* is far more imaginatively demanding, more dense in its layering, than the work of Marion. The problem is, then, that *The Erotic Phenomenon* too quickly allows the theologian to translate it into theological terms. Theology is too easily entertained by the body (the flesh too quickly made into the Word), and Marion moves rapidly from the loving couple to divine love in the final pages. The imagination stops short.

However, I have spent some time with this work for good reason. Marion at least offers his reader the opportunity of dwelling within his text, something approaching a liturgical dwelling with a fluidity that embraces theological understanding with the complexities of the body, and a body that comes to know, within the erotic phenomenon, at least something like the divinized body of the resurrection. What I have been discussing is not so very far removed from the metaphysical personalism of Austin Farrer, with its sense of the "becoming" of being, and that is not so far either from the thought of Edmund Husserl and Heidegger,[43] and its acknowledgment of the divinity within us. But the deep roots of my discussion are, I think, very different from those of the philosopher Farrer, for they lie in the reading and the consuming of texts, texts that consume and are realized in our bodies in a Word made flesh, that flesh disciplined and tempered by an asceticism that is a full realization of the body in a generous and humane "discourse of resistance."[44]

I conclude, then, with an example of how such discourse is found finally in the depths of the body itself, depths of the spirit as well as of the body and evoked only in the most profound of negations, truly a desert of salvation. Nicholas of Cusa's brief *Dialogus de Deo abscondito* (*Dialogue on the Hidden God*; 1444/5) begins with a Pagan addressing a Christian who is prostrate and weeping tears of love from the heart.[45] It is in the body that we worship God. What follows is a theological conversation, which begins with the remarkable assertion by the Christian who does not know whom he worships, but yet "it is because I do not know that I worship."[46] But what he dismisses are the dangers inherent in the one who actually "thinks he knows." What then is true knowledge? In fact, the dialogue is more a meditation on the two kinds of "not knowing." They are described succinctly in the words of one commentator on Nicholas of Cusa, Morimichi Watanabe:

1. not knowing what can be known and perhaps should be known; and
2. not knowing by possessing something other than knowing, something greater, and fuller and utterly transcendent.[47]

It is the latter form of not-knowing that Cusa calls a "being in truth" (or sometimes the "desire to be in truth"), a manner of being that I relate closely to Heideggerian poetic dwelling and what lies beyond it. Its expression is the act of worship in the body by prostration and tears, and it is beyond all possible either knowing or not knowing. Finally, we rejoice in the utter hiddenness of God, for only thus can we be said to be in God, beyond any act of knowing or experience, but in the body that is at once, absolutely profane and wholly sacred. Thus, to conclude with the words of Thomas Altizer to me: "Ultimately I think this can only be an evocation of the depths of the Body of the Godhead, and if that Body is a Crucified Body, perhaps it can be most real to us through everything that [is called] forth as an absolute desert and not simply a sacred desert in the common sense, but a sacred desert that is an absolutely profane desert." It is this pure desert, at once sacred and profane, that we have been exploring through the geography of the ascetic body, most perfectly prefigured in the figure of the crucified Christ and at once utterly broken and perfectly fulfilled, unbearable to the gaze in its dark suffering and dazzling beauty, the body of the resurrection, yet here with us as a Total Presence in pure, surrendered simplicity.

> And knowe you not, sayes Love, who bore the blame?
> My deare, then I will serve.
> You must sit down, sayes Love, and taste my meat:
> So I did sit and eat.[48]

NOTES

Preface

1. One might mention, for example, Frank Burch Brown, *Religious Aesthetics: A Theological Study of Making and Meaning* (1980); David Bentley Hart, *The Beauty of the Infinite: The Aesthetics of Christian Truth* (2003); and Graham Howes, *The Art of the Sacred: An Introduction to the Aesthetics of Art and Belief* (2007).
2. Quoted in Arthur C. Danto, *The Abuse of Beauty: Aesthetics and the Concept of Art* (Chicago: Open Court, 2003), 148.
3. Quoted in Danto, *The Abuse of Beauty*, 159.
4. Gavin Flood, *The Ascetic Self: Subjectivity, Memory and Tradition* (Cambridge: Cambridge University Press, 2004), 163.
5. T. E. Lawrence, Seven Pillars of Wisdom: A Triumph (vol. 1; London: World Books, 1939), 40.
6. James C. Edwards, *The Plain Sense of Things: The Fate of Religion in an Age of Normal Nihilism* (University Park: Pennsylvania State University Press, 1997), 184. In what follows, I am much indebted to Edwards.
7. "Building Dwelling Thinking," "The Thing," "Poetically Man Dwells," and "The Question Concerning Technology" are all reprinted in Martin Heidegger, *Poetry, Language, Thought* (trans. Albert Hofstader; New York: Harper & Row, 1971).
8. Norman Russell, trans., *The Lives of the Desert Fathers* (Kalamazoo: Cistercian, 1981), 50.
9. Heidegger, *Poetry, Language, Thought*, 150.
10. Chapter 1 in this volume further extends this preliminary discussion of Heidegger and the idea of "poetic dwelling."
11. Pseudo-Dionysius, *The Complete Works* (trans. C. Luibheid; NewYork: Paulist, 1987), 137.
12. LXX: φωνη αυρας λεπτης. Vulgate: *Sibilus aurae tenuis.*

13. I was given this quotation on a card during a conference on Meister Eckhart. I have never been able to trace its origin in Edmond Jabès works.

14. David Jasper, *The Sacred Desert: Religion, Literature, Art, and Culture* (Oxford: Blackwell, 2004), vi.

15. Gregory McNamee, ed., *The Desert Reader: A Literary Companion* (Albuquerque: University of New Mexico Press, 1995), 103.

16. Jim Crace, *Quarantine* (Harmondsworth: Penguin, 1997), preface.

17. Crace, *Quarantine*, 193.

18. See the longer discussion of Eckhart in chapter 8 in this volume.

19. Crace, *Quarantine*, 243.

20. Bill Viola, *Reasons for Knocking at an Empty House: Writings 1973–1994* (London: Thames and Hudson, 1995), 54.

21. Paul Ricoeur, *The Symbolism of Evil* (trans. Emerson Buchanan; Boston: Beacon, 1969), 349.

22. Meister Eckhart, *Selected Writings* (trans. Oliver Davies; Harmondsworth: Penguin, 1994), 108.

23. Jasper, *The Sacred Desert*, v.

Chapter 1

1. Quoted in Arthur C. Danto, *The Abuse of Beauty* (Chicago: Open Court, 2003), 158–60.

2. See chapter 10 in this volume, pp. 176–78, and especially Jean-Yves Lacoste, *Experience and the Absolute: Disputed Questions on the Humanity of Man* (trans. Mark Raftery-Skehan; New York: Fordham University Press, 2004), and Jean-Luc Marion, *God Without Being* (trans. Thomas A. Carlson; Chicago: Chicago University Press, 1991).

3. Thomas J. J. Altizer, *Total Presence: The Language of Jesus and the Language of Today* (New York: Seabury, 1980).

4. This was written in a personal letter to me. It is quoted at more length in chapter 2 in this volume, p. 21.

5. Such liturgical dwelling is a constant theme of this book but is finally explored in chapter 10 in this volume, pp. 171–85.

6. Sarah Coakley, ed., *Religion and the Body* (Cambridge: Cambridge University Press, 1997), 6. The recent *Oxford Companion to the Body* (ed. Colin Blakemore and S. Jennett; Oxford: Oxford University Press, 2001), v, begins its preface with these words: "We are our bodies. The evolution of humanity is the adaptation of bodies. Bodies are the tangible material of being. Bodies contain us, restrain us, perplex us, attract us, disgust us. They are the objects of most of the thoughts and actions of human beings. Scientists, writers, artists and poets are bodies with a mission." No mention is made of theologians or an anthropology that acknowledges the religious dimension in human existence.

7. An important issue of the journal *CrossCurrents* (Winter 2008) was dedicated to the study of asceticism in contemporary religious practice, but it was published after the writing of this book was completed. Its concerns, however, were not specifically theological.

8. Danto, *The Abuse of Beauty*, 25.

9. Russell, *The Lives of the Desert Fathers*, 50.

10. See Douglas Burton-Christie, "Part III: The Word Realized," in his book *The Word in the Desert: Scripture and the Quest for Holiness in Early Christian Monasticism* (Oxford: Oxford University Press, 1993), 181–296.

11. Bernard of Clairvaux, *Sermones super cantica canticorum*, quoted in Anna Harrison, "Community Among the Dead: Bernard of Clairvaux's *Sermons for the Feast of All Saints*," in *Last Things: Death and the Apocalypse in the Middle Ages* (ed. Caroline Walker. Bynum and Paul Freedman; Philadelphia: University of Pennsylvania Press, 2000), 194.

12. See Caroline Walker Bynum, *Holy Feast and Holy Fast: The Religious Significance of Food to Medieval Women* (Berkeley: University of California Press, 1987).

13. See chapter 7 in this volume, pp. 128–33.

14. See also Flood, *The Ascetic Self*, 4: "Asceticism is the reversal of the flow of the body, which is also an attempt to reverse the flow of time."

15. The earliest surviving Christian commentary on the Song of Songs is by St. Hippolytus of Rome (fl. 200 C.E.), a work certainly known to Origen, who wrote his own commentary, and to St. Jerome and St. Augustine. The Cappadocian Father Gregory of Nyssa also wrote an influential work on the Song of Songs.

16. I am grateful here to the final, unpublished, chapter of Altizer's "Theological Memoir," in *Living the Death of God* (Albany: State University of New York Press, 2006).

17. See Flood, *The Ascetic Self*, 146.

18. See also Vincent L. Wimbush and Richard Valantasis, eds., "Part 4: Aesthetics of Asceticism," in *Asceticism* (Oxford: Oxford University Press, 1998), 267–371.

19. Patricia Cox Miller, "Dreaming the Body: An Aesthetics of Asceticism" in *Asceticism* (ed. V. L. Wimbush and R. Valantasis; Oxford: Oxford University Press, 1998), 287.

20. See chapter 3 in this volume, pp. 44–45, and chapter 5, pp. 69–80.

21. Quoted in Flood, *The Ascetic Self*, 154.

22. Georges Bernanos, *The Diary of a Country Priest* (trans. Pamela Morris; New York: Carroll & Graf, 2002), 104. See reference in Adam G. Cooper, *The Body in St. Maximus the Confessor: Holy Flesh, Wholly Deified* (Oxford: Oxford University Press, 2005), 208. See chapter 4 in this volume on Bernanos and the priest's death, pp. 54–57. For another moment of transcendent, eucharistic beauty in death, see Walter Pater, *Marius the Epicurean: His Sensations and Ideas* (1885; New York: New American Library, 1970): "In the moments of his extreme helplessness their mystic bread had been placed, had descended like a

snow-flake from the sky, between his lips. . . . It was the same people, who in the gray, austere evening of that day took up his remains, and buried them secretly with their accustomed prayers; but with joy also, holding his death, according to their generous view in this matter, to have been of the nature of a martyrdom, and martyrdom, as the church had always said, a kind of sacrament with plenary grace" (285–86).

23. Bernard McGinn describes Meister Eckart's style as "'stretching the envelope,' creating new fields of meaning." McGinn, *The Mystical Thought of Meister Eckhart: The Man From Whom God Hid Nothing* (New York: Herder and Herder, 2001), 32. See chapter 8 in this volume, pp. 135–48.

24. G. W. F. Hegel, *Aesthetics: Lectures on Fine Art* (vol. 1; trans. T. M. Knox; Oxford: Clarendon, 1988), 30–32. See also Danto, *The Abuse of Beauty*, 12–13.

25. See Harrison, "Community Among the Dead," 201.

26. See Caroline Walker Bynum, *The Resurrection of the Body in Western Christianity, 200–1336* (New York: Columbia University Press, 1995).

27. This is a collection of ascetic and mystical writings of the fourth to the fifteenth centuries, first published in Venice in 1782, and quickly translated into Slavonic and Russian.

28. See above on Danto, *The Abuse of Beauty*, 3. I remain indebted to Danto in the discussion that follows.

29. See above, pp. xiii–xiv.

30. Edwards, *The Plain Sense of Things*, 172.

31. See Geoffrey Galt Harpham, *The Ascetic Imperative in Culture and Criticism* (Chicago: University of Chicago Press, 1987), xii.

32. For a more detailed discussion of this question, see Danto, *The Abuse of Beauty*, ix–xi.

33. See Arthur C. Danto, *The Transfiguration of the Commonplace* (Cambridge: Harvard University Press, 1981).

34. See David Morgan, *The Sacred Gaze: Religious Visual Culture in Theory and Practice* (Berkeley: University of California Press, 2005), 26: "Theory is interesting and useful as a way of reflecting on the practice of studying religious visual culture. But theory for its own sake is not what motivates my scholarship or the work I find most influential and productive."

35. St. Gregory of Sinai, "Instructions to Hesychasts," *Writings from the Philokalia: On Prayer of the Heart* (trans. E. Kadloubovksy and G. E. H. Palmer; London: Faber and Faber, 1992), 74–94.

36. Albert Schweitzer, *The Quest of the Historical Jesus* (trans. W. Montgomery, J. R. Coates, Susan Cupitt, and John Bowden; London: SCM Press, 2000), 487.

37. Quoted in Andrew Bowie, *Aesthetics and Subjectivity from Kant to Nietszche* (Manchester: Manchester University Press, 1990), 129. Friedrich Wilhelm Joseph von Schelling objected to Hegel inasmuch as "he places the most abstract concepts first, becoming, existence, etc.; but abstractions cannot of course be there, be taken for realities, before that from which they are abstracted." Schelling here

deeply influenced the thought of Ludwig Feuerbach and Karl Marx. My own argument, in a different way, turns back to Hegel's insight.

38. Marion, *God Without Being*, 148–49.

39. Harrison, "Community Among the Dead," 192–94.

40. For the perverse opposite of this, see Patrick Süskind, *Perfume: The Story of Murderer* (trans. John E. Woods; Harmondsworth: Penguin, 1987), p. 263: "For the first time they had done something out of Love." These are the last words of the novel after the crowd, driven mad by the odor of his perfume, distilled from the bodies of the women whom he has murdered, have literally consumed the body of Grenouille.

41. Bernard of Clairvaux, *Sermones super cantica canticorum*, quoted in Harrison, "Community Among the Dead."

42. Nadia Tazi, "Celestial Bodies: A Few Stops on the Way to Heaven," in *Fragments for a History of the Human Body* (eds. Michel Feher with Ramona Naddaff and Nadia Tazi; New York: Zone, 1989), 542.

43. D. G. Leahy, *Novitas Mundi: Perception of the History of Being* (New York: SUNY University Press, 1994), 378.

44. Thomas J. J. Altizer, an unpublished review article of D. G. Leahy, *Novitas Mundi* and *Foundation: Matter the Body Itself* (New York: SUNY University Press, 1996).

45. See Harpham, *The Ascetic Imperative*, xii.

46. Paul Virilio, *The Aesthetics of Disappearance* (trans. Philip Beitchman; NewYork: Semiotexte, 1991), quoted in Jim Harold, ed., *Desert* (Southampton: John Hansard Gallery, 1996), 41.

Chapter 2

1. One of the most beautiful and troubling depictions of such ambiguities in modern fiction is in Ron Hansen's *Mariette in Ecstasy* (1991), a novel that is, as Robert Detweiler suggests, powerful in its "unfamiliar ordinariness." See Detweiler, *Uncivil Rites: America Fiction, Religion, and the Public Sphere* (Urbana: University of Illinois Press, 1996), 81. The novel explores the themes of sexuality and transcendence, the ambiguities of a nun's "kind of love affair with Jesus," an incorporation of the flesh made Word.

2. See Bynum, *Holy Feast and Holy Fast*. "As the writings of Catherine of Siena make clear, to eat Christ is to become Christ. The Christ one becomes, in the reception of communion and in the *imitatio* of asceticism, is the bleeding and suffering Christ of the cross. The flesh of Christ—both flesh as body and flesh as food—is at the very center of female piety. And this flesh is simultaneously pleasure and pain" (245).

3. Harpham, *The Ascetic Imperative*, xii.

4. Harpham, *The Ascetic Imperative*, xii.

5. Michel Foucault, "Introduction" to Gustave Flaubert, *The Temptation of Saint Anthony* (New York: Modern Library, 2001), xxx.

6. Thomas J. J. Altizer, *The Self-Embodiment of God* (New York: Harper & Row, 1977), 96: "The real ending of speech is the dawning of resurrection, and the final ending of speech is the dawning of a totally present actuality. That actuality is immediately at hand when it is heard, and it is heard when it is enacted. And it is enacted in the dawning of the actuality of silence, and actuality ending all disembodied and unspoken presence."

7. Paul de Man, *The Resistance to Theory* (Manchester: Manchester University Press, 1986), 19.

8. See Wolfgang Iser, "The Reading Process: A Phenomenological Approach," in *The Implied Reader: Patterns of Communication in Prose Fiction from Bunyan to Beckett* (Baltimore: Johns Hopkins University Press, 1974), 274–94.

9. John Updike, *In the Beauty of the Lilies* (London: Hamish Hamilton, 1996), 52–54.

10. Friedrich Hölderlin, *Poems and Fragments* (trans. Michael Hamburger; London: Anvil Press Poetry, 1994), 399. The German lines translated here read:

Den falschen Priester, ins Dunkel, daß ich
Das warnende Lied den Gelehrigen singe,
Dort

See also chapter 4 in this volume, on Georges Bernanos' *Diary of a Country Priest*.

11. Leo Tolstoy, *Resurrection* (trans. Rosemary Edmonds; Harmondsworth: Penguin, 1966), 561.

12. Fyodor Dostoevsky, *The Idiot* (trans. David Magarshack; Harmondsworth: Penguin, 1955), 447.

13. McGinn, *The Mystical Thought of Meister Eckhart*, 105.

14. See Edith Wyschogrod, *Saints and Postmodernism: Revisioning Moral Philosophy* (Chicago: Chicago University Press, 1990), 6. See also Peter Brown, "Potentia," in *The Cult of the Saints: Its Rise and Function in Latin Christianity* (Chicago: Chicago University Press, 1982), 106–27.

15. Harpham, *The Ascetic Imperative*, 185–88. See more on Mathias Grünewald in chapter 3 in this volume, pp. 142–43.

16. Gustave Flaubert, *The Temptation of Saint Anthony* (trans. Lafcadio Hearn; New York: Modern Library, 2001), 190.

17. Foucault, "Introduction," xliv. *Bouvard et Pécuchet* (1881) was Flaubert's final and unfinished work.

18. Evelyn Waugh, *Brideshead Revisited* (Harmondsworth: Penguin, 1962), 351.

19. Waugh, *Brideshead Revisited*, 352.

20. Robert Murray, S.J., "Philippians," in *The Oxford Bible Commentary* (ed. John Barton and John Muddiman; Oxford: Oxford University Press, 2001), 1185. *Kenosis* is also central to the radical theology "after the end of metaphysics," of

the Italian philosopher Gianni Vattimo, whose thinking has much influenced my own.

21. See Marie-José Baudinet, "The Face of Christ, The Form of the Church," in *Fragments for a History of the Human Body* (ed. Michel Feher with Ramona Naddaff and Nadia Tazi; New York: Zone Books, 1989), 151.

22. Nicephorus the Patriarch, *Antirrhetic II*, in *Fragments for a History of the Human Body* (trans. Anna Cancogne; New York: Zone Books, 1989), 157–59.

23. Baudinet, "The Face of Christ," 152.

24. Jean-Luc Marion, *God Without Being*, 17.

25. For a further discussion on this, see chapter 10, pp. 179–84.

26. See, for example, in the context of Victorian portrayals of women's bodies, Helena Michie, *The Flesh Made Word: Female Figures and Women's Bodies* (Oxford: Oxford University Press, 1987). Michie further explores the body's capacity to elude such definitions. "If the tropes that entrap women's bodies are examined both in their power and in their ability to dissolve themselves, if women's bodies are seen to appear and to disappear at particular moments in the text and in history, this liberation, based on the energy of movement and subversion, will become a possibility" (8).

27. See Thomas J. J. Altizer, *The Contemporary Jesus* (London: SCM Press, 1998), x.

28. William Blake, *Jerusalem*, Plate 3, "To the Public," in *The Complete Works* (ed. Geoffrey Keynes; Oxford: Oxford University Press, 1966), 621.

29. Miller, "Dreaming the Body," 282.

30. Peter Brown, *The Body and Society: Men, Women and Sexual Renunciation in Early Christianity* (New York: Columbia University Press, 1988), 31. See also chapter 1 in this volume, pp. 4–8.

31. See Benedicta Ward, trans., *Sayings of the Desert Fathers* (Kalamazoo: Cistercian, 1975), 197.

32. See Miller, "Dreaming the Body," 282.

33. Thomas Laqueur, *Making Sex: Body and Gender from the Greeks to Freud* (Cambridge, Mass: Harvard University Press, 1990), 114.

34. In Ernest Renan, *La Vie de Jésus* (1863), quoted in Schweitzer, *The Quest of the Historical Jesus*, 158.

35. Baudinet, "The Face of Christ," 151.

36. Camille Paglia, *Sexual Personae: Art and Decadence from Nefertiti to Emily Dickinson* (London: Penguin, 1992), 298.

37. Leo Steinberg, *Leonardo's Incessant Last Supper* (New York: Zone Books, 2001), 193–94.

38. See Martin Hengel, *Crucifixion in the Ancient World and the Folly of the Message of the Cross* (trans. John Bowden; Philadelphia: Fortress, 1977); Stephen D. Moore, *God's Gym: Divine Male Bodies of the Bible* (New York: Routledge, 1996).

39. Elaine Pagels, *Beyond Belief: The Secret Gospel of Thomas* (London: Macmillan, 2003), 19; emphases added.

40. See Pagels, *Beyond Belief*, 20, and N. T. Wright, *Jesus and the Victory of God* (Minneapolis: Fortress Press, 1992).

41. Thomas J. J. Altizer, *Godhead and the Nothing* (Albany: State University of New York, 2003), 111.

42. Süskind, *Perfume*, 263. See also chapter 1 in this volume, p. 11n40.

43. Altizer, *The Contemporary Jesus*, 6.

44. St. Athanasius, *The Life of St. Antony* (trans. Robert C. Gregg; New York: Paulist, 1980), 42.

45. See Peter Brooks, *Body Work: Objects of Desire in Modern Narrative* (Cambridge, Mass: Harvard University Press, 1993), 281–83; Laqueur, *Making Sex*, 243.

46. G. W. F. Hegel, *The Philosophy of History* (trans. J. Shibree; New York: Wiley, 1944), 377. See also Brown, *The Cult of the Saints*, 86.

47. Brooks, *Body Work*, 280. See also chapter 1 in this volume, pp. 9–10, on when a work of art is art, and the "demonic possibility" at the heart of theology.

48. Hengel, *Crucifixion in the Ancient World*, 87.

49. T. Todorov, *La Conquista de América: El Problema del Otro* (México: Siglo XXI, 1987), 151, quoted in Marcella Althaus-Reid, *Indecent Theology: Theological Perversions in Sex, Gender and Politics* (London: Routledge, 2000), 11.

50. Catherine Kerr, *The Face of the Deep: A Theology of Becoming* (London: Routledge, 2003), 220.

51. See Pagels, *Beyond Belief*, 25–26.

52. The deeply perplexing, even profane nature of such images was revived when Salvador Dali's great painting of *Christ of St. John of the Cross* (1951), an image of Christ crucified but triumphant and bursting from the tomb, was damaged and slashed as it hung in the Kelvingrove Art Gallery in Glasgow.

53. Thomas J. J. Altizer, "William Blake and the Role of Myth," in Altizer and Hamilton, *Radical Theology and the Death of God* (London: Penguin, 1968), 177.

54. William Blake, *Complete Writings* (ed. Geoffrey Keynes; Oxford: Oxford University Press, 1966), 221.

55. Altizer, *The Contemporary Jesus*, 8.

56. Leo Steinberg, *The Sexuality of Christ in Renaissance Art and in Modern Oblivion* (2nd ed.; Chicago: University of Chicago Press, 1996), 106.

57. See also Gilles Deleuze, *The Fold: Leibniz and the Baroque* (trans. Tom Conley; London: Continuum, 2003), xii.

58. Tom Conley, "A Plea for Leibniz," foreword to Deleuze, *The Fold*, xii. On the theme of scarring, see further Mark Ledbetter, *Victims and the Postmodern Narrative, or Doing Violence to the Body* (London: Macmillan, 1996).

59. The phrase is taken from the title of Denys Turner's book, *The Darkness of God: Negativity in Christian Mysticism* (Cambridge: Cambridge University Press, 1995).

60. Jean-Luc Marion, *The Erotic Phenomenon* (trans. S. E. Lewis; Chicago: Chicago University Press, 2007), 9.

Chapter 3

1. I am indebted to Tom Altizer for this insight, which is crucial for a proper understanding of the spirituality of the desert fathers and mothers. See also Adolf von Harnack's treatment of Origen in his *History of Dogma* (1894–1999).
2. John Donne, *The Complete English Poems* (ed. A. J. Smith; Harmondsworth: Penguin, 1971), 55–56.
3. Dostoevsky, *The Idiot*, quoted in Julia Kristeva, *Black Sun: Depression and Melancholia* (New York: Columbia University Press, 1980), 109. See also chapter 2 in this volume, p. 18. On the theme of dismemberment, see the essay by Robert Detweiler, "Torn by Desire: Sparagmos in Greek Tragedy and Recent Fiction," in *Postmodernism, Literature and the Future of Theology* (ed. David Jasper; London: Macmillan, 1993), 60–77.
4. Julian of Norwich, *Revelations of Divine Love* (trans. Clifton Wolters; Harmondsworth: Penguin, 1966), 66.
5. Richard Rolle, *Meditations on the Passion*, quoted in Gabriele Finaldi, *The Image of Christ* (London: National Gallery, 2000), 148.
6. Isaac Watts, "Crucifixion to the World by the Cross of Christ," in *The New Oxford Book of Christian Verse* (ed. Donald Davie; Oxford: Oxford University Press, 1981), 146.
7. It is quite opposite to the perverse readings of Christianity offered by Slavoj Žižek in his in his much-discussed book *The Puppet and the Dwarf: The Perverse Core of Christianity* (2003), which is simply a flight from the spiritual.
8. Kristeva, *Black Sun*, 113.
9. Margaret R. Miles, *The Word Made Flesh: A History of Christian Thought* (Oxford: Blackwell, 2005), 391.
10. Jorie Graham, *Erosion* (Princeton: Princeton University Press, 1983), 74. See a more detailed discussion in chapter 6 in this volume, pp. 103–4.
11. Drawing on the work of J. H. Eaton, *Kingship and the Psalms* (2nd ed.; Sheffield: JSOT Press, 1986), 176.
12. C. S. Rodd, "Psalms," in *The Oxford Bible Commentary* (ed. John Barton and John Muddiman; Oxford: Oxford University Press, 2001), 375.
13. For an excellent discussion of the novel, see Thomas M. Dicken, "God and Pigment: John Updike on the Conservation of Meaning," *Religion and Literature* 36, no. 3 (2004): 69–87.
14. John Updike, *Seek My Face* (Harmondsworth: Penguin, 2003), 272.
15. Updike, *Seek My Face*, 276.
16. Elie Wiesel, *Night* (trans. Stella Rodway; Harmondsworth: Penguin, 1981), 126.
17. Joseph Heller, *God Knows* (London: Black Swan, 1985), 446.
18. Dostoevsky, *The Idiot*, quoted in Kristeva, *Black Sun*, 109.
19. *Duchess of Malfi*, act 2, scene 1.
20. "Stabat Mater Dolorosa," vv. 4, 6 in *The English Hymnal* (trans. Bishop Mant et al.; London: Oxford University Press, 1933), 158. The origins of the hymn

are unknown, but it is probably from the late thirteenth century and taken into liturgical use in the later Middle Ages.

21. Rowan Williams, *Resurrection: Interpreting the Easter Gospel* (London: Darton, Longman & Todd, 1982), 106.

22. "I am according to my *flesh*. Contrary to the formal abstraction that makes objects, my flesh allows itself to be affected without end by the things of the world." Marion, *The Erotic Phenomenon*, 13.

23. See also chapter 1 in this volume, p. 4.

24. Rowan A. Greer, introduction to *Origen: Selected Works* (New York: Paulist, 1979), 28.

25. See Don Cupitt, *Mysticism after Modernity* (Oxford: Blackwell, 1998), 44–45.

26. Bernard of Clairvaux, *Selected Works* (trans. G. R. Evans; New York: Paulist, 1987), 222. On the kisses, see chapter 4 in this volume, p. 48.

27. Rowan Williams, *The Wound of Knowledge: Christian Spirituality from the New Testament to St. John of the Cross* (London: Darton, Longman & Todd, 1979), 108–33.

28. See chapter 8 in this volume, pp. 135–48.

29. Quoted in Miles, *The Word Made Flesh*, 150.

30. Bernard of Clairvaux, *Selected Works*, 223. See also Melvyn Matthews, *Both Alike to Thee: The Retrieval of the Mystical Way* (London: SPCK, 2000), 33–37.

31. Donne, *The Complete English Poems*, 60.

32. St. John of Damascus, *Three Treatises on the Divine Images* (trans. Andrew Louth; New York: St. Vladimir's Seminary, 2003), 10.

33. St. John of Damascus, *Treatise* 1:7, 27.

34. St. John of Damascus, *Treatise* 1:4, 22.

35. The best meditation on the term "co-inherence" remains Charles Williams' study of the Holy Spirit, *The Descent of the Dove* (London: Longmans, Green and Co., 1939). Williams begins, "The history of Christendom is the history of an operation. It is an operation of the Holy Ghost towards Christ, *under the conditions of our humanity; and it was our humanity which gave the signal, as it were, for that operation*" (1; emphases added).

36. See also chapter 2 in this volume, p. 18.

37. See note 23 in chapter 2.

38. St. Athanasius, *The Life of Antony*, 42.

39. T. S. Eliot, "Journey of the Magi," in *Complete Poems and Plays* (London: Faber and Faber, 1969), 104. On Edith Wyschogrod, see also chapter 2 in this volume, pp. 19–20.

40. On the "*noli me tangere*," see also chapter 2 in this volume, p. 24.

41. Wyschogrod, *Saints and Postmodernism*, 10.

42. Harold Bloom, *The Anxiety of Influence: A Theory of Poetry* (Oxford: Oxford University Press, 1973), 87–88.

43. Harpham, *The Ascetic Imperative*, 191.

44. See further chapter 6 in this volume, pp. 101–3.

45. Polly Toynbee, *The Guardian*, December 5, 2005.
46. Peter Brown, *The Body and Society*, 218.
47. The quote is from Benedicta Ward, S.L.G., *Harlots of the Desert: A Study of Repentance in Early Monastic Sources* (Kalamazoo: Cistercian Publications, 1987), 33–34.

Chapter 4

1. R. Aqiba at the Council of Jamnia (90 C.E.) described the Song as "the Holy of Holies," and warned against the singing of it at feasts. See David Lyle Jeffrey, ed., *A Dictionary of Biblical Tradition in English Literature* (Grand Rapids: Eerdmans, 1992), 727.
2. See chapter 1 in this volume, p. 14n15.
3. Origen, *The Prologue to the Commentary on the Song of Songs*, in *Selected Works* (trans. Rowan A Greer; New York: Paulist, 1979), 217.
4. Origen, *The Prologue*, 218.
5. Bernard of Clairvaux, *Selected Works*, 210.
6. Bernard of Clairvaux, *Selected Works*, 226. See also chapter 3 in this volume, pp. 37–38.
7. Marion, *The Erotic Phenomenon*, 222.
8. J. Cheryl Exum, *Song of Songs: A Commentary*. The Old Testament Library (Louisville: Westminster John Knox, 2005), 92.
9. See chapter 8 in this volume, p. 155.
10. Psalm 33:6.
11. See further Joanne Snow-Smith, "Michelangelo's Christian Neoplatonic Aesthetics of Beauty in His Early *Oeuvre*: The *Nuditas Virtualis* Image," in *Concepts of Beauty in Renaissance Art* (ed. Francis Ames-Lewis and Mary Rogers; Aldershot: Ashgate, 1998), 147.
12. "The primary Imagination I hold to be the living Power and prime Agent of all human Perception, and as a repetition in the finite mind of the eternal act of creation in the infinite I AM." Samuel Taylor Coleridge, *Biographia Literaria* (1817) in *The Collected Works* (vol. 7; ed. James Engell and W. Jackson Bate; Princeton: Princeton University Press, 1983), ch. 13. The reference is to the "I am" sayings of Exodus and the Fourth Gospel (Exod 3:14, John 8:58). On Coleridge, see further below, Chap.9.
13. See further Frank Kermode, *The Genesis of Secrecy: On the Interpretation of Narrative* (Cambridge, Mass.: Harvard University Press, 1979). See also David Jasper, "On Reading the Scriptures as Literature," *History of European Ideas* 3, no. 8 (1982): 311–34.
14. See also Ezekiel 3:3. "He said to me, Mortal, eat this scroll that I give you and fill your stomach with it. Then I ate it; and in my mouth it was as sweet as honey."
15. On the *Philokalia*, see chapter 1, note 27.

16. Walter Ong, *Orality and Literacy: The Technologizing of the Word* (London: Methuen, 1982), 32–33. See also Walter Ong, *Interfaces of the Word* (Ithaca: Cornell University Press, 1977), 230–71; and Coleridge, *Biographia Literaria*, chap. 10, on words as living things.

17. See Douglas Burton-Christie, *The Word in the Desert: Scripture and the Quest for Holiness in Early Christian Monasticism* (New York: Oxford University Press, 1993), 20–23.

18. St. Athanasius, *The Life of Antony*, 31.

19. Burton-Christie, *The Word in the Desert*, 40–43.

20. See Jasper, *The Sacred Desert*, 78; and Lawrence, *Seven Pillars of Wisdom*, 1:38.

21. See the story of the idiotic scullery maid in the fourth-century *Lausiac History* of Bishop Palladius. Jasper, *The Sacred Desert*, 11–12.

22. See chapter 8 in this volume, pp. 142–43, and chapter 5 on Martha and Mary, especially in Meister Eckhart's great sermon on Luke 10:38–42 (DW 86). Eckhart, *Selected Writings*, 193–202.

23. See chapter 1 in this volume, p. 3.

24. See Lawrence M. Wills, "Ascetic Theology Before Asceticism? Jewish Narratives and the Decentering of the Self," *Journal of the American Academy of Religion* 74, no. 4 (December 2006): 902–25. Wills examines ascetic "decentering" in the texts of the Qumran community. The same has been observed of T. E. Lawrence by Edward Said in *Reflections on Exile and Other Literary and Cultural Essays* (London: Granta Books, 2001), 31–40.

25. Flood, *The Ascetic Self*, 4.

26. Owen Chadwick notes rather soberly of John Cassian, who adapted Egyptian ideals and methods for Latin use in the fifth century and, in a sense, made them possible, that "he set western monasticism on sane lines and. . . . was the first guide to the contemplative ideal in the history of western thought." Owen Chadwick, *John Cassian* (2nd ed.; Cambridge: Cambridge University Press, 1968), 162.

27. *Writings from the "Philokalia,"* 23.

28. Marion, *The Erotic Phenomenon*, 193.

29. For a fuller account, see the publisher's note to Irina Ratushinskaya's poems in *Pencil Letter* (Newcastle: Bloodaxe Books, 1988), 9. Her own account of her arrest and imprisonment is published as *Grey is the Colour of Hope* (trans. Alyona Kojevnikov; London: Hodder & Stoughton, 1988).

30. Ratushinkshaya, *Pencil Letter*, 13.

31. Quoted in Rémy Rougeau, introduction to *The Diary of a Country Priest*, by Georges Bernanos (trans. Pamela Morris; New York: Carroll & Graf, 2002), ix. Compare with chapter 2 in this volume, p. 17, on Hölderlin's "As on a holiday."

32. Bernanos wrote an essay titled "Sermon of an Agnostic on the Feast of St. Thérèse," in *The Heroic Face of Innocence: Three Stories* (Grand Rapids: William B. Eerdmans, 1999).

33. Bernanos, *The Diary of a Country Priest*, 1.

34. Bernanos, *The Diary of a Country Priest*, 5–6.
35. Bernanos, *The Diary of a Country Priest*, 298. Bernanos, as author (though not his young priest), is using the words of St. Thérèse, "Grace is everywhere."
36. St. Bernard of Clairvaux, *Selected Works*, 226.
37. Compare this with the dying Simone Weil; see chapter 7 in this volume, pp. 128–33.
38. The question of reading is finally dealt with in some detail in chapter 10 in this volume.
39. We might compare the insight of R. S. Thomas on his own work as a parish priest in his poem "The Priest," written as a dialogue with the reader:

"Crippled soul," do you say? Looking at him
From the mind's height; "limping through life
On his prayers. There are other people
In the world, sitting at table
Contented, though the broken body
And the shed blood are not on the menu."

"Let it be so," I say. "Amen and amen." (R. S. Thomas, *Selected Poems 1946–1968* [Newcastle: Bloodaxe Books, 1986])

Thomas moves beyond the considered superiority of the "mind's height" to the actuality of the priest's bodily presence in his parish, picking his way among the people whose "flesh rejects him," his thoughts "icicles."
40. Bernanos, *The Diary of a Country Priest*, 279.
41. See the chapter 1 in this volume on Hegel's *Aesthetics*, p. 7.
42. Rougeau, Introduction, *The Diary of a Country Priest*, vii.
43. Milorad Pavić, *Landscape Painted with Tea* (trans. Christina Pribićević-Zorić; New York: Alfred A. Knopf, 1990), 6.
44. Pavić, *Landscape Painted with Tea*, 7.
45. See also St. Mary of Egypt, chapter 5 in this volume, p. 74.
46. Pavić, *Landscape Painted with Tea*, 192; cf. Wolfgang Iser, *The Implied Reader: Patterns of Communication in Prose Fiction from Bunyan to Beckett* (Baltimore: Johns Hopkins University Press, 1974), and see chapter 2 in this volume, p. 16.
47. Pavić, *Landscape Painted with Tea*.
48. Pavić, *Landscape Painted with Tea*, 338.
49. Pavić, *Landscape Painted with Tea*, 339.
50. Tazi, "Celestial Bodies," 519.
51. Paul Celan, *Selected Poems* (trans. Michael Hamburger; Harmondsworth: Penguin, 1990), 60–61.
52. Geoffrey Hill, *New and Collected Poems, 1952–1992* (New York: Houghton Mifflin Harcourt, 1994).
53. Franz Kafka, *Metamorphoses and Other Stories* (trans. Willa Muir and Edwin Muir; Harmondsworth: Penguin, 1961), 169.

Chapter 5

1. Thomas Traherne, *Centuries* (The Second Century: 66, 68), from *Poetry and Prose*, selected and introduced by Denise Inge (London: SPCK, 2002), 14–15.
2. Compare Meister Eckhart as a "literalist"; see chapter 8 in this volume, p. 138.
3. Ward, *Harlots of the Desert*, 91.
4. The phrase "myth and metaphor" is taken from the title of Susan Haskins, *Mary Magdalen: Myth and Metaphor* (London: HarperCollins, 1993).
5. John 20:17. This is during the episode when Mary meets the risen Lord in the garden. The NRSV suggests that it should read, "Do not hold on to me." See chapter 2 in this volume, p. 24, and chapter 6 in the discussion of the art of Velázquez.
6. *The Gospel of Philip*, c.63, quoted in Elaine Pagels, *The Gnostic Gospels* (London: Weidenfeld and Nicolson, 1984), 84.
7. Michèle Roberts, *The Wild Girl* (London: Minerva, 1991), 181.
8. For the most authoritative text, see *Vita Sanctae Pelagiae, Meretricis*, in J. P. Migne, *Patrologiae cursus completus: series Latina* (vol. 73; Paris, 1857–66), cols. 663–72.
9. Ward, *Harlots of the Desert*, 66.
10. Ward, *Harlots of the Desert*, 67–68.
11. For further and more complex readings of this traditional contrast between the active and the contemplative ways, see chapters 6 and 9 in this volume.
12. Benedicta Ward, trans., *The Wisdom of the Desert Fathers* (London: SLG Press,1983), 46. See also chapter 3 in this volume, p. 45 for another story of John the Dwarf.
13. Migne, *Patrologiae*, cols. 661–62.
14. The story is reproduced in English in Ward, *Harlots of the Desert*, 83–84.
15. Quoted in the introduction to *The Dramas of Hrotsvit of Gandersheim* (trans. Katharina M. Wilson; Matrologia Latina Saskatoon: Peregrina, 1985), 1. The text is translated from Hrotsvitha, *Hrotsvithae Opera* (ed. Helena Homeyer; München: Schoningh, 1970).
16. *The Dramas of Hrotsvit of Gandersheim*, 93–111.
17. *The Dramas of Hrotsvit of Gandersheim*, 110–11.
18. *The Dramas of Hrotsvit of Gandersheim*, 104.
19. *The Dramas of Hrotsvit of Gandersheim*, 104.
20. For a full discussion of this, see David Chamberlain, "Musical Learning and Dramatic Action in Hrotsvit's *Pafnutius*," *Studies in Philology* 77, no. 4 (1980): 319–43.
21. St. Sophronius' *Life of St. Mary of Egypt* is prefaced by words from Tobit 2, "It is good to keep close the secret of a king, but to reveal gloriously the works of God."
22. Michel Foucault, *The Care of the Self* (vol. 3 of *The History of Sexuality*; trans. Robert Hurley; Harmondsworth: Penguin, 1990), 238.
23. Foucault, *The Care of the Self*, 239.

24. See Julia Reinhard Lupton, *Citizen-Saints: Shakespeare and Political Theology* (Chicago: University of Chicago Press, 2005), 125–57.

25. The most accessible English version of St. Sophronius' *Life* can be found in Ward, *Harlots of the Desert*, 35–56.

26. See chapter 2 in this volume, pp. 19–20.

27. Wyschogrod, *Saints and Postmodernism*, 9–10.

28. For a development of this phrase, see chapter 10 in this volume, pp. 171–85.

29. Sophronius, *Life*, in Ward, *Harlots of the Desert*, 51.

30. Sophronius, *Life*, in Ward, *Harlots of the Desert*, 56.

31. See Stanley Fish, *Is There a Text in This Class? The Authority of Interpretive Communities* (Cambridge, Mass.: Harvard University Press, 1980).

32. See especially Gregory of Nyssa, *The Life of Moses* (trans. Abraham J. Malherbe and Everett Ferguson; New York: Paulist, 1978).

33. Abbot Isaiah of Scetis, *Ascetic Discourses* (trans. John Chryssavgis and Pachomios [Robert] Penkett; Kalamazoo: Cistercian, 2002), 161. On the question of the lives of contemplation and activity in Mary and Martha, see also chapter 6 in this volume, and, in the thought of Meister Eckhart, see chapter 8.

34. 1 Cor 13:1, 3–5. See also Abbot Isaiah of Scetis, *Ascetic Discourses*, 160.

35. Harpham, *The Ascetic Imperative*, 223.

36. See Jacques Derrida, *Of Grammatology* (trans. Gayatri Chakravorty Spivak; Baltimore: Johns Hopkins University Press, 1976), 6–26.

37. See Ward, *Harlots of the Desert*, 33.

38. By the eighth century, the myth had developed that Mary Magdalene, like St. Mary of Egypt, spent the last years of her life on earth as a contemplative in the desert, covered only by her hair and fed by angels. Typically, she was occupied not in penitence but reflecting on her life in sorrow and love. See Haskins, *Mary Magdalene*, 111.

39. This is in direct contrast to the Gnostic aspiration to primordial asexuality. In the *Gospel of Thomas*, Jesus informs Mary Magdalene that even she may become male, which is to say "spiritual." In the *Gospel of Mary*, she herself announces that "he has prepared us [and] made us into men." Later, St. Augustine in *De Civitate Dei*, book 22, ch. 17, allows women to retain their female characteristics in the resurrection body, yet not for sexual purposes, but only to "arouse the praises of God." St. Augustine, *The City of God* (trans. Henry Bettenson; Harmondsworth: Penguin, 1972), 1057.

40. For a fine reading of this episode from the *Lausiac History*, see Michael de Certeau, *The Mystic Fable* (vol. 1 of *The Sixteenth and Seventeenth Centuries*; trans. Michael B. Smith; Chicago: University of Chicago Press, 1992), 32–34.

41. Ward, *Harlots of the Desert*, 40.

42. S. Brent Plate, *Walter Benjamin, Religion, and Aesthetics: Rethinking Religion Through the Arts* (New York: Routledge, 2005), 51. Plate relates this distinction between the metaphorical (vertical) and the metonymic (horizontal) with Julia Kristeva's distinction between the "horizontal function" of the sign with

the "hierarchical and hierarchizing" functions of the symbol in her 1970 essay, "From Symbol to Sign," reprinted in Toril Moi, ed., *The Kristeva Reader* (Oxford: Blackwell, 1986), 62–73.

43. For more on the horizontal planes of the desert landscape, see Jasper, *The Sacred Desert*.

44. Ward, *Harlots of the Desert*, 36.

45. The phrase is from Coleridge's *Biographia Literaria*: "that willing suspension of disbelief for the moment, which constitutes poetic faith."

46. The distinction, of course, is from Aristotle. See Jean-Luc Marion's "impossible impossibility in Marion, *The Erotic Phenomenon*, 193.

47. Ward, *Harlots of the Desert*, 38.

48. Ward, *Harlots of the Desert*, 40.

49. Ward, *Harlots of the Desert*, 41.

50. Ward, *Harlots of the Desert*, 41.

51. Ward, *Harlots of the Desert*, 43.

52. Ward, *Harlots of the Desert*, 46.

53. See letter to the author from Thomas J. J. Altizer, in chapter 2 in this volume, p. 21.

54. Ward, *Harlots of the Desert*, 49.

55. Ward, *Harlots of the Desert*, 52.

56. Ward, *Harlots of the Desert*, 53.

57. Ward, *Harlots of the Desert*, 54.

58. Ward, *Harlots of the Desert*, 56.

59. Painted in 1618, the picture is in the National Gallery of Scotland, Edinburgh. For further reflections on the art of Velázquez, see chapter 6 in this volume.

60. For a further description of this painting, see Norbert Wolf, *Velázquez, 1599–1660: The Face of Spain* (Köln: Taschen, 2005), 10–11.

61. Michèle Roberts, *Impossible Saints* (London: Virago, 1998), 292.

62. Roberts, *Impossible Saints*, 297.

63. Ward, *Harlots of the Desert*, 40.

64. Psalm 84:1–2, from the Coverdale version of the psalms in *The Book of Common Prayer*.

65. Roberts, *Impossible Saints*, 29.

66. Roberts, *Impossible Saints*, 301.

67. Origen, *The Prologue*, 217.

68. Roberts, *Impossible Saints*, 303.

69. George Newlands, *The Transformative Imagination: Rethinking Intercultural Theology* (Aldershot: Ashgate Publishing, 2004), 169.

70. Richard F. Patteson, *A World Outside: The Fiction of Paul Bowles* (Austin: University of Texas Press, 1987), x–xi.

71. Paul Bowles, *The Sheltering Sky* (Harmondsworth: Penguin, 1969), 79.

72. "I think of myself as an existentialist. My mind works like that. I live in the present. I don't think about the future. Whatever happens is what happens." Paul

Bowles, 1988, quoted in Gena Dagel Caponi, *Paul Bowles* (New York: Twayne Publishers, 1998), 18.

73. Bowles, *The Sheltering Sky*, 100.

74. Bowles, *The Sheltering Sky*, 22.

75. Bowles, *The Sheltering Sky*, 217–18.

76. Bowles, *The Sheltering Sky*, 202.

77. See further Wayne Pounds, *Paul Bowles: The Inner Geography* (New York: Peter Lang, 1985).

78. Bowles, *The Sheltering Sky*, 237.

79. Bowles, *The Sheltering Sky*, 231.

80. Gena Dagel Caponi, *Paul Bowles: Romantic Savage* (Carbondale: Southern Illinois University Press, 1994), 132.

81. Bowles, *The Sheltering Sky*, 302.

82. Quoted in Bowles, *The Sheltering Sky*, 132–33.

83. Tennessee Williams, "An Allegory of Man and His Sahara," *New York Times Book Review*, December 4, 1949, p. 7.

84. Pounds, *Paul Bowles: The Inner Geography*; Patteson, *A World Outside*; Caponi, *Paul Bowles: Romantic Savage*.

85. Marion, *God Without Being*, 153–58.

86. Marion, *God Without Being*, 140.

87. Caponi, *Paul Bowles: Romantic Savage*, 222; Paul Bowles, *Next to Nothing: Collected Poems 1926–1977* (Santa Barbara: Black Sparrow, 1981), 71.

Chapter 6

1. Anatole France, *Thaïs* (trans. Robert B. Douglas (Wildside, 2005), 141.

2. Altizer, "William Blake and the Role of Myth," 182.

3. Jean-Luc Marion, *Prolegomena to Charity* (trans. Stephen Lewis; New York: Fordham University Press, 2002), 71.

4. For a more detailed description of the incident, see Simon Schama, *Rembrandt's Eyes* (Penguin: London, 2000), 383–86.

5. See Mieke Bal, *Reading "Rembrandt": Beyond the Word-Image Opposition* (Cambridge: Cambridge University Press, 1991), 21.

6. Bal, *Reading "Rembrandt,"* 20–23, 336–46.

7. In 1671, Jan de Bisschop criticized Rembrandt for abandoning the classical ideal of the female form, giving us instead "a Leda or a Danaë. . . . as a naked woman with swollen belly, hanging breasts and garter marks on the legs." See Seymour Slive, *Rembrandt and His Critics* (Hague, 1953; repr., New York, 1988), 83.

8. Louis Viardot, *Les Musées d'Angleterre, de Belgique, de Hollande et de Russie* (Paris, 1860), 319.

9. Schama, *Rembrandt's Eyes*, 387.

10. See further Hidda Hoekstra, *Rembrandt and the Bible* (Utrecht: Magna Books, 1990), 362–63.

11. See chapter 5 in this volume, pp. 72–73.

12. See McGinn, *The Mystical Thought of Meister Eckhart*, 67. See also chapter 8 in this volume, pp. 142–43.

13. This painting is now in the National Gallery of Art in Washington, D.C.

14. See further W. J. T. Mitchell, *Iconology: Image, Text, Ideology* (Chicago: Chicago University Press, 1986).

15. Jane Boyd and Philip Esler, *Visuality and the Biblical Text: Interpreting Velázquez' "Christ with Martha and Mary" as a Test Case* (Leo S. Olschki Editore, 2004), 128.

16. Jacques Lacan, *The Four Fundamental Concepts of Psycho-Analysis* (trans. A. Sheridan; Harmondsworth: Penguin, 1979).

17. See Joseph Leo Koerner, *The Reformation of the Image* (London: Reaktion Books, 2004).

18. See further Nelson Goodman, *Problems and Projects* (New York: Bobbs-Merrill, 1976) on the move from the "picture theory of language" to the "language theory of pictures."

19. Compare her with the mad scullery maid of the *Lausiac History* (see chapter 5 in this volume, p. 74), who "takes upon herself the body's most humble functions; she loses herself in the unassertable, below the level of all language. But this 'disgusting' castaway makes possible for the other women the sharing of meals, the community of the vestiary and corporeal signs indicating that hey have been chosen, the communication of words. The excluded one renders possible an entire circulation." de Certeau, *The Mystic Fable*, 34.

20. Boyd and Esler, *Visuality and the Biblical Text*, 128.

21. Abbot Isaiah of Scetis, *The Ascetic Discourses*; see chapter 5 in this volume, pp. 72–73.

22. Norbert Wolf, *Diego Velázquez (1599–1660): The Face of Spain* (Taschen: Cologne, 2005), 19.

23. Wolf, *Velázquez, 1599–1660*, 19–20.

24. Boyd and Esler, *Visuality and Biblical Text*, 33.

25. This painting is now in the Detroit Institute of Arts.

26. Boyd and Esler, *Visuality and the Biblical Text*, 97.

27. Steinberg, *The Sexuality of Christ*, 106.

28. Eckhart, *Selected Writings*, 193.

29. See Ernst van Wetering, "The Multiple Functions of Rembrandt's Self-Portraits," in *Rembrandt by Himself* (ed. Christopher White and Quenti Buvelot; London: National Gallery Publications, 1999), 17–19.

30. Van Wetering, "The Multiple Functions," 19. Perhaps the greatest model for this is Montaigne in his *Essais* of 1580–88.

31. Baudinet, "The Face of Christ," 151.

32. See Marion, *God Without Being*, 20.

33. Thomas J. J. Altizer, "Van Gogh's Eyes," an unpublished essay in honor of Patrick A. Heelan, pp. 3–4 (emphases added).

34. Quoted in *Guide: Van Gogh Museum* (Amsterdam: Van Gogh Museum, 1996), 54.

35. Mark Roskill, ed., *The Letters of Vincent van Gogh* (London: Fontana Paperbacks, 1963), 335.

36. Roskill, *The Letters of Vincent van Gogh*, 340.

37. Miles, *The Word Made Flesh*, 228.

38. Jorie Graham, "At Luca Signorelli's Resurrection of the Body," in *Erosion* (Princeton: Princeton University Press, 1983), 74. See chapter 3 in this volume, p. 34.

39. Flood, *The Ascetic Self*, 4. See also chapter 1 in this volume, p. 4.

40. G. Vasari, *The Lives of the Artists* (1568), quoted in Miles, *The Word Made Flesh*, on CD-ROM, notes to fig. 6.6.

41. Graham, "At Luca Signorelli's Resurrection of the Body," 77.

42. Miles, *The Word Made Flesh*, 228.

43. St. Augustine, *The City of God*, 1057. For a slightly different reading of this passage, see chapter 5 in this volume, p. 201n39.

44. See also Altizer, "The Eyes of Van Gogh," 14.

45. See chapter 8 in this volume, pp. 148–56.

46. Arthur C. Danto, *The Body/Body Problem: Selected Essays* (Berkeley: University of California Press, 1999), 184–205.

47. Danto, *The Body/Body Problem*, 185. The phrase "by whom the world is kept in being," referring to the early Christian monks of the Egyptian desert, is drawn from Russell, *The Lives of the Desert Fathers*, 50. See also Jasper, *The Sacred Desert*.

48. Descartes, quoted in Danto, *The Body/Body Problem*, 194.

49. Don Cupitt, "How Mystical Writing Produces Religious Happiness," in *Mysticism after Modernity* (Oxford: Blackwell, 1998), 71.

50. Danto, *The Body/Body Problem*, 205.

51. James Joyce, *Ulysses* (Harmondsworth: Penguin, 1968), 704. See further chapter 8 in this volume, p. 152.

52. Danto, *The Body/Body Problem*, 205 (emphases added).

Chapter 7

1. Tertullian, *Apology*, 8, quoted in Pagels, *Beyond Belief*, 18.

2. Terry Eagleton, *The Ideology of the Aesthetic* (1990), quoted in Detweiler, "Torn by Desire," in *Postmodernism, Literature and the Future of Theology* (ed. David Jasper; London: Macmillan, 1993), 60.

3. I am referring here to Ippolit in *The Idiot* and his description of Hans Holbein the Younger's painting of *The Body of the Dead Christ in the Tomb* (1522). See also chapter 2 in this volume, p. 18.

4. George Eliot, *Adam Bede*, quoted in Martin Laird, *Into a Silent Land: The Practice of Contemplation* (London: DLT, 2006), 31.

5. Graham Greene, *Monsignor Quixote* (London: Penguin, 1983), 250.

6. Pater, *Marius the Epicurean*, 283.

7. Hill, "Canticle for Good Friday," in *New and Collected Poems*. See also chapter 4 in this volume, p. 61.

8. Michael Ondaatje, *The English Patient* (London: Picador, 1993), 3–4.

9. Compare the Oxford theologian Austin Farrer's sermon for Christmas Day, describing the infant Christ, "A Grasp of the Hand." "We will not lift our hands to pull the love of God down to us, but he lifts his hands to pull human compassion down upon his cradle." Farrer, *Said or Sung* (London: Faith, 1960), 35. The comparison with the body in Ondaatje's novel is intended to be disturbing.

10. Michael Ondaatje, *Anil's Ghost* (London: Picador, 2000), 307.

11. See Tomas Kulka, *Kitsch and Art* (University Park: Pennsylvania State University Press, 1996), 33.

12. Emile Zola, *Nana*. 1871. (trans. George Holden; London: Penguin, 1972), 469.

13. See Thomas J. J. Altizer, *The Descent into Hell: A Study of the Radical Reversal of the Christian Consciousness* (Philadelphia: J. B. Lippincott Company, 1970).

14. See Detweiler, "Torn by Desire," 75. Compare also the women running, awestruck, from the tomb in their recognition of the resurrected Christ in St. Mark's Gospel, speechless—"for they were afraid" ("ἐφοβοῦντο γάρ").

15. Wilfred Owen, quoted in C. Day Lewis, introduction to *The Collected Poems of Wilfred Owen* (London: Chatto & Windus, 1963), 23.

16. Pat Barker, *Regeneration* (London: Penguin, 1992), 180.

17. See also chapter 4 in this volume, p. 56n39.

18. See Cooper, *The Body in St. Maximus the Confessor*.

19. Miles, *The Word Made Flesh*, 391. See further chapter 3 in this volume, p. 33.

20. Richard Hoggart, introduction to *Lady Chatterley's Lover*, by D. H. Lawrence (London: Penguin, 1961), v.

21. Brooks, *Body Work*, 261.

22. Updike, *Seek My Face*, 272. See also chapter 3 in this volume, pp. 34–35.

23. Reprinted in Susan Rubin Suleiman, ed., *The Female Body in Western Culture: Contemporary Perspectives* (Cambridge, Mass.: Harvard University Press, 1985), 193–208.

24. See further chapter 8 in this volume, pp. 152, 155, on James Joyce and Anna Livia Plurabelle.

25. Miles, *The Word Made Flesh*, 204.

26. John Steinbeck, *The Grapes of Wrath* (London: Penguin, 1951), 416.

27. Guy de Maupassant, *Selected Short Stories* (trans. Roger Colet; London: Penguin, 1971), 264. I am grateful here to the insights of Rachel Andrea Kent in her brilliant, unpublished thesis, *"Pieta": Theological Contemplations of Interdisciplinary Pieta Figurations* (University of Glasgow, 2006).

28. See, for example, Eleanor J. McNees, *Eucharistic Poetry: The Search for Presence in the Writings of John Donne, Gerard Manley Hopkins, Dylan Thomas and Geoffrey Hill* (Lewisburg: Bucknell University Press, 1992).

29. See Michie, *The Flesh Made Word*, and chapter 2 in this volume, p. 23n26.

30. See Timothy Clark, *Martin Heidegger* (London: Routledge, 2002), 118. On Heidegger, see chapter 9 in this volume, pp. 161–63.

31. James Boyd White, *"This Book of Starres": Learning to Read George Herbert* (Ann Arbor: University of Michigan Press, 1994), 29.

32. George Herbert, "Affliction (1)," lines 55–59. All quotations from Herbert are taken from the now standard work *The English Poems of George Herbert* (ed. Helen Wilcox; Cambridge: Cambridge University Press, 2007), hereafter cited as *EP*.

33. Samuel Johnson, *The Lives of the Poets* (vol. 1; 1781; Oxford: Oxford University Press, 1952), 204.

34. See White, *"This Book of Starres,"* 34.

35. Joan Bennett, *Five Metaphysical Poets* (Cambridge: Cambridge University Press, 1966), 56.

36. David L. Edwards, *Poets and God* (London: Darton, Longman & Todd, 2005), 103.

37. Izaak Walton, *The Life of Mr. George Herbert* (1670), in *The Complete English Poems* (ed. John Tobin; Harmondsworth: Penguin, 1991), 295.

38. Maurice Blanchot, *The Space of Literature* (trans. Ann Smock; Lincoln: University of Nebraska Press, 1982), 21.

39. "The Glimpse," *EP*, 145.

40. Blanchot, *The Space of Literature*, 22.

41. White, *"This Book of Starres,"* 43.

42. Dominic Baker-Smith, "Exegesis: Literary and Divine," in *Images of Belief in Literature* (ed. David Jasper; London: Macmillan, 1984), 175.

43. Robert Carroll and Stephen Prickett, *The Bible: Authorized King James Version with Apocrypha* (Oxford: Oxford University Press, 1997), "The Translators to the Reader," lvi.

44. Baker-Smith, "Exegesis," 175.

45. John Donne, *Devotions Upon Emergent Occasions* (ed. Anthony Raspa; Montreal: McGill-Queens University Press, 1975), 100.

46. Sir Philip Sidney, *An Apology for Poetry* (1595), in *English Critical Essays XVI–XVIII Centuries* (ed. Edmund D. Jones; Oxford: Oxford University Press, 1947), 15.

47. Samuel Taylor Coleridge, *Collected Letters* (ed. Earl Leslie Griggs; Oxford: Oxford University Press, 1956, 1971), vol., p. 352. Also, see chapter 9 in this volume, pp. 158–59.

48. Coleridge, *Collected Letters*, vol. 1, p. 626; vol. 5, p. 228.

49. D. J. Enright, *Collected Poems* (Oxford: Oxford University Press, 1987), 206.

50. See Paul A. Welsby, *Lancelot Andrewes, 1555–1626* (London: SPCK, 1958), 107–9.

51. George Herbert, *A Priest to the Temple, or, The Country Parson, His Character, and Rule of Holy Life* (1652), repr. in *The Complete English Poems*, 213.

52. This is not, of course, the *Prayer Book* of 1662, which is still used in churches today, but essentially, with some minor changes, the *Prayer Book* of 1552, to which the Articles were added.

53. Article 25 of the Articles of Religion, agreed upon by Convocation in 1562 and reprinted in the 1662 *Book of Common Prayer*. See further William J. McGill, *Poets' Meeting: George Herbert, R. S. Thomas and the Argument with God* (Jefferson, N.C.: McFarland & Co, 2004), 78–82.

54. See further on Heidegger's notion of "poetic dwelling" in Edwards, *The Plain Sense of Things*, 151–94, and the preface of this book.

55. *EP*, 143.

56. *EP*, 94.

57. Clark, *Martin Heidegger*, 101. For more reflections on Heidegger and Hölderlin, see chapter 9 in this volume, pp. 161–63.

58. Heidegger, *Poetry, Language, Thought*, 29.

59. Martin Heidegger, *Elucidations of Hölderlin's Poetry* (trans. Keith Hoeller; New York: Humanity Books, 2000), 22.

60. Clark, *Martin Heidegger*, 105.

61. Heidegger, *Elucidations*, 43, 47.

62. *EP*, 290.

63. See chapter 9 in this volume, p. 158.

64. See Donald Gray, "Cranmer and the Collects," in *The Oxford Handbook of English Literature and Theology* (ed. Andrew Hass, David Jasper, and Elisabeth Jay; Oxford: Oxford University Press, 2007), 561–74.

65. The final two words of the poem "Prayer (I)," *EP*, 178.

66. See Gianni Vattimo, "The Age of Interpretation," in *The Future of Religion* (ed. Santiago Zabala; New York: Columbia University Press, 2005), 43–54.

67. Gianni Vattimo, *Belief* (trans. Luca D'Isanto and David Webb; Cambridge: Polity, 1999), 77.

68. Vattimo, *Belief*, 79.

69. Vattimo, "The Age of Interpretation," 52.

70. "The Holy Scriptures (I)," in *EP*, 208.

71. Examples may be found in Shakespeare's *Hamlet* and Webster's *The Duchess of Malfi*.

72. See Helen Wilcox, "'Heaven's Lidger Here': Herbert's *Temple* and Seventeenth Century Devotion," in *Images of Belief in Literature*, 153–68.

73. See also Robert P. Scharlemann, *The Reason of Following: Christology and the Ecstatic I* (Chicago: University of Chicago Press, 1991).

74. Simone Weil, *Waiting on God* (trans. Emma Craufurd; London: Fount, 1977), 35

75. Julian of Norwich, *Revelations of Divine Love*, 65.

76. Weil, *Waiting on God*, 23.

77. Weil, *Waiting on God*, 119.

78. Simone Weil, *Écrits de Londres* (Paris: Gallimard, 1957), 187, quoted in Alexander Irwin, *Saints of the Impossible: Bataille, Weil and the Politics of the Sacred* (Minneapolis: University of Minnesota Press, 2002), 183.

79. Simone Weil, *First and Last Notebooks* (trans. R. Rees; London: Oxford University Press, 1970), 244. See further, and for a rather different reading, Ann Loades, "Simone Weil—Sacrifice: A Problem for Theology," in *Images of Belief in Literature*, 122–37.

80. Quoted in Irwin, *Saints of the Impossible*, 186.

81. Simone Weil, *Intimations of Christianity among the Ancient Greeks* (London: Routledge, 1957), 70.

82. Simone Weil, *La Pesanteur et la grâce* (Paris: Agora/Pocket, 1991), quoted in Irwin, *Saints of the Impossible*, 173.

83. Simone Weil, *L'Enracinement* (Paris: Gallimard, 1990), 271–72, quoted in Irwin, *Saints of the Impossible*, 181 (emphases added).

84. Irwin, *Saints of the Impossible*, 203.

85. H. Oppenheimer, "Life after Death," *Theology* 82 (1979), 335. See also Loades, "Simone Weil—Sacrifice," 133.

86. Weil, *Intimations of Christianity among the Ancient Greeks*, 24–55.

87. Weil, *Intimations of Christianity among the Ancient Greeks*, 55.

88. See further chapter 8 in this volume, p. 139, on Meister Eckhart.

89. Weil, "God's Quest for Man," in *Intimations of Christianity among the Ancient Greeks*, 8.

90. See chapter 2 in this volume, p. 17.

91. Weil, *Waiting on God*, 130, 133.

92. St. Simeon the New Theologian, "Practical and Theological Precepts," in *Writings from the Philokalia: On Prayer of the Heart* (trans. E. Kadloubovsky and G. E. H. Palmer; London: Faber and Faber, 1992), 109.

93. Weil, *Waiting on God*, 141.

94. See Irwin, *Saints of the Impossible*.

95. Weil, *Waiting on God*, 62.

96. See Marion, *God Without Being*, 140.

Chapter 8

1. Jean-Michel Rabaté, *James Joyce, Authorized Reader* (Baltimore: Johns Hopkins University Press, 1991).

2. Friedrich Nietzsche, *The Genealogy of Morals* (trans. Francis Golffing; New York: Doubleday, 1956), 298–99.

3. On the semantics and sources of the term *grunt* in Eckhart's teaching, see Bernard McGinn, *The Mystical Thought of Meister Eckhart*, 38–44.

4. McGinn, *The Mystical Thought of Meister Eckhart*, 115.

5. See Frank Tobin, *Meister Eckhart: Thought and Language* (Philadelphia: University of Pennsylvania Press, 1986), 158–67.

6. See chapter 9 in this volume, on the language of Henry James and Jean-Luc Marion.

7. Miles, *The Word Made Flesh*, 193.

8. Anon., *The Cloud of Unknowing* (trans. Clifton Wolters; Harmondsworth: Penguin, 1961), 51.

9. See chapter 9 in this volume, pp. 163–64, on God's first utterance.

10. See Marion, *Prolegomena to Charity*, 23–26. "More than every other soul, Satan suffers from hell, the ultimate circle of which binds him in a solitude so absolute, an identity so perfect, a consciousness so lucid and a sincerity so transparent to itself, that he becomes there the absolute negative of the person—the perfect idiot" (26).

11. Pseudo-Dionysius, *The Complete Works*, 137. The last phrase is perhaps more familiar in English as *The Cloud of Unknowing*.

12. For the full quotation, see the preface of this book, p. xvi.

13. Eckhart, *Selected Writings*, 39.

14. Maximus the Confessor, *Selected Writings* (trans. George C. Berthold; New York: Paulist, 1985), 160–61. On Eckhart, Maximus and "pan-Christic ontology," see McGinn, *The Mystical Thought of Meister Eckhart*, 119.

15. See chapter 3 in this volume, pp. 40–41, for the full quotation from Athanasius, *Life of Antony*.

16. Thomas Merton, *The Wisdom of the Desert: Sayings from the Desert Fathers of the Fourth Century* (London: Sheldon, 1961), 8.

17. See McGinn, *The Mystical Thought of Meister Eckhart*, 53–70.

18. An anecdote referred to by G. K. Chesterton in his book *Saint Thomas Aquinas* nicely illustrates the dialectical relationship between body and soul, which finally emerges in the oneness and liberation of infinite freedom, and the irrepressible vitality and humor that characterizes the tradition we have been pursuing (and will spill over in the second half of this chapter, in James Joyce). Chesterton writes, "There is one casual anecdote about St. Thomas which illuminates him. . . . It. . . . shows him as a character, and even as a comedy character . . . They steered that reluctant bulk of reflection to a seat in the royal banquet hall; and . . . he. . . . was soon forgotten in the most brilliant and noisy clatter in the world: the noise of French talking. . . . and then suddenly the goblets leapt and rattled on the board and the great table shook, for the friar. . . . had cried out in a strong voice. . . . 'And that will settle the Manichees!'" Quoted in Francesca Murphy, *God Is Not a Story: Realism Revisited* (Oxford: Oxford University Press, 2007), 334.

19. For a discussion on the significance of this in contemporary radical theology, see Don Cupitt, *Taking Leave of God* (London: SCM Press, 1980).

20. A useful review of the thought of Nicholas of Cusa can be found in F. L. Cross and E. A. Livingstone, ed., *The Oxford Dictionary of the Christian Church* (3rd ed.; Oxford: Oxford University Press, 1997), 1149–50.

21. St. Augustine, *Confessions* (trans. R. S. Pine-Coffin; Harmondsworth: Penguin, 1961), 273.

22. It is a theme oft repeated in love poetry. As a modern example, we might recall Louis MacNeice's "Meeting Point":

> Time was away and somewhere else,
> There were two glasses and two chairs
> And two people with the one pulse
> (Somebody stopped the moving stairs):
> Time was away and somewhere else. (*Poetry of the Thirties* [ed. Robin Skelton; Harmondsworth: Penguin, 1964], 192–93)

23. In William Dalrymple's *From the Holy Mountain* (London: HarperCollins, 1998), a contemporary revisiting of the journey of the sixth-century John Moschos as recorded in *The Spiritual Meadow*, there is a delightful photograph of Father Dioscorus discussing with two fellow monks their latest sighting of St. Antony.

24. Frederick Frank, trans., *The Book of Angelus Silesius* (London: Wildwood House, 1976), 43.

25. E. M. Forster, *Aspects of the Novel* (Harmondsworth: Penguin, 1962), 16. The reference, of course, is to Isaac Watt's hymn, "O God, our help in ages past."

26. Raman Selden, ed., *The Theory of Criticism: A Reader* (London: Longman, 1988), 41.

27. Marion, *The Erotic Phenomenon*, 193; see also chapter 4 in this volume, pp. 179–84.

28. Lawrence, *Seven Pillars of Wisdom: A Triumph*, 1:40.

29. Russell, *The Lives of the Desert Fathers*, 50.

30. Eckhart, *Selected Writings*, 151.

31. Angelus Silesius, *The Cherubinic Wanderer* (trans. Maria Shrady; New York: Paulist, 1986), 39. The closest contemporary writings to this classic text are in the works of Thomas J. J. Altizer, especially his *Godhead and the Nothing*. Altizer also refers to the Buddhist tradition to which Silesius has been compared. "So it would not be amiss to pose the question if it is possible that the Buddhist Sangha knows Jesus more deeply than does the Christian Church, and perhaps truly knows the original Jesus by knowing the original Gotama." Altizer, *The Contemporary Jesus*, 163–64. See also, Frank, *The Book of Angelus*.

32. Denys Turner, *The Darkness of God: Negativity in Christian Mysticism* (Cambridge: Cambridge University Press, 1995), 179.

33. Russell, *The Lives of the Desert Fathers*, 66.

34. Eckhart, *Selected Writings*, 193–202. See also chapter 5 in this volume on Abba Isaiah of Scetis and St. Mary of Egypt, and chapter 6 on Velázquez.

35. Dietmar Mieth, *Die Einheit von Vita Activa und Vita Passiva in den deutschen Predigten und Traktaten Meister Eckharts und bei Johannes Tauler* (Regensburg:

Pustet, 1969), 190, quoted in McGinn, *The Mystical Thought of Meister Eckhart*, 158.

36. McGinn, *The Mystical Thought of Meister Eckhart*, 157 (emphasis added).

37. Eckhart, *Selected Writings*, 199.

38. See further on Eckhart's biblical hermeneutics in McGinn, *The Mystical Thought of Meister Eckhart*, 27.

39. Gertrude Bell, *The Desert and the Sown* (1907; New York: Cooper Square, 2001), on the valleys in Judaea, which, to this day, are peopled "by a race of gaunt and starved ascetics, clinging to a tradition of piety that common sense has found it hard to discredit" (10).

40. Robert Detweiler, *Breaking the Fall: Religious Readings of Contemporary Fiction* (San Francisco: Harper and Row, 1989), 35.

41. The arresting phrase is from Ward Blanton's brilliant book, *Displacing Christian Origins: Philosophy, Secularity, and the New Testament* (Chicago: Chicago University Press, 2007), 126. Blanton shares with Altizer a recognition of Albert Schweitzer as the central figure in the last two hundred years of New Testament scholarship.

42. Schweitzer, *The Quest of the Historical Jesus*, 487. See also chapter 1 in this volume, p. 11.

43. Eckhart, *Selected Writings*, 149. See also chapter 3 in this volume, p. 38.

44. C. S. Lewis, *A Grief Observed* (London: Faber and Faber, 1966), 64.

45. See chapter 3 in this volume, pp. 42–43.

46. Isaiah 52:14. See also chapter 2 in this volume, p. 22, on St. John Chrysostom.

47. See also McNamee, *The Desert Reader*, 103.

48. Lawrence, *Seven Pillars of Wisdom*, 1:38.

49. Jasper, *The Sacred Desert*, 187.

50. Even Lawrence wrote of the "death in life" in the desert.

51. Eckhart, *Selected Writings*, 258.

52. See Andrew Marvell, "On Mr. Milton's Paradise Lost," in *The Poems of Andrew Marvell* (ed. Hugh MacDonald; London: Routledge and Kegan Paul, 1952), 64.

53. William Blake, "A Memorable Fancy," in *The Marriage of Heaven and Hell* (1790–93), in *The Complete Works* (ed. Geoffrey Keynes; Oxford: Oxford University Press, 1966), 153.

54. Samuel Taylor Coleridge, *The Statesman's Manual* (1816), in *Lay Sermons*. R. J. White, ed., *The Collected Works* (vol. 6; Princeton: Princeton University Press, 1972), 29. For more detail on this passage, see chapter 9 in this volume, pp. 158–59.

55. On March 30, 1820, Coleridge wrote to Thomas Allsop of his "GREAT WORK, to the preparation of which more than twenty years of my life have been devoted, and on which my hopes of extensive and permanent Utility, of Fame in the noblest sense of the word, mainly rest." Coleridge, *Collected Letters*, 5:27–28.

56. Coleridge's father was an Anglican priest.

57. *The First Prayer Book of Edward VI* (1549), in F. E. Brightman, *The English Rite* (vol. 1; Rivingtons: London, 1915), 204–6.

58. Altizer, *The Self-Embodiment of God*, 96.

59. Seamus Deane, introduction to *Finnegans Wake*, by James Joyce (Harmondsworth: Penguin, 1992), xviii.

60. Thomas J. J. Altizer, *History as Apocalypse* (Albany: State University of New York Press, 1985), 238.

61. Joyce, *Finnegans Wake*, 83.

62. John Milton, *Paradise Lost*. 1667. (ed. Douglas Bush; Oxford: Oxford University Press, 1966), 212.

63. Leahy, *Novitas Mundi*, 360.

64. John Henry Newman, *Apologia Pro Vita Sua* (London: Fontana, 1959), 21.

65. Bell, *The Desert and the Sown*. See p. 212n39.

66. Joyce, *Finnegans Wake*, 3.

67. See James S. Atherton, *The Books at the Wake* (London: Faber, 1959).

68. Rabaté, *James Joyce, Authorized Reader*, 146–48.

69. Steinberg links this statement with "rare and psychologically troubling images" in Renaissance art indicating the Father's "intrusive gesture" on the Son's loins. Steinberg, *The Sexuality of Christ*, 105.

70. Joyce, *Finnegans Wake*, 380–82.

71. See chapter 1 in this volume, p. 191n40, on Süskind's novel *Perfume* and the dark and monstrous reversal of this in the consumption of Grenouille. See also Ledbetter, *Victims and the Postmodern Narrative*.

72. Joyce, *Finnegans Wake*, 381.

73. Nietzsche, *The Genealogy of Morals*, 151, 298–89.

74. Joyce, *Finnegans Wake*, 628.

75. Joyce, *Ulysses*, 704.

76. See Roland Barthes, "The Death of the Author," in *Image Music Text* (trans. Stephen Heath; London: Fontana, 1977), 142–48. Barthes, probably unwittingly, anticipates the death of God—the necessary death in creation—as the great author, when he asserts that "writing is the destruction of every voice, of every point of origin" (142).

77. Joyce, *Finnegans Wake*, 3, 628.

78. Thomas J. J. Altizer, *Genesis and Apocalypse: A Theological Voyage Toward Authentic Christianity* (Louisville: Westminster/John Knox Press, 1990), 172.

79. Rabaté, *James Joyce, Authorized Reader*, 179.

80. See further on "creative joy" in George Dekker, "The All-Animating Joy Within," in *Coleridge and the Literature of Sensibility* (London: Vision, 1978), ch. 4.

81. Thomas Goddard Bergin and Max Harold Fisch, trans. and eds., *The New Science of Giambattista Vico* (3d ed.; Ithaca: Cornell University Press, 1968), 105.

82. Joyce, *Finnegans Wake*, 628 (emphases added).

83. Richard Ellman, *James Joyce* (Oxford: Oxford University Press, 1966) 5.

84. "He doth bestride the narrow world / Like a Colossus" (Shakespeare, *Julius Caesar*, 1.1.135–36). The image is used also of Mark Antony in *Antony and Cleopatra*.
85. Joyce, *Finnegans Wake*, 381 (emphases added).
86. Coleridge, *Biographia Literaria*, 304, and ch. 4 on the secondary imagination.
87. Altizer, *Godhead and the Nothing*, 93.
88. Altizer, *The Self-Embodiment of God*, 96.
89. Joyce, *Finnegans Wake*, 377–78.
90. Joyce, *Ulysses*, 55–56.
91. Leahy, *Novitas Mundi*, 345.

Chapter 9

1. Richard Kearney, *The Wake of Imagination: Toward a Postmodern Culture* (London: Routledge, 1988).
2. J. S. Mill, "Coleridge," *London and Westminster Review* (March 1840); repr. in *Mill's Essays on Literature and Society* (ed. J. B. Schneewind; New York: Collier Books, 1965), 294.
3. Coleridge, *The Statesman's Manual*, 29. See also chapter 8 in this volume, p. 149.
4. William Wordsworth, *Poetical Works* (ed. Thomas Hutchinson; rev. Ernest de Selincourt; Oxford: Oxford University Press, 1969), 744.
5. See also Thomas J. J. Altizer, *The New Apocalypse: The Radical Christian Vision of William Blake* (Aurora, Co.: The Davies Group, 2000), xi.
6. E. S. Shaffer, *"Kubla Khan" and the Fall of Jerusalem: The Mythological School in Biblical Criticism and Secular Literature, 1770–1880* (Cambridge: Cambridge University Press, 1975), 32.
7. G. H. Lewes, *The Life and Works of Goethe* (vol. 1; 2nd ed.; Leipzig, 1858), 227.
8. Coleridge once remarked in a letter to William Mudford of May 28, 1822, that "Words are not *Things*; but they are *Spirits* and *living Agents*." Coleridge, *Collected Letters*, 5:228. In his Preface to *Aids to Reflection* (1825), Coleridge also wrote that "if words are not THINGS, they are LIVING POWERS, by which the things of most importance to mankind are actuated, combined and humanized." Coleridge, *Aids to Reflection* (London: G. Bell and Sons, 1913), xix.
9. Samuel Taylor Coleridge, *Logic*, in *The Collected Works* (ed. J. R. de J. Jackson; Princeton: Princeton University Press, 1981), vol. 13, p. 282. See also Alice D. Snyder, ed. *Coleridge on Logic and Learning* (New Haven: Yale University Press, 1929), 78–79, and Emerson R. Marks, *Coleridge on the Language of Verse* (Princeton: Princeton University Press, 1981), 9–10.
10. Coleridge, *Collected Letters*, 1:625.
11. Coleridge, *The Statesman's Manual*, 30.
12. Goethe, *Faust, Part I* (trans. Philip Wayne; Harmondsworth: Penguin, 1949), 71.

13. Quoted in Clark, *Martin Heidegger*, 112, from Heidegger, *Gesamtausgabe* [*Collected Works*] (Frankfurt: Klosterman, 1975), 39:79 (emphases added).

14. Clark, *Martin Heidegger*, 107.

15. The translation used is that of Michael Hamburger in *Friedrich Hölderlin: Poems and Fragments* (London: Anvil, 1994), 423.

16. Blanchot, *The Space of Literature*, 143.

17. See Clark, *Martin Heidegger*, 105.

18. Hamburger, *Friedrich Hölderlin*, 281.

19. Hamburger, "As on a Holiday" [*Wie Wenn am Feiertage*], in *Friedrich Hölderlin*, 395.

20. Hamburger, Friedrich Hölderlin, 423. See also chapter 2 in this volume, p. 17, on the "false priest," and chapter 4 on Bernanos' *The Diary of a Country Priest*, pp. 54–57.

21. Hamburger, *Friedrich Hölderlin*, 427.

22. Clark, *Martin Heidegger*, 120. See also chapter 7 in this volume, p. 124.

23. Samuel Taylor Coleridge, "Kubla Khan," in *Poetical Works* (ed. Ernest Hartley Coleridge; Oxford: Oxford University Press, 1969), 298.

24. Hamburger, "As on a Holiday," in *Friedrich Hölderlin*, 399.

25. See chapter 6 in this volume, especially on Van Gogh, pp. 101–3.

26. Quoted in William Vaughan, *German Romantic Painting* (2nd ed.; New Haven: Yale University Press, 1994), 93.

27. See, for more detail, Joseph Leo Koerner, *Caspar David Friedrich and the Subject of Landscape* (London: Reaktion Books, 1995), 119.

28. Quoted in Koerner, *Caspar David Friedrich*, 116.

29. See Vaughan, *German Romantic Painting*, 8: Ramdohr's heartless pursuit of good taste in aesthetic experience had already earned him the approbation of Friedrich Wackenroder in his celebrated work *Heartfelt Effusions of an Art-Loving Monk* (1797).

30. Quoted in Vaughan, *German Romantic Painting*, 8.

31. Koerner, *Caspar David Friedrich*, 100.

32. Quoted in Koerner, *Caspar David Friedrich*, 59.

33. The Greek phrase is from Coleridge's *The Statesman's Manual*, 30.

34. Coleridge, "Limbo," *Poetical Works*, 430. See further David Jasper, "S. T. Coleridge. The Poet as Theologian: Two Late Poems," *The Modern Churchman* 26, no. 1 (1983): 35–43.

35. G. W. F. Hegel, *Phenomenology of Spirit* (trans. A. V. Miller; Oxford: Oxford University Press, 1977), 19–20.

36. Hegel, *Phenomenology of Spirit*, 21.

37. See Altizer, *The New Apocalypse*, 64.

38. See also Heidegger, *Poetry, Language, Thought*.

39. Hegel, *Phenomenology of Spirit*, 485.

40. Coleridge, "Limbo," in *Poetical Works*, 431.

41. Blake, *Complete Works*, 153.

42. Coleridge, *The Statesman's Manual*, 30.
43. See Koerner, *Caspar David Friedrich*, 59.
44. See further Alison Jasper, *The Shining Garment of the Text: Gendered Readings of John's Prologue* (Sheffield: Sheffield Academic Press, 1998), 13–32.
45. Susan A. Handelman, *The Slayers of Moses: The Emergence of Rabbinic Interpretation in Modern Literary Theory* (Albany: State University of New York Press, 1982), 38.
46. Coleridge, *The Statesman's Manual*, 30.
47. Koerner, *Caspar David Friedrich*, 96.
48. Blanchot, *The Space of Literature*, 269.

Chapter 10

1. Regis J. Armstrong and Ignatius C. Brady, trans., *Francis and Clare: The Complete Works* (New York: Paulist, 1982), 165–66. See also Lacoste, *Experience and the Absolute*, 193–94.
2. Derek Krueger, *Writing and Holiness: The Practice of Authorship in the Early Christian East* (Philadelphia: University of Pennsylvania Press, 2004), 104.
3. For a fine, recent reading of Henry James and his "convoluted later style," see Terry Eagleton, *The English Novel: An Introduction* (Oxford: Blackwell, 2005), 214–31.
4. Henry James, *The Wings of the Dove* (Harmondsworth: Penguin, 1971), 5.
5. Henry James, *The Art of the Novel: Critical Prefaces* (New York: Charles Scribner's Sons, 1962), 332 (first emphasis added).
6. James, *The Art of the Novel*, 348.
7. Henry James, *The Golden Bowl* (Harmondsworth: Penguin, 1972), 29.
8. James, *The Golden Bowl*, 547.
9. J. Hillis Miller, *The Disappearance of God: Five 19th Century Writers* (New York: Schocken, 1965), 271.
10. Hans Urs von Balthasar, *The Glory of the Lord: A Theological Aesthetics* (vol. 3 of *Studies in Theological Style: Lay Styles*; trans. Andrew Louth et al.; Edinburgh: T & T Clark, 1986), 353–99.
11. John Henry Newman, *An Essay in Aid of a Grammar of Assent* (London: Burns, Oates, & Co., 1870), 343.
12. G. M. Hopkins, from the "terrible" sonnets: "And my lament / Is cries countless, cries like dead letters sent / To dearest him that lives alas! Away." Hopkins, *Selected Poems and Prose* (ed. W. H. Gardner; Harmondsworth: Penguin, 1953), 62.
13. The words are those of Altizer in a private letter to me.
14. Hopkins, "My own heart let me more have pity on," in *Selected Poems and Prose*, 63.
15. J. Hillis Miller, "Naming and Doing: Speech Acts in Hopkins's Poems," *Religion and Literature* 22, nos. 2–3 (1990): 188.

16. Hopkins, "That Nature Is a Heraclitean Fire and of the Comfort of the Resurrection," in *Selected Poems and Prose*, 66. See further David Jasper, "God's Better Beauty: Language and the Poetry of Gerard Manley Hopkins," *Christianity and Literature* 34, no. 3 (Spring 1985), 9–22. This article is now over twenty years old, and I would now want to move away from its triumphalist tone in reading Hopkins, indeed, to *read* Hopkins in a very different way.

17. Edwards, *The Plain Sense of Things*, 184, and see also the preface to this volume, pp. xiii–xiv.

18. Lacoste, *Experience and the Absolute*, 19.

19. Throughout these reflections I am heavily indebted to the work of Lacoste and of Marion.

20. See Lacoste, *Experience and the Absolute*, 44–45.

21. Matthew Arnold, "Stanzas from the Grande Chartreuse," in *The Poems of Matthew Arnold, 1849–1867* (Oxford: Oxford University Press, 1924), 260.

22. Nicholas of Cusa, *De Docta Ignorantia* (1440), in *Selected Spiritual Writings* (trans. H. Lawrence Bond; New York: Paulist, 1997). "The simply and absolutely maximum, than which there cannot be anything greater, is greater than we can comprehend, for it is infinite truth; therefore, we can attain it only incomprehensibly" (91).

23. Iris Murdoch, *Under the Net* (London: Triad/Panther, 1979), 255.

24. Russell, *The Lives of the Desert Fathers*, 50.

25. Lacoste, *Experience and the Absolute*, 194.

26. Edwards, *The Plain Sense of Things*. The term "normal nihilism" is taken from the subtitle of Edwards' *The Plain Sense of Things: The Fate of Religion in an Age of Normal Nihilism*.

27. See also Thomas J. J. Altizer, "William Blake and the Role of Myth in the Radical Christian Vision," in T. J. J. Altizer and William Hamilton, *Radical Theology and the Death of God* (Harmondsworth: Penguin, 1966), 169–88.

28. In his essay "Poetically Man Dwells," in *Poetry, Language and Thought*, 219, Heidegger quotes from Hölderlin:

> As long as Kindness,
> The Pure, still stays with his heart, man
> Not unhappily measures himself
> Against the godhead. Is God unknown?
> Is he manifest like the sky? I'd sooner
> Believe the latter. It's the measure of man.

29. Clark, *Martin Heidegger*, 99.

30. Quoted in Don Cupitt, *Mysticism after Modernity*, 73.

31. See also chapter 2 in this volume, p. 16.

32. Werner G. Jeanrond, "Love Enlightened: The Promises and Ambiguities of Love," in *Faith in the Enlightenment? The Critique of the Enlightenment Revisited* (ed. Lieve Boeve et al.; Amsterdam: Rodopi, 2006), 283.

33. Marion, *The Erotic Phenomenon*, 215.
34. Marion, *The Erotic Phenomenon*, 210.
35. John Donne, "The Sun Rising," in *The Complete English Poems*, 80. Louis Mac-Neice, "Meeting Point" (1939).
36. Hamburger, *Friedrich Hölderlin*, 280–81.
37. Don Cupitt, *The Long Legged Fly: A Theology of Language and Desire* (London: SCM Press, 1987).
38. Marion, *The Erotic Phenomenon*, 187.
39. See Mark 9:24.
40. Marion, *The Erotic Phenomenon*, 184–222.
41. Marion, *The Erotic Phenomenon*, 198 (emphases added).
42. Marion, *The Erotic Phenomenon*, 201.
43. See Charles Conti, *Metaphysical Personalism: An Analysis of Austin Farrer's Theistic Metaphysics* (Oxford: Oxford University Press, 1995), 172.
44. See, again, Harpham, *The Ascetic Imperative*.
45. Nicholas of Cusa, *Selected Spiritual Writings*, 209–13.
46. Nicholas of Cusa, *Selected Spiritual Writings*, 209.
47. Morimichi Watanabe, introduction to *Selected Spiritual Writings*, by Nicholas of Cusa, 38.
48. Herbert, "Love (III)," in *The English Poems of George Herbert*, 661.

BIBLIOGRAPHY

What follows is not intended to be a comprehensive bibliography of all the works referred to in this book. Details may be found in the footnotes to each chapter. Rather, this is a list of the most important texts used.

Biblical references are generally from the New Revised Standard Version, except where circumstances dictate preferable alternative versions.

Altizer, Thomas J. J. *Genesis as Apocalypse: A Theological Voyage Toward Authentic Christianity.* Louisville: Westminster/John Knox Press, 1990.

———. *Godhead and the Nothing.* Albany: SUNY Press, 2003.

———. *History as Apocalypse.* Albany: SUNY Press, 1985.

———. *The Contemporary Jesus.* London: SCM, 1998.

———. *The Descent into Hell: A Study of the Radical Reversal of the Christian Consciousness.* Philadelphia: J. B. Lippincott, 1970.

———. *The New Apocalypse: The Radical Vision of William Blake.* Aurora, Colo.: The Davies Group, 2000.

———. *The Self-Embodiment of God.* New York: Harper & Row, 1977.

———. *Total Presence: The Language of Jesus and the Language of Today.* New York: Seabury Press, 1980.

Altizer, Thomas J. J., and William Hamilton. *Radical Theology and the Death of God.* Harmondsworth, England: Penguin, 1968.

Angelus Silesius. *The Cherubinic Wanderer.* Translated by Maria Shrady. New York: Paulist Press, 1986.

Armstrong, Regis J., and Ignatius C. Brady, trans. *Francis and Clare: The Complete Works.* New York: Paulist Press, 1982.

Athanasius. *The Life of St. Antony and the Letter to Marcellinus.* Translated by Robert C. Gregg. New York: Paulist Press, 1980.

Augustine of Hippo. *The City of God*. Translated by Henry Bettenson. Harmondsworth, England: Penguin, 1972.

Bal, Mieke, *Reading "Rembrandt": Beyond the Word-Image Opposition*. Cambridge: Cambridge University Press, 1991.

Balthasar, Hans Urs von. *Studies in Theological Style: Lay Styles*. Vol. 3 of *The Glory of the Lord: A Theological Aesthetics*. Translated by Andrew Louth et al. Edinburgh: T & T Clark, 1986.

Barker, Pat. *Regeneration*. Harmondsworth, England: Penguin, 1992.

Bernanos, Georges. *The Diary of a Country Priest*. Translated by Pamela Morris. New York: Carroll & Graf, 2002.

Bernard of Clairvaux. *Selected Works*. Translated by G. R. Evans. New York: Paulist Press, 1987.

Blake, William. *The Complete Works*. Edited by Geoffrey Keynes Oxford: Oxford University Press, 1966.

Blakemore, Colin, and Sheila Jennett, eds. *The Oxford Companion to the Body*. Oxford: Oxford University Press, 2001.

Blanchot, Maurice, *The Space of Literature*. Translated by Ann Smock. Lincoln: University of Nebraska Press, 1982.

Bowie, Andrew. *Aesthetics and Subjectivity from Kant to Nietszche*. Manchester: Manchester University Press, 1990.

Bowles, Paul. *The Sheltering Sky*. Harmondsworth, England: Penguin, 1969.

Boyd, Jane, and Philip Esler. *Visuality and the Biblical Text: Interpreting Velázquez' "Christ with Martha and Mary" as a Test Case*. Florence, Italy: Leo S. Olschki, 2004.

Brooks, Peter. *Body Work: Objects of Desire in Modern Narrative*. Cambridge, Mass.: Harvard University Press, 1993.

Brown, Frank Burch. *Religious Aesthetics: A Theological Study of Making and Meaning*. London: Macmillan, 1980.

Brown, Peter. *The Body and Society: Men, Women and Sexual Renunciation in Early Christianity*. New York: Columbia University Press, 1988.

———. *The Cult of the Saints: Its Rise and Function in Latin Christianity*. Chicago: University of Chicago Press, 1982.

Burrus, Virginia. *The Sex Lives of the Saints: An Erotics of Ancient Hagiography*. Philadelphia: University of Pennsylvania Press, 2004.

Burton-Christie, Douglas. *The Word in the Desert: Scripture and the Quest for Holiness in Early Christian Monasticism*. Oxford: Oxford University Press, 1993.

Bynum, Caroline Walker. *Holy Feast, Holy Fast: The Religious Significance of Food to Medieval Women*. Berkeley: University of California Press, 1987.

Bynum, Caroline Walker. *The Resurrection of the Body in Western Christianity, 200–1336*. New York: Columbia University Press, 1995.

Bynum, Caroline Walker, and Paul Freedman, eds. *Last Things: Death and the Apocalypse in the Middle Ages*. University Park: University of Pennsylvania Press, 2000.

Caponi, Gena Dagel. *Paul Bowles: Romantic Savage*. Carbondale: Southern Illinois University Press, 1994.

Celan, Paul. *Selected Poems*. Translated by Michael Hamburger. Harmondsworth, England: Penguin, 1990.

Clark, Timothy. *Martin Heidegger*. London: Routledge, 2002.

Coakley, Sarah, ed. *Religion and the Body*. Cambridge: Cambridge University Press, 1997.

Coleridge, S. T. *Biographia Literaria*. Vol. 7 of *The Collected Works*. Edited by James Engell and W. Jackson Bate, 1817. Repr. Princeton: Princeton University Press, 1983.

———. *The Collected Letters*. Edited by Earl Lesle Griggs. 7 vols. Oxford: Oxford University Press, 1956–1971.

———. *The Statesman's Manual*, in *Lay Sermons*. Vol. 6 of *The Collected Works*. Edited by R. J. White. Princeton: Princeton University Press, 1972.

Cooper, Adam G. *The Body in St. Maximus the Confessor: Holy Flesh, Wholly Deified*. Oxford: Oxford University Press, 2005.

Crace, Jim. *Quarantine*. Harmondsworth, England: Penguin, 1997.

Cupitt, Don. *Mysticism after Modernity*. Oxford: Blackwell, 1998.

———. *Taking Leave of God*. London: SCM, 1980.

Danto, Arthur C. *The Abuse of Beauty: Aesthetics and the Concept of Art*. Chicago: Open Court, 2003.

———. *The Body/Body Problem: Selected Essays*. Berkeley: University of California Press, 1999.

———. *The Transfiguration of the Commonplace*. Cambridge, Mass.: Harvard University Press, 1981.

De Certeau, Michel. *The Sixteenth and Seventeenth Centuries*. Vol. 1, *The Mystic Fable*. Translated by Michael B. Smith. Chicago: University of Chicago Press, 1992.

Detweiler, Robert. *Breaking the Fall: Religious Readings of Contemporary Fiction*. San Francisco: Harper & Row, 1989.

Donne, John. *The Complete English Poems*. Edited by A. J. Smith. Harmondsworth, England: Penguin, 1971.

Dostoevsky, Fyodor. *The Idiot*. Translated by Rosemary Edmonds. Harmondsworth, England: Penguin, 1966.

Eckhart, Meister. *Selected Writings.* Translated by Oliver Davies. Harmondsworth, England: Penguin, 1994.

Edwards, James C. *The Plain Sense of Things: The Fate of Religion in an Age of Normal Nihilism.* University Park: Pennsylvania State University Press, 1997.

Feher, Michel, Ramona Naddaff, and Nadia Tazi, eds. *Fragments for a History of the Human Body.* Part 2. New York: Zone Books, 1989.

Fish, Stanley. *Is There a Text in This Class? The Authority of Interpretive Communities.* Cambridge, Mass.: Harvard University Press, 1980.

Flaubert, Gustave. *The Temptation of Saint Anthony.* Translated by Lafcadio Hearn. New York: The Modern Library, 2001.

Flood, Gavin. *The Ascetic Self: Subjectivity, Memory and Tradition* Cambridge: Cambridge University Press, 2004.

Foucault, Michel. Introduction to *The Temptation of Saint Anthony*, by Gustave Flaubert. New York: The Modern Library, 2001.

———. *The Care of the Self.* Vol 3 of *The History of Sexuality.* Translated by Robert Hurley. Harmondsworth, England: Oenguin, 1990.

France, Anatole. *Thaïs.* Translated by Robert B. Douglas, 1920. Repr. Rockville, MD: Wildside Press, 2005.

Goethe, Johann Wolfgang. *Faust. Part One.* Translated by Philip Wayne. Harmondsworth, England: Penguin, 1949.

Graham, Jorie. *Erosion.* Princeton: Princeton University Press, 1983.

Greene, Graham. *Monsignor Quixote.* Harmondsworth, England: Penguin, 1983.

Gregory of Nyssa. *The Life of Moses.* Translated by Abraham J. Malherbe and Everett Ferguson. NewYork: Paulist Press, 1978.

Harpham, Geoffrey Galt. *The Ascetic Imperative in Culture and Criticism* Chicago: University of Chicago Press, 1987.

Hegel, G. W. F. *Aesthetics: Lectures on Fine Art.* Vol. 1. Translated by T. M. Knox. Oxford: Clarendon Press, 1988.

———. *Phenomenology of Spirit.* Translated by A. V. Miller. Oxford: Oxford University Press, 1977.

Heidegger, Martin. *Poetry, Language, Thought.* Translated by Albert Hofstader. New York: Harper & Row, 1971.

Herbert, George. *The Complete English Poems.* Edited by John Tobin. Harmondsworth, England: Penguin, 1991.

———. *The English Poems.* Edited by Helen Wilcox. Cambridge: Cambridge University Press, 2007.

Hill, Geoffrey. *New and Collected Poems, 1952–1992*. New York: Houghton Mifflin Harcourt, 1994.

Hoekstra, Hidda. *Rembrandt and the Bible*. Utrecht: Magna Books, 1990.

Hölderlin, Friedrich. *Poems and Fragments*. Translated by Michael Hamburger. London: Anvil Press, 1994.

Hopkins, G. M. *Selected Poems and Prose*. Edited by W. H. Gardner. Harmondsworth, England: Penguin, 1953.

Howes, Graham. *The Art of the Sacred: An Introduction to the Aesthetics of Art and Belief*. London: I. B. Tauris, 2007.

Hrotsvit. *The Dramas of Hrotsvit of Gandersheim*. Translated by Katharina M. Wilson. Saskatoon, Saskatchewan: Peregrina Publishing, 1985.

Irwin, Alexander. *Saints of the Impossible: Bataille, Weil and the Politics of the Sacred*. Minneapolis: University of Minnesota Press, 2002.

Isaiah of Scetis. *Ascetic Discourses*. Translated by John Chryssavgis and Pachomios (Robert) Penkett. Kalamazoo: Cistercian Publications, 2002.

Iser, Wolfgang. *The Implied Reader: Patterns of Communication in Prose Fiction from Bunyan to Beckett*. Baltimore: Johns Hopkins University Press, 1974.

James, Henry. *The Art of the Novel: Critical Prefaces*. New York: Charles Scribner's Sons, 1962.

———. *The Golden Bowl*. Harmondsworth, England: Penguin, 1972.

———. *The Wings of the Dove*. Harmondsworth, England: Penguin, 1971.

Jasper, David, ed. *Images of Belief in Literature*. London: Macmillan, 1984.

———, ed. *Postmodernism, Literature and the Future of Theology*. London: Macmillan, 1993.

———. *The Sacred Desert: Religion, Literature, Art, and Culture*. Oxford: Blackwell, 2004.

John of Damascus. *Three Treatises on the Divine Images*. Translated by Andrew Louth. New York: St. Vladimir's Press, 2003.

Joyce, James. *Finnegans Wake*. Harmondsworth, England: Penguin, 1992.

———. *Ulysses*. Harmondsworth, England: Penguin, 1968.

Julian of Norwich. *Revelations of Divine Love*. Translated by Clifton Wolters. Harmondsworth, England: Penguin, 1966.

Kadloubovsky, E., and G. E. H. Palmer, trans. *Writings from the Philokalia: On the Prayer of the Heart*. London: Faber & Faber, 2000.

Kearney, Richard. *The Wake of Imagination: Toward a Postmodern Culture*. London: Routledge, 1988.

Koerner, Joseph Leo. *Caspar David Friedrich and the Subject of Landscape*. London: Reaktion Books, 1995.

Kristeva, Julia. *Black Sun: Depression and Melancholia*. New York: Columbia University Press, 1980.

Krueger, Derek. *Writing and Holiness: The Practice of Authorship in the Early Christian East*. Philadelphia: University of Pennsylvania Press, 2004.

Lacoste, Jean-Yves. *Experience and the Absolute: Disputed Questions on the Humanity of Man*. Translated by Mark Raftery-Skehan. New York: Fordham University Press, 2004.

Laqueur, Thomas. *Making Sex: Body and Gender from the Greeks to Freud*. Cambridge, Mass.: Harvard University Press, 1990.

Lawrence, T. E. *Seven Pillars of Wisdom*. London: World Books, 1939.

Leahy, D. G. *Novitas Mundi: Perception of the History of Being*. New York: SUNY Press, 1994.

Ledbetter, Mark. *Victims and the Postmodern Narrative, or Doing Violence to the Body*. London: Macmillan, 1996.

Marion, Jean-Luc. *God Without Being*. Translated by Thomas A. Carlson. Chicago: University of Chicago Press, 1991.

———. *Prolegomena to Charity*. Translated by Stephen Lewis. New York: Fordham University Press, 2002.

———. *The Erotic Phenomenon*. Translated by Stephen E. Lewis. Chicago: University of Chicago Press, 2007.

Maximus Confessor. *Selected Writings*. Translated by George C. Berthold. New York: Paulist Press, 1985.

McGinn, Bernard. *The Mystical Thought of Meister Eckhart: The Man From Whom God Hid Nothing*. New York: Herder & Herder, 2001.

McNamee, Gregory, ed. *The Desert Reader: A Literary Companion*. Albuquerque: University of New Mexico Press, 1995.

Merton, Thomas. *The Wisdom of the Desert: Sayings from the Desert Fathers of the Fourth Century*. London: Sheldon Press, 1961.

Michie, Helena. *The Flesh Made Word: Female Figures and Women's Bodies*. Oxford: Oxford University Press, 1987.

Miles, Margaret R. *The Word Made Flesh: A History of Christian Thought*. Oxford: Blackwell, 2005.

Miller, J. Hillis. *The Disappearance of God: Five Nineteenth Century Writers*. New York: Schocken Books, 1965.

Morgan, David. *The Sacred Gaze: Religious Visual Culture in Theory and Practice*. Berkeley: University of California Press, 2005.

Nicholas of Cusa, *Selected Spiritual Writings*. Translated by H. Lawrence Bond. New York: Paulist Press, 1997.

Nietzsche, Friedrich, *The Genealogy of Morals*. Translated by Francis Golffing. New York: Doubleday, 1956.

Ondaatje, Michael. *The English Patient*. London: Picador, 1993.

Oppenheimer, Helen. "Life after Death." *Theology* 82 (1979): 328–35.

Origen, *Selected Works*. Translated by Rowan A. Greer New York: Paulist Press, 1979.

Owen, Wilfred. *The Collected Poems*. Edited by C. Day Lewis. London: Chatto & Windus, 1963.

Pagels, Elaine. *Beyond Belief: The Secret Gospel of Thomas*. London: Macmillan, 2003.

Pater, Walter. *Marius the Epicurean*. New York: New American Library, 1970.

Pavić, Milorad. *Landscape Painted with Tea*. Translated by Christina Pribićević-Zorić. New York: Knopf, 1990.

Plate, S. Brent. *Walter Benjamin, Religion and Aesthetics: Rethinking Religion through the Arts*. New York and London: Routledge, 2005.

Pseudo-Dionysius. *The Complete Works*. Translated by Colm Luibheid. New York: Paulist Press, 1987.

Rabaté, Jean-Michel. *James Joyce, Authorized Reader*. Baltimore: Johns Hopkins University Press, 1991.

Ratuskinskaya, Irina. *Pencil Letter*. Newcastle: Bloodaxe Books, 1988.

Ricoeur, Paul. *The Symbolism of Evil*. Translated by Emerson Buchanan. Boston: Bacon Press, 1969.

Roberts, Michèle. *Impossible Saints*. London: Virago Press, 1998.

———. *The Wild Girl*. London: Minerva, 1991.

Roskill, Mark, ed. *The Letters of Vincent van Gogh*. London: Fontana, 1963.

Russell, Norman, trans. *The Lives of the Desert Fathers* (*Historia Monachorum*). Kalamazoo: Cistercian Publications, 1981.

Schama, Simon. *Rembrandt's Eyes*. London: Penguin, 2000.

Schweitzer, Albert. *The Quest of the Historical Jesus*. Translated by W. Montgomery, J. R. Coates, Susan Cupitt, and John Bowden. London: SCM, 2000.

Steinberg, Leo. *The Sexuality of Christ in Renaissance Art and in Modern Oblivion*. 2d ed. Chicago: University of Chicago Press, 1996.

Suleiman, Susan Rubin, ed. *The Female Body in Western Culture: Contemporary Perspectives*. Cambridge, Mass.: Harvard University Press, 1985.

Turner, Denys, *The Darkness of God: Negativity in Christian Mysticism*. Cambridge: Cambridge University Press, 1995.

Updike, John. *In the Beauty of the Lilies*. London: Hamish Hamilton, 1996.

———. *Seek My Face*. Harmondsworth, England: Penguin, 2003.

Vattimo, Gianni. *Belief.* Translated by Luca D'Isanto and David Webb. Cambridge: Polity Press, 1999.

Vaughan, William. *German Romantic Painting.* 2d ed. New Haven: Yale University Press, 1994.

Viola, Bill. *Reasons for Knocking at an Empty House: Writings, 1973–1994.* London: Thames & Hudson, 1995.

Ward, Benedicta. *Harlots of the Desert: A Study of Repentance in Early Monastic Sources.* Kalamazoo: Cistercian Publications, 1987.

———, trans. *The Wisdom of the Desert Fathers (Apophthegmata Patrum).* Oxford: SLG Press, 1986.

Weil, Simone. *Intimations of Christianity Among the Ancient Greeks.* London: Routledge, 1957.

———. *Waiting on God.* Translated by Emma Craufurd. London: Fount, 1977.

White, James Boyd, *"This Book of Starres": Learning to Read George Herbert.* Ann Arbor: University of Michigan Press, 1994.

Wills, Lawrence M. "Ascetic Theology before Asceticism? Jewish Narratives and the Decentering of the Self." *JAAR* 74, no. 4 (2006): 902–25.

Wimbush, Vincent L., and Richard Valantasis, eds. *Asceticism.* Oxford: Oxford University Press, 1998.

Wolf, Norbert. *Velázquez, 1599–1660: The Face of Spain.* Köln: Taschen, 2005.

Wolters, Clifton, trans. *The Cloud of Unknowing.* Harmondsworth, England: Penguin, 1961.

Wordsworth, William. *Poetical Works.* Edited by Thomas Hutchinson. Revised, Ernest de Selincourt. Oxford: Oxford University Press, 1969.

Wyschogrod, Edith. *Saints and Postmodernism: Revisioning Moral Philosophy.* Chicago: University of Chicago Press, 1990.

Zabala, Santiago, ed. *The Future of Religion.* New York: Columbia University Press, 2005.

INDEX

Note: Bold page numbers indicate where detailed and central discussions of the person or subject appear.

Abbey in the Oak Forest (Friedrich), 165
Abstract Expressionism, 164
Abuse of Beauty, The (Danto), 2, 5
Adam Bede (George Eliot), 110
Adoration of the Magi, The (Velázquez), 92
Adorno, Theodore, 59
Aesthetics (Hegel), 7
Aids to Reflection (Coleridge), 214
Alexander the Great, 66
Allsop, Thomas, 212
Althaus-Reid, Marcella, 28
Altizer, Thomas J. J., 1–2, 21, 28–29, 87–88, 102, 149, 153, 155, 185
Ambigua (*Difficulties*) (Maximus), 5
Ambrose, St., 64
Andrewes, Lancelot, 121
Angelus Silesius, 131, 140, 142, 174, 211
Anil's Ghost (Ondaatje), 112
Anna Livia Plurabelle, 143, 152
Antigone (Sophocles), 183
Antony of Egypt, St., xii, xiii, 5, 10, 16, 19, 20–21, 40–41, 42, 44, 50, 64, 67, 71, 75, 82, 88, 90, 100, 129, 137, 138, 140, 143, 147–48, 172

Antony, St., *Life of* (Athanasius), 40–41, 44, 50, 172
Apocalypse of Peter, 28
Apollo of Piombino, 105
Apologia Pro Vita Sua (Newman), 150
Apology for Poetry, An (Sidney), 120–21
Apophthegmata Patrum. See *Wisdom (Sayings) of the Desert Fathers, The (Apophthegmata Patrum)*
Aquinas, St. Thomas, 154, 210
Arabian Nights, The, 143
Arnold, Matthew, 177
Art of the West, The (Focillon), 29
"As on a holiday" (*Wie wenn am Feiertage*) (Hölderlin), 162
Ascent of Mount Carmel (St. John of the Cross), 180
Ascetic Discourses (Abbot Isaiah), 72
Ascetic Imperative in Culture and Criticism, The (Harpham), 2
Ascetic Self, The (Flood), 2
Aspects of the Novel (Forster), 140
"At Luca Signorelli's Resurrection of the Body" (Graham), 34, 103–4
Athanasius, St., xii, 10, 40–41, 50, 114, 118, 137, 138, 146, 147, 172
Athos, Mount, 10, 52, 57

Augustine of Hippo, St., 47, 88, 91,
103, 104–5, 139, 141, 151, 182

Bacchae, The (Euripides), 26
Bach, J. S., 60
Bacon, Francis, 118
Baker-Smith, Dominic, 120
Bal, Mieke, 89, 94, 100, 104
Balthasar, Hans Urs von, xi, 174
Barker, Pat, 113
Bataille, Georges, 133
Baudinet, Marie-José, 40
Beckett, Samuel, 153
Being and Time (Sein und Zeit), 8, 173
Bernanos, Goerges, 6, **54–57**
Bernard of Clairvaux, St., 3, 7, 11–12,
37–39, 40, 45, 48, 99, 123
Bertolucci, Bernado, 83
Beyond Belief (Pagels), 25–26
Bhagavad Gita, 130
Biographia Literaria (Coleridge), 153,
158, 197
Bisschop, Jan de, 203
Blake, William, 23, 24, 26–27, 28–29,
148–49, 151, 155, 168, 181
Blanchot, Maurice, 119, 169–70
Blanton, Ward, 212
Bloch, Ernst, 138
Bloom, Harold, 43
Bloom, Molly, 106, 143, 152, 154, 156
bodegónes, 92, 95, 99
*Body of the Dead Christ in the Tomb,
The* (Holbein), 18, 32, 36, 39, 41,
43, 61, 112
Body Work (Brooks), 27
Body/Body Problem, The (Danto), 105–6
Book of Commn Prayer, The, 17, 119,
122–23, 125, 149
Bowles, Paul, **80–85**
Boyd, Jane, 91, 92, 94
Brideshead Revisited (Waugh), 21
Brillo Box (Warhol), 9
Brooks, Peter, 27
Brown, Peter, 23, 44

Bultmann, Rudolf, 126
Burroughs, William, 83
Burton-Christie, Douglas, 51
Bynum, Caroline Walker, 19

Cage, John, 9
Camus, Albert, 81
"Canticle for Good Friday" (Hill), 61
Caponi, Gena Dagel, 82–83
Caravaggio, Michelangelo Merisi da,
92, 100
Carceri d'Invenzione (Piranesi), 62
Care of the Self, The (*History of Sexuality
3*) (Foucault), 70
Cassian, John, 198
Celan, Paul, **59–60**
Cézanne, Paul, 87
Cherubinic Wanderer, The (Angelus
Silesius), 142
Chesterton, G. K., 210
Christ of St. John of the Cross (Dali), 194
Christ with Martha and Mary
(Velázquez), **91–101**
"Christmas" (Herbert), 125
Chrysostom, St. John, 22, 64, 119
Civitate Dei, De (*The City of God*)
(Augustine), 103, 104–5
Clark, Timothy, 124, 161, 163
Clement of Alexandria, 138
Cloud of Unknowing, The, 136–37
Coakley, Sarah, 2
coincidentia oppositorum, 10, 139,
140, 145, 146, 163
Coleridge, Samuel Taylor, 121, 149,
153, 154, 157, 158–60, 163, 165,
166, 168–69
Colossians, Epistle to, 123
Colour Beginning (Turner), 164
Commentary on the Song of Songs (Ori-
gen), 47, 79
Confessions (Augustine), 139, 182
Conley, Tom, 29
Cooper, Adam G., 6
Copland, Aaron, 83

Corinthians I, Epistle to, 12, 52, 72, 73
Corinthians II, Epistle to, 39
Correggio, Antonio, 89
Crace, Jim, xvi
Cranmer, Thomas, 123, 125, 149
Crime and Punishment (Dostoevsky), 18
Critique of Judgement, The (*Third Critique*) (Kant), xii, 8, 132, 168
Critique of Practical Reason (Kant), xii
Cross on the Mountains, The (Friedrich), 165
Cunningham, Martin, 154
Cupitt, Don, 37–38, 182

Da Vinci, Leonardo, 24–25
Danaë (Rembrandt), **88–90**, 106
Daniel, 28, 49
Dante, Alighieri, 105
Danto, Arthur C., xii, 2, 5, 105–6, 107
De Andrea, John, 27–28
De Docta Ignorantia (*On Learned Ignorance*) (Nicholas of Cusa), 139
De Man, Paul, 16
Deane, Seamus, 149
Deleuze, Gilles, 29
Derrida, Jacques, 4, 138, 139
Descartes, René, 106, 174, 182
Descent of the Dove, The (Williams), 196
desert absolu, xviii, 27, 82, 139
Desert Fathers, The (Waddell), 65
Detweiler, Robert, 144
Deus unus est (Eckhart), 147
Devotions Upon Emergent Occasions (Donne), 120
Dialogus de Deo abscondito (*Dialogue on the Hidden God*) (Nicholas of Cusa), 184–85
Diary of a Country Priest, The (Bernanos), 6, **54–57**
Dickens, Charles, 79
Didache, 28
Dillenberger, Jane, 94
Divided Self, The (Laing), 83
Dix, Dom Gregory, 148

Donne, John, 31, 39, 120, 181, 182
Dostoevsky, Fyodor, 18, 32–33, 36, 39, 40, 43, 61, 103, 110
Drury, John, 94
Duchamp, Marcel, 9
Duchess of Malfi, The (Webster), 36
Duns Scotus, 174

Eagleton, Terry, 109
East of Eden (Steinbeck), 155
"Easter-Wings" (Herbert), 123
Eckhart, Meister, xvii, xix, 6, 8, 19, 20, 27, 33, 38, 51, 72, 91, 101, **135–48**, 183
"Ecstacy, The" (Donne), 31
Edwards, David L., 118
Edwards, James C., xiii, 171
Eichhorn, Johann Gottfried, 159
Elijah, xv, 75
Eliot, George, 110
Eliot, T. S., 154
Ellmann, Richard, 154
Emmaus road, 10–11, 51, 167
English Patient, The (Ondaatje), 111–12
Enright, D. J., 121
Ephesians, Epistle to, 52
Erasmus, Desiderius, 120
Erotic Phenomenon, The (Marion), 31, **179–84**
Esler, Philip, 91, 93, 94
"Essay, Supplementary to the Preface to *The Lyrical Ballads*" (Wordsworth), 159
Eucharist, 109–12, 116–17, 122–23, 128, 130, 131, 133, 151, 156
Euripides, 26
Eustochius, 65
Exodus, 158
Ezekiel, 148, 149, 158

Farrer, Austin, 184, 206
Faust, Part I (Goethe), 60, 160–61
Fear and Trembling (Kierkegaard), 178
Felix culpa, 151, 152, 155

Finnegans Wake (Joyce), 7, 105, 106, 136, 143, 144, **148–56**, 173
Flaubert, Gustave, 16, 20–21, 73
Flesh Made Word, The (Michie), 193
Flood, Gavin, 2
Fold, The (Deleuze), 29
Forster, E. M., 140
Foucault, Michel, 16, 70
Foundation: Matter the Body Itself (Leahy), 12
Fragmenta in Cantica Canticorum (Hippolytus), 47
France, Anatole, 66, 87, 144
Francis of Assissi, St., 171–72, 174, 176, 178
Freedberg, David, 83
Freud, Sigmund, 83
Friedrich, Caspar David, 161, **164–66**, 167, 168

Galatians, Epistle to, 139, 147
Gelassenheit, 144–45
Genealogy of Morals, The (Nietzsche), 135, 152
Generosity and the Christian Future (Newlands), 69
Genesis, xviii, 44, 48, 144, 146, 148, 154, 155
"Germania" (Höldelin), 161, 162–63
Gill, Eric, 114–15
Glory of the Lord, The (von Balthasar), xi, 174
Gnosticism, 201
God Knows (Heller), 35–36
God Without Being (Marion), 22
Godhead and the Nothing (Altizer), 155
Godwin, William, 121, 160
Goethe, J. W. von, 60, 159, 160–61, 166
Golden Bowl, The (James), 173–74
Golden Legend, The (Voragine), 66
"Good Morrow, The" (Donne), 39
Gorgonia, 5
Graham, Jorie, 34, 103–4

"Grand Inquisitor, The" (Dostoevsky), 103
Grapes of Wrath, The (Steinbeck), 116
Great Expectations (Dickens), 79
Greco, El (Domenikos Theotocopoulos), 91, 92
Greene, Graham, 110–11
Gregory Nazianzen, 5
Gregory of Nyssa, 5, 72, 135, 137, 175
Gregory of Sinai, St., 10
Grief Observed, A (Lewis), 145
Grünewald, Mathias, 20, 33, **42–43**, 61, 112, 146, 165

Handelman, Susan, 169
Harlots of the Desert (Ward), 64
Harpham, Geoffrey Galt, 2, 15, 20, 43–44
Hebrews, Epistle to, 72
Hegel, G. W. F., 6, 7–8, 10, 11, 153, 154, 159, 161, 162, 166–68, 178
Heidegger, Martin, xiii–xiv, xix, 1, 3, 7, 8–9, 117, 124, 126, 137, 153, 161–63, 173, 175, 180, 184, 185, 217
Heller, Joseph, 35–36
Hengel, Martin, 25
Herbert, George, 39, 116, **117–28**, 135, 150, 161, 182
Herder, Johann Gottfried, 159
Hermitage Museum, St. Petersburg, 88, 89
Hill, Geoffrey, 61, 117
Hippolytus of Rome, St., 47
Historia Monachorum. See *Lives of the Desert Fathers, The* (*Historia Monachorum*)
"History of World Languages" (Enright), 121
Hitler, Adolf, 129
Hoggart, Richard, 114
Holbein, Hans the Younger, 18, 32–33, 39, 41, 43, 61, 112
"Holbein's Dead Christ" (Kristeva), 32

Hölderlin, Friedrich, 17, 124, 161–63,
165, 167, 169–70, 180, 182, 217
"Hölderlin's Itinerary" (Blanchot),
169–70
Holocaust, 9
"Holy Scriptures (I), The" (Herbert),
127–28
"Homecoming" (Hölderlin), 161–62,
182
Homer, 132
Hopkins, Gerard Manley, 117, 174–75
Hosea, xvi, 34, 137, 143
Hrotsvit of Gandersheim, 66–68, 87
Huebner, Douglas, 2–3
Huis Clos (Sartre), 81
Hunt, Holman, 111
Husserl, Edmund, 184
Hyperion (Hölderlin), 169

Ideology of the Aesthetic, The (Eagleton),
109
Idiot, The (Dostoevsky), 18, 2–33, 40,
43
"Idyll" (Maupassant), 116
Ignatius Loyola, St., 174
Iliad, The (Homer), 132
Immaculate Conception, The
(Velázquez), 92
Impossible Saints (Roberts), 78–80
In the Beauty of the Lilies (Updike), 17
In the Penal Settlement (Kafka), 61–62
Incarnatio continua, 130, 136, 139, 149
Inquisition, Holy, 99
Irwin, Alexander, 131
Isaiah, xvi, 21, 146, 148
Isaiah, Abbot of Scetis, 72, 90, 98,
100–101
Iscariot, Judas, 176–77
Isenheim Altarpiece (Grünewald),
42–43, 146, 165

Jabès, Edmond, xv
Jacob, 44, 59
Jakobson, Roman, 74

James, Deacon, 65
James, Henry, 172–75, 179, 180
Jeanrond, Werner, G., 181
Jerome, St., 47, 116
Jerusalem (Blake), 23
Jesus and the Adulterous Woman (Rembrandt), 90
Joan of Arc, St., 131
Job, Book of, 33
John Climacus, St., 133
John of Damascus, St., 39, 40
John of the Cross, St., 7, 45, 132, 180
John the Baptist, xvi, 42
John the Dwarf, 45, 66
John, Gospel of, xiii, 6, 7, 8, 23, 24, 42,
48–49, 56, 57, 65, 90, 97, 124,
130, 145, 149, 158, 159–60, 177,
182, 183
Johnson, Samuel, 118
Jonah, 28
Joyce, James, 7, 105, 110, 135, 136,
148–56, 173, 179
Julian of Norwich, 32, 129
Justin Martyr, 26

Kafka, Franz, 61–62
Kant, Immanuel, xii, 7, 8, 132, 168
Kazantzakis, Nikos, 18
Kearney, Richard, 157
Kenosis, 17, 19, 22, 23, 25, 26, 33, 40,
42–43, 49, 56, 59, 101, 122, 124,
126, 146, 152, 163, 167, 172,
192
Kierkegaard, Søren, 178
King James Bible, 120
Kings I, Book of, xv, 60
Kitchen Maid, The (Velázquez), 92
Kleist, Heinrich von, 164
Koerner, Joseph, 94, 165
Kristeva, Julia, 32
Krueger, Derek, 172
"Kubla Khan" (Coleridge), 163
Kügelgen, Gerhard von, 165

La Tour, Georges de, 91, 92
Lacan, Jacques, 93
Lacoste, Jean-Yves, 1, 175–76, 178
Lady Chatterley's Lover (Lawrence), 114
Laing, R. D., 83
Landscape Painted with Tea (Pavić), **57–59**
Laqueur, Thomas, 24, 27
Lorraine, Claude, 165
Las Meninas (*The Maids of Honour*) (Velázquez), 92
Last Supper, The (da Vinci), 24–25
Last Temptation, The (Kazantzakis), 18
Lausiac History (Palladios), 74, 80, 143, 204
Lawrence, D. H., 114
Lawrence, T. E., xiii, 51, 141, 146
Leahy, D. G., 12, 150
Lessing, Gotthold Ephraim, 159–60
Levinas, Emmanuel, 4
Lewes, G. H., 159
Lewis, C. S., 44, 145
Libri Tres Antirrhetici (Nicephorus), 2, 40
"Limbo" (Coleridge), 166, 168
Lives of the Desert Fathers, The (*Historia Monachorum*), iv, xviii, 3, 44, 141, 142
living liturgically, 1, **171–78**
Logic (Coleridge), 159–60
Logic (Hegel), 11
Logos, 48–49, 149, 167, 172, 175
"Love (III)" (Herbert), 116, 123, 128–29, 150, 185
Luke, Gospel of, 10–11, 66, 73, 90–91, 93, 94, 97, 99, 156
Luther, Martin, 94
Luxury and Fashion, Journal of, 164

MacNeice, Louis, 181
Macrina, 5
Madame Bovary (Flaubert), 16
Making Sex (Laqueur), 24

Malkovich, John, 83
Mariette in Ecstacy (Hansen), 191
Marion, Jean-Luc, 1, 11, 22, 31, 48, 84, 88, 140, **179–84**
Marius the Epicurean (Pater), 111, 189
Mark, Gospel of, 41, 49–50, 139, 183, 206
Martha and Mary, **90–101**, 142
Martha and Mary Magdalene (Caravaggio), 100
Mary Magdalene, 24, 41, 42, 64, 73, 80, 91, 97
Mary of Egypt, St., 5, 41, 44, 45, 50, **69–80**, 82, 84, 89, 100, 106, 116, 143, 147, 175
Mary of Egypt, St., Life of (Sophronius), **71–77**, 184
Massenet, Jules, 87
Matthew, Gospel of, 50, 139
Maupassant, Guy de, 116
Maximus the Confessor, St., xii–xiii, 1, 5–6, 8, 19, 114, 137
Meditations (Descartes), 106
Meditations on the Life of Christ (Pseudo-Bonaventura), 92
"Meeting Point" (MacNeice), 181, 211
"Memorable Fancy, A" (Blake), 148–49, 168, 181
Merton, Thomas, xix, 138
Michelangelo, Buonarroti, 103
Miles, Margaret, 3, 104, 105, 115–16, 136–37
Mill, J. S., 158
Miller, J. Hillis, 174, 175
Milton, John, 106, 148, 150
Monk by the Sea, The (Friedrich), **164–66**, 167
Monsignor Quixote (Greene), 110–11, 113
Moore, Stephen D., 25
Moschos, John, 143
Moses, xiv, 44, 64, 137, 147, 151, 155, 158

Moses, Life of (Gregory of Nyssa), 137
Murdoch, Iris, 177
Mystical Theology (Pseudo-Dionysius), xiv, 137
Mysticism after Modernity (Cupitt), 37–38

Nabokov, Vladimir, xi, 1
Nag Hammadi, 28
Nana (Zola), 112
Narnia, 44
National Gallery, London, 90, 91, 92, 95
National Gallery of Art, Washington, D.C., 101
Neoplatonism, 4, 138
New Science, The (Vico), 154
New York Times, 83
Newlands, George, 69
Newman, Barnett, 8, 10
Newman, John Henry, 150, 174
Nicephorus the Solitary, 52
Nicephorus, St., 22, 30, 40, 41
Nicholas of Cusa, 10, 139, 184–85
Nietzsche, Friedrich, 135, 150, 152, 179, 182
Night (Wiesel), 35
Novalis (Friedrich von Hardenberg), 168
Novitas Mundi (Leahy), 150
Nuptials of God, The (Gill), 114–15

Old Woman Cooking Eggs, The (Velázquez), 77–78, 92
"On Art and the Spirit of Art" (Friedrich), 168
On the Epistle of John to the Parthians (Augustine), 141
On the Noble Man (Eckhart), xix, 137
On Virginity (Gregory of Nyssa), 135
Ondaatje, Michael, 111–12
Onement I (Newman), 8
Ong, Walter, 50
Oppenheimer, Helen, 131

Origen, 4, 12, 31, 37, 45, 47–48, 79, 138
Orvieto, Chapel, 103–4
Owen, Wilfred, 113
Oxford Bible Commentary, The (Barton and Muddiman), 34
Oxford Companion to the Body, The (Blakemore and Jennett), 188
Oxford English Dictionary, The, 157

Pafnutius (or, *The Conversion of the Harlot Thaïs*) (Hrotsvit), 68
Pagels, Elaine, 25
Paglia, Camille, 24
Paradise Lost (Milton), 150
Paris, Texas (Wenders), 145
Parsifal, 154
Pascal, Blaise, 143
Pater, Walter, 111, 189
"Patmos" (Hölderlin), 163
Patteson, Richard F., 83
Pavić, Milorad, **57–59**
Pelagia, St., **64–66**, 69, 71, 72, 89
"Pencil Letter" (Ratushinskaya), 53
Perfume (Süskind), 26, 191
Phenomenology of Spirit, The (Hegel), 7–8, 159, 166–68
Philip IV of Spain, 99
Philip, Gospel of, 64
Philippians, Epistle to, 126, 146
Philokalia, 8, 10, 133, 138, 147
Pieta, 114, 116
Piranesi, Giovanni Battista, 62
Plain Sense of Things, The (Edwards), 171
Pollock, Jackson, 10, 34
Pounds, Wayne, 83
Power of Images, The (Freedberg), 117
Prescott, Orville, 83
"Priest, The" (Thomas), 199
Priest to the Temple, A (Herbert), 122
Prolegomena to Charity (Marion), 88
Psalm 27, 34, 38
Psalm 84, 78

Pseudo-Bonaventura, 91–92
Pseudo-Dionysius, xiv, 137, 139

Quarantine (Crace), xvi–xvii
Qui audit me (Eckhart), 139
Quia Amore Langeo, 48
Qur'an, xvi, 143

Rabaté, Jean-Michel, 135, 151, 153–54
Rachel and Leah, 91
Ramdohr, Freiherr von, 165–66
Ratushinskaya, Irina, 53
Regeneration (Barker), 113
Rembrandt, van Ryn, 44, **88–90**, 100, 101, 102
Renan, Ernest, 24
Repentant Magdalen (La Tour), 91–92
Resurrection (Tolstoy), 18
Revelation, Book of, 49, 50, 143
Ricoeur, Paul, xviii–xix
Roberts, Michèle, 64, **78–80**
Rokeby Venus, The (*Venus at her Toilet*) (Velázquez), 92
Rolle, Richard, 32, 35
Romeo and Juliet (Shakespeare), 183
Rothko, Mark, 164
Rougeau, Rémy, 57
Royce, Josiah, 7

Sacred Desert, The (Jasper), xi, 1, 51, 136, 147, 179
Sacred Gaze, The (Morgan), 190
Sartre, Jean Paul, 81
Scapegoat, The (Hunt), 111
Schelling, Friedrich Wilhelm Joseph von, 162, 190
Schlegel, Friedrich, 168
Schleiermacher, Friedrich, 165
Schopenhauer, Joanna, 164
Seek My Face (Updike), 34–35, 114
Selden, Raman, 140
Self-Embodiment of God, The (Altizer), 192

Self-Portrait with Beret and Turned-up Collar (Rembrandt), 101
Sermons for the Feast of All Saints (Bernard of Clairvaux), 3, 7, 11–12
Sermons on the Song of Songs (Bernard of Clairvaux), 40
Seven Pillars of Wisdom (Lawrence), xiii, 51, 141, 146
Seville, 99
Sexuality of Christ in Renaissance Art and in Modern Oblivion, The (Steinberg), 100, 115
Shaffer, Eleanor, 159
Shakespeare, William, 248, 154, 182
Shape of the Liturgy, The (Dix), 148
Sheltering Sky, The (Bowles), **80–85**
Sidney, Sir Philip, 120–21
Signorelli, Luca, 34, 88, 103–5
Sistine Chapel, 103
Sitwell, Osbert, 113
Snyder, Alice D., 159–60
Song of Songs, 4, 6–7, 37–39, 40, 47–48, 70, 123, 183
Songs of Innocence (Blake), 28–29
Sophronius, St., 71, 184
Spinoza, Baruch, 159
Spiritual Meadow, The (John Moschos), 143
Stabat Mater, 36
"Stanzas from the Grande Chartreuse" (Arnold), 177
Statesman's Manual, The (Coleridge), 158, 160, 165, 169
Stein, Gertrude, 83
Steinbeck, John, 116, 155
Steinberg, Leo, 25, 29, 100, 115
Sterne, Laurence, 151
Stockhausen, Karlheinz, 9
Süskind, Patrick, 26, 191
Swift, Jonathan, 151
Symbolism of Evil, The (Ricoeur), xviii–xix

Tate Gallery, London, 164
Tempest, The (Shakespeare), 148, 156

Temple, The (Herbert), 122, 128
Tentation de saint Antoine, La (Flau-
    bert), 16, 73
Terence, 67
Tertullian, 25–26, 109
Thaïs, **66–69**, 71, 72, 87, 88, 89, 100,
    143
Thaïs (France), 66, 87, 106
Thaïs (Massenet), 87, 144
Thérèse de Lisieux, St., 54
Thesiger, Wilfred, 36, 140
Thirty-Nine Articles of Religion,
    122–23
Thomas, R. S., 114, 117, 199
Three Treatises on the Divine Images
    (John of Damascus), 39
Tieck, Ludwig, 168
Tillich, Paul, 126
Tintoretto, Jacopo, 89
Titian, 89
Tobit, 78
"Todesfuge" ("Death Fugue") (Celan),
    60
Tolstoy, Leo, 18
Torah, 169
Total Presence, 1, 5, 6, 20, 45, 57, 84,
    128, 133, 147, 149, 155, 156,
    158, 185
Toynbee, Polly, 44
Traherne, Thomas, 63
Trent, Council of, 96, 99
Turner, Denys, 142
Turner, J. M. W., 164

Ulysses (Joyce), 144, 150, 151, 152
Under the Net (Murdoch), 177
Updike, John, 17, 34–35, 114

Valantasis, Richard, 2
van Gogh, Vincent, 10, 44, 87, 88,
    101–3
Vasari, Giorgio, 104
Vattimo, Gianni, 125–27, 192

Velázquez, Diego Rodriguez de Silva,
    41, 73, 77–78, 88, **91–101**, 106
vita contemplativa/*vita activa*, 80, 90–101
Viardot, Louis, 89
Vico, Giambattista, 153–54
Vidal, Gore, 83
Viola, Bill, xviii
"Virgin's One Bare Breast, The" (Miles),
    11
Virilio, Paul, 12
Visuality and Biblical Text (Boyd and
    Esler), 91
Voragine, Jacobus de, 66

Waddell, Helen, 65
Walton, Izaak, 118–19, 121
Ward, Benedicta, 64, 75
Warhol, Andy, 9, 34
Watanabe, Morimichi, 184
Water Seller of Seville, The (Velázquez),
    92
Watts, Isaac, 32
Webster, John, 36
Weil, Simone, 3, 6, 122, **128–33**, 135,
    174
Wenders, Wim, 145
Weyden, Roger van der, 91
Wheatfield with Crows (van Gogh), 102
White, James Boyd, 118, 119–20
Wiesel, Elie, 35
Wild Girl, The (Roberts), 64
William of St. Thierry, 99
Williams, Rowan, 37–38
Williams, Tennessee, 83
Wimbush, Vincent L., 2
Winger, Debra, 83
Wings of the Dove, The (James), 172–75
*Wisdom (Sayings) of the Desert Fathers,
    The* (*Apophthegmata Patrum*),
    44–45, 50, 66, 138
Wolf, Norbert, 98
Word in the Desert, The (Burton-
    Christie), 51
Word Made Flesh, The (Miles), 33

Wordsworth, William, 159, 166
Wound of Knowledge, The (Williams), 38
Writing and Holiness (Krueger), 172
Wyschogrod, Edith, 19, 71

Yeats, W. B., 182

Zola, Emile, 112
Zossimus (Zossima), 5, 69–80, 89, 100, 116